THE UAE & OMAN
ULTIMATE
EXPLORER

Ultimate Explorer 2012/1st Edition

ISBN 978-9948-450-61-0

Printed and bound by Emirates Printing Press, Dubai, United Arab Emirates.

Explorer Publishing & Distribution
PO Box 34275, Dubai
United Arab Emirates
Phone   +971 (0)4 340 8805
Fax   +971 (0)4 340 8806
Email   info@askexplorer.com
Web   www.askexplorer.com

WELCOME...

THE WEEKEND HAS FINALLY LANDED - WHAT ARE YOU GOING TO DO WITH YOURS?

More malls and bigger brunches? Plough through another boxset? Hit the sunlounger? Or do you have your tent, mountain bike, harness and hiking boots at the ready?

Think you can 4WD your way up Fossil Rock, hike to the Hanging Gardens, explore deep down in the 7th Hole or pitch a tent on Jabal Shams? Can you cycle up the climbs to Tayyibah, spot lionfish at Octopus Rock, take to the air in a hot air balloon… and then dive out of a plane?

In short, do you have what it takes to become a UAE & Oman Ultimate Explorer? If you're constantly eager to break free from the city limits and are simply itching for adventure, then this book is just what you've been waiting for. There's a whole rugged, action-packed, adventure-soaked world out there, and it's time you dived right in.

After all, would you rather spend another day shopping, or spend nights gazing up at the bright stars as you fall asleep under a brilliant sky amongst the endless dunes of Al Gharbia, grab a lazy bite in the shade of a ghaf tree before cooling off under a waterfall, or discover the amazing creatures that call the local waters home? With the help of *The UAE & Oman Ultimate Explorer* guide, you'll soon be swapping swimming pools for skydives and giving up taxi rides for boat trips.

Whether you're an experienced wadi-basher, boater, biker, or a first time adventurer, you'll find everything you need, from easy-to-use maps for navigation to directional tips and GPS points covering everything from the heights of Jabal Shams to the depths of Al Hoota caves.

If one day of adventure just isn't enough, check out our itineraries (p.8), Camping section (p.59) and the Weekend Breaks chapter (p.187) which reveal where, when and how to spend the night. For snap-happy adventurers, there is more than enough to point your lens at, from Dubai skyscrapers to abandoned villages, unexpected oases and imposing forts.

There are literally hundreds of experiences contained within these pages but this book is about more than **explorer** telling you what to do. We want you to come back from your adventures and visit askexplorer.com – let us know where you've been, post images of your trips, and tell us if you met any other explorers out there, or if there are any top tips that we missed out.

Happy (and, most importantly, safe) exploring.

there's more to life...
ask**explorer**.com

CONTENTS

USING THIS GUIDE

By activity

In this guide, you will find activities grouped into colour-coded sections; in the Off-roading Chapter, for example, you can learn all about driving off-road throughout the UAE and Oman, from dune-bashing in Liwa, to wadi bashing in Musandam. Each chapter explains how to get started, where to pick up all the gear and where to go to practise the activity, as well as extra information on clubs and groups.

The UAE and Oman are outdoor adventure 'free zones' with very few restrictions on where you can drive, camp, ride, dive, climb or sail. For the more adventurous, it's as simple as making it up as you go along. However, in certain chapters, such as Off-roading, Hiking, Diving and Cycling, we've included some specific sites and routes. In these chapters, you'll find maps, directions, GPS points, or a combination of several to point you in the right direction.

By area

If you've got a destination in mind and would like to know exactly which activities are available there, take a look at the map on p.4 and the table on p.6. These highlight a few of the main areas within the UAE and Oman, and let you know exactly which activities you can find there, as well as the page on which you can find all the relevant information. The Distance Chart below is also useful, letting you know the driving distance between all of the main activity hubs featured in the guide.

Inspiration

If all these hundreds of activities, adventures, routes and destinations leave you a little spoiled for choice, fear not; you'll find plenty of inspiration in this guidebook too. We have a range of multi-day itineraries on p.8-p.12 according to your preferred destination, how long you have or the types of activities you prefer.

And then there's also the Weekend Breaks (p.187) chapter which highlights a number of the most popular one or two night getaways, along with a few hotel options, if you've tired of nights under canvas.

Maps

Bear in mind that, due to the length and detail of different routes and itineraries, the maps used in this guide all follow different scales. Equally, some maps are detailed enough to be followed precisely, while others are there purely to give you an idea of where the activity takes place.

Back of the book

Wherever relevant, the details of companies, activity providers, equipment suppliers and accommodation options have been included in the activity chapters themselves, but you'll also find details in the Directory at the back of this book (p.238). In fact, you'll find all manner of other useful numbers that aren't featured in the rest of the book there too, along with some basic First Aid advice.

DISTANCE CHART

	ABU DHABI	AL AIN	DIBBA	DUBAI	FUJAIRAH	HATTA	JABAL SHAMS (WESTERN HAJJAR)	JEBEL YIBIR	LIWA	MUSANDAM	MUSCAT	PEARL COAST (MIRFA)	RAS AL KHAIMAH	UMM AL QUWAIN
1 ABU DHABI		159	145	145	315	244	435	300	228	340	500	140	248	190
2 AL AIN	159		205	125	215	143	275	225	269	310	340	300	221	165
3 DIBBA	306	205		146	60	170	505	90	496	170	410	445	79	115
4 DUBAI	145	125	146		150	146	400	115	335	195	480	285	103	50
5 FUJAIRAH	315	215	60	150		62	415	52	505	170	295	435	110	115
6 HATTA	244	143	170	146	62		410	135	470	60	325	385	123	120
7 JABAL SHAMS (WESTERN HAJJAR)	435	275	505	400	415	410		480	545	610	225	575	500	525
8 JEBEL YIBIR	300	225	90	115	52	135	480		480	200	480	440	130	105
9 LIWA	228	269	496	335	505	470	545	480		530	720	135	438	380
10 MUSANDAM	340	310	170	195	170	60	610	200	530		525	480	90	145
11 MUSCAT	500	340	410	480	295	325	225	480	720	525		645	540	410
12 PEARL COAST (MIRFA)	140	300	445	285	435	385	575	440	135	480	645		390	445
13 RAS AL KHAIMAH	248	221	79	103	110	123	500	130	438	90	540	390		55
14 UMM AL QUWAIN	190	165	115	50	115	120	525	105	380	145	410	445	55	

Take Care

Make sure you evaluate all advice, comments, opinions and directions for yourself. Use your common sense, know your limits and use descriptions with EXTREME CAUTION.

For hikes and climbs in particular, we strongly recommend that you go accompanied by an experienced hiker or climber or, better still, a professional tour group.

Explorer Publishing accepts no responsibility for any accidents, injuries, loss, inconvenience, disasters or damage to persons or property that may occur while you are out and about or using this guidebook. **Ultimately, you are responsible for determining your own limitations based on the conditions you encounter.**

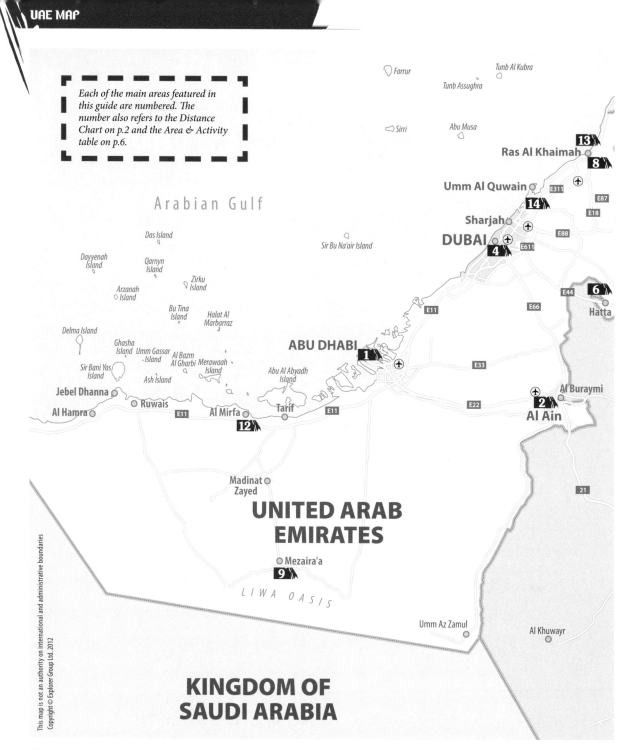

Each of the main areas featured in this guide are numbered. The number also refers to the Distance Chart on p.2 and the Area & Activity table on p.6.

Arabian Gulf

Farrur

Tunb Al Kubra

Tunb Assughra

Sirri

Abu Musa

13

Ras Al Khaimah

8

Umm Al Quwain

E311

E87

14

E18

Sharjah

E88

DUBAI

4

E611

E44

6

Das Island

Sir Bu Na'air Island

Dayyenah Island

Qarnyn Island

Zirku Island

E11

E66

Hatta

Arzanah Island

Bu Tina Island

Halat Al Marbarraz

Delma Island

Ghasha Island

Umm Gassar Island

Al Bazm Al Gharbi

Merawaah Island

Abu Al Abyadh Island

ABU DHABI

1

Sir Bani Yas Island

Ash Island

E33

Al Buraymi

Jebel Dhanna

Ruwais

E11

Al Mirfa

Tarif

E11

E22

2

Al Ain

Al Hamra

12

Madinat Zayed

UNITED ARAB EMIRATES

21

Mezaira'a

9

L I W A   O A S I S

Umm Az Zamul

Al Khuwayr

KINGDOM OF SAUDI ARABIA

WHAT TO DO WHERE

		OFF-ROADING	CAMPING	HIKING & CLIMBING	CYCLING	DIVING	WATERSPORTS	BOATING & YACHTING	WEEKEND BREAKS	EXPERIENCES	INDOOR
1	ABU DHABI	P.48	P.62	P.98	P.117	P.130	P.148	P.178	P.189	P.211	P.228
2	AL AIN	P.32		P.86	P.121		P.150		P.196	P.211	
3	DIBBA	P.38	P.62	P.83	P.110	P.132		P.183	P.198		
4	DUBAI	P.26	P.67	P.98	P.116	P.131	P.146	P.178	P.189	P.211	P.228
5	FUJAIRAH		P.62	P.83		P.138	P.155		P.198	P.217	P.227
6	HATTA		P.67	P.87	P.121		P.161		P.190	P.213	
7	JABAL SHAMS (WESTERN HAJJAR)		P.66	P.92							
8	JEBEL YIBIR		P.66	P.84	P.114				P.201		
9	LIWA	P.48	P.67						P.195		
10	MUSANDAM		P.66	P.88	P.106	P.135		P.183	P.204		
11	MUSCAT		P.72	P.90	P.119	P.143		P.178	P.206		
12	PEARL COAST (MIRFA)		P.63				P.154		P.192		
13	RAS AL KHAIMAH	P.44		P.85			P.169		P.200	P.211	
14	UMM AL QUWAIN		P.72				P.161	P.178	P.203	P.217	

SIMPLY CROSS-REFERENCE THE AREA YOU ARE INTERESTED IN WITH THE VARIOUS ACTIVITIES COVERED IN THIS BOOK TO DISCOVER FROM WHICH PAGE YOU'LL BE ABLE TO FIND THE INFORMATION YOU NEED TO PLAN YOUR NEXT ULTIMATE ADVENTURE IN THE UAE OR OMAN!

HOME TO YOUR FAVOURITE SPORT BRANDS.

Catering to all sport professionals and enthuthiast's needs from clothing and footwear to equipement, accessories and much more.

ITINERARY 1: 2-4 DAYS
FINDING NORTH

Whether leaving from Abu Dhabi or Dubai, you'd do well to make a stop-off along the E311 as it passes through Ajman and towards Umm Al Quwain. On the north side of the road here, you'll see a number of off-road centres offering adventures on quads and dune buggies – the perfect pre-lunch pick-me-up.

If that gives you a taste for more dune adventures, take the truck road off the E311 (signposted to the various Al Aqah beach hotels) and continue for a few kilometres until you see the turnoff for the Banyan Tree Al Wadi. Pull off into the wild here; there are plenty of tracks and dunes that make this area ideal for an afternoon of 4WD off-roading.

Once finished, head back towards RAK and, more specifically, to the Al Hamra Fort Hotel (p.162) which is home to an excellent watersports centre that offers banana boating, tube rides, wakeboarding, fishing trips and sailing lessons. But the most fun of all just might be the high-octane jetskiing.

Stay the night at the Al Hamra Fort Hotel or drive a little inland to the west coast entrance to Wadi Bih where there are plenty of locations to pitch your tent at. Although Wadi Bih may no longer offer a coast-to-coast route due to border checkpoints, you can still spend much of the following day trying out the Ainee Village and Hibs Village hikes.

Late afternoon, head back into RAK and then south and east towards Fujairah, pulling off along the way to make for the heights of the towering Jebel Yibir; near the top, you'll discover some of the best barbecue and camping spots in the Emirates. Rise early and begin the day on one of the most thrilling all-terrain

bike descents anywhere (p.114). After tackling the hard climb back up, you can try a spot of rock climbing or, if that sounds just too strenuous, embark on a number of challenging hikes.

All these activities may have you feeling wiped out – and there's no shame in making for home at the end of the day. But, for the real hardcore adventurers, continue the drive to Dibba where you can jump on an overnight dhow safari along the Musandam. Spend the night sleeping on deck beneath the stars, and the next day either scuba diving, snorkelling, fishing or sea kayaking. If you make special arrangements beforehand, you may even be able to try some cliff diving or deep water solo bouldering (p.136). By which point, you'll definitely be ready for home!

> **IN THIS PART OF THE WORLD, ADVENTURE IS EVERYWHERE BUT, FOR A HUGE VARIETY OF THRILLS AND SPILLS, YOU SHOULD LOOK NORTH.**

WADI BIH: ONE OF THE REGION'S MOST FAMOUS WADIS, WADI BIH (RIGHT) IS AN ADVENTURE HOTSPOT, ATTRACTING OFF-ROADERS, CAMPERS, HIKERS, BIKERS AND CLIMBERS IN THEIR DROVES.

FAMILY ITINERARY

With so many family-friendly activities to choose from, you're spoiled for choice and most itineraries can be made pretty child-suitable, but one destination stands above the rest when it comes to planning an action-packed weekend away with the youngsters: Al Ain.

Begin your weekend by stopping off at Hili Fun City (p.218), which is the ideal place for enjoying a picnic or barbecue in between bouts of bumper car racing and all manner of rides. From there, make for Al Ain Zoo (p.215), where you get to admire exotic animals from white lions to gorillas and penguins. Later, get back in the car and make the short drive to, and up, Jebel Hafeet to treat the kids – not to mention yourself – to one of the most exciting and most scenic drives in the world. There are several roadside play areas and picnic tables to choose from, and all come with stunning vistas to boot.

Al Ain of course boasts plenty of hotels (p.242) and the chalets at Green Mubazzarrah are also an option but, if it's a night under the stars you want, then head through the border to Buraimi (the Omani side of Al Ain) where you'll find some amazing off-road routes and hikes (p.86). Camp in Wadi Madbah and, when you wake in the morning, you can start the day with a nice but not-too-hard hike to the pools and waterfall. On the way home, make time for another wadi – Wadi Adventure (p.150) – where the whole family can enjoy thrilling white-water rafting, kayaking, climbing and zip lines.

ITINERARY 2: 3 DAYS

SANDS OF TIME

This trip will take you west, but also back in time, deep into the Rub Al Khali, where you'll get an intrepid taste of traditional Bedouin desert life before returning east and to the modern UAE. It's a taste of just how far things have come in a short space of time.

Start the first day early and get the longest drive of the trip out of the way – 190km from Abu Dhabi and 320km from Dubai. Follow the E11 west out of Abu Dhabi (signposted Tarif) until you reach the road that heads straight inland (signposted Madinat Zayed). The town of Mezaira'a is your last opportunity to make sure you've all the food, water, firewood and petrol you're going to need for the next couple of days – no matter what's in the tank, it's worth filling up! You may even like to grab some lunch in Mezaira'a or around the pool at the Liwa Hotel. In Mezaira'a (after the petrol station on the left) you'll come to a T-junction where you should take the right (heading west). At the next roundabout, take a left (signposted Moreeb), which takes you on to a magnificent, winding road that leads deeper and deeper into the desert. The road ends with Moreeb Dune on the left and here is where your ultimate off-roading adventure begins. Spend the afternoon surfing up and down the huge dunes and speeding across the vast salt flats in your 4WD. Before the sun sets, set up camp and start the barbecue – and soak up the most remote, noiseless night you'll have ever experienced.

In the morning, after enjoying the blood red sun rising over this alien lunarscape, there's plenty of opportunity for more serious off-roading action (you'll want to take loads of photos), before finding your way back to the road and heading back to Mezaira'a. Book an evening safari through one of the local hotels and you'll be whisked back out into the dunes, getting to see how the experts do it, before being delivered to a Bedouin style base camp for camel rides, quad biking and shisha, followed by a traditional Emirati buffet and entertainment from a belly dancer.

That night, camp again or take advantage of the local hotels (p.242) for something a bit more glamorous, before making the drive back towards civilisation in the morning. If you're in no rush, once you hit the coast road, stop off at Tarif or Mirfa for breakfast or lunch on the beach – and you can even try your hand at some watersports. Finally, it's back to the modern face of Abu Dhabi – and where could encapsulate the changing face of the emirate more than Yas Island, where fast-paced go-karting and an afternoon at the state-of-the-art Ferrari World should bring your trip to an epic close.

GET READY FOR THE ULTIMATE WILD WEST ADVENTURE INTO THE PAST AND FUTURE.

**RUB AL KHALI:
COVERING LARGE PARTS OF THE
UAE, OMAN, SAUDI ARABIA AND
YEMEN, THE 'EMPTY QUARTER'
IS OFFICIALLY THE WORLD'S
LARGEST SAND DESERT. IT'S
ALSO AN OFF-ROAD MUST-DO.**

WATER ITINERARY

Flanked by water along the length of both countries, the UAE and Oman are blessed with superb watersports scenes. If you long for the life aquatic, then your explorations have to begin in Musandam. Day dives are, of course, possible but, given the variety of dive sites and rich marine life, you may need more than 24 hours – stay on board a dhow (p.182) or opt for a comfy eco-lodge if you want a couple of days of diving. It doesn't all have to be about scuba; dive operators in this neck of the woods can provide kayaking, snorkelling, fishing and even whale and dolphin watching in the Straits of Hormuz. After all that marine exploration, head back south via stop-offs at Ice Land Waterpark in Ras Al Khaimah and Dreamland Aquapark in Umm Al Quwain. To round-off the water-based fun, why not try some wet and wild thrills, like parasailing (p.146) or Zapcatting (p.159) in Dubai or taking a white-knuckle RIB tour around The Palm or along Abu Dhabi Corniche.

ITINERARY 3: 4-7 DAYS
OH MAN, OMAN!

A THRILLING ITINERARY IN THE WORLD'S NEW ADVENTURE CAPITAL.

This route takes in the most attractive sights of the east coast, with beaches, wadis, mountains, deep pools and even the possibility of some desert. The main town in the region is Sur, which you'll conveniently reach half way through this itinerary.

Coming from the UAE, it can be nice to make the first day's drive down to Muscat a fairly leisurely one, giving you time to explore the city in the afternoon; however, if you're dead-set on diving straight into adventure, either stop en route to Muscat and spend a couple of hours tackling The Chains (p.99) or discovering the Omani capital by foot on the Riyam-Mutrah hike (p.91).

End the first day by checking into one of Muscat's many delightful hotels (p.247), or you can set up camp at one of the beaches around Muscat or Yiti, which is a little further south along the coast road. Better still, camp in style at the Oman Dive Center and you can rise in the morning to face a whole day of spectacular scuba, as well as a variety of other water-based activities such as kayaking or even whale spotting trips.

If you're a keen cyclist, and you're in no rush, you might like to add an extra day in Muscat for a spot of riding. Spend the morning tackling The Hotels (an easy 58km) or the flat Al Seeb (73km) loops, or dedicate a full day to the tough Col De Al Amarat (115km) or extremely challenging All In One (165km) routes (see muscatcyclingclub.com for route breakdowns). If they sound a bit too demanding, simply hire a bike and enjoy the easy ride along Mutrah's corniche and some of the city's oldest sections.

Allow for a full day of driving to make the trip from Muscat down to Ras al Jinz, which includes time for exploring the

wadis along the way, as well as a swim or two in the pools. Wadi ash Shab and Tiwi both offer hiking and exploring.

After passing through the ancient shipbuilding town of Sur, it's just over an hour to Ras Al Jinz where a number of accommodation options await (p.247), as do hundreds of turtles that come up on to the beach to lay their eggs. The largest numbers visit in July but, if you go between September and November, you'll be able to see both adults laying and hatchlings making their way down to the sea. Summer is generally a good time to visit this area, as the ever-present winds and eastern exposure keep it a good 10-15°C cooler than other parts of Oman.

The following day, you can begin your journey home and you can choose to retrace your route along the coast, or head inland via Ibra and Nizwa. If you opt for the latter, there's really no end of adventure still in store, and you could extend your trip from an extra day to an extra three days.

Between Sur and Ibra lies Wadi Bani Khalid, which makes the ideal place for a short hike, a picnic lunch and a cooling splash in the pools, before continuing

the journey through the Wahiba Sands – pull off just about anywhere for some serious dune-bashing fun. Spend the night camping on the dunes, try out one of the luxurious 'glamping' options (p.72) or continue to Ibra where you'll find some basic hotels.

It's a couple of hours on to the ancient Omani capital, Nizwa, which has plenty of cultural attractions but, as the gateway to the Western Hajars, it also has plenty to offer the more adventurous. Try the Al Qannah hike and via ferrata climb, for spectacular views of the 'Grand Canyon of Oman'. Jabal Akhdar is popular with hikers, canyons and cavers, while there's also a back-breaking 70km ride (road bike or MTB) from Al Sheif, climbing more than 2,000m in total up to the Sayq Plateau.

On the other side of Nizwa lies the region's highest peak, Jabal Shams, and its incredible array of hikes, with the highlight arguably being the trek to the almost mythical looking village of Bilad Sayt. For something a little different, try a mountain biking tour from The View eco lodges, or head for Al Hoota Cave for an underground expedition. And then, finally, it's time for the long journey home.

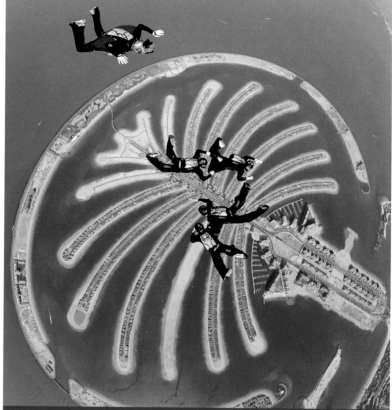

DESERT STORMERS

No matter where you live in the UAE or Oman, the desert is never far away and learning to drive on sand is an experience no UAE or Oman dweller should go without. If you don't have your own 4WD, you can look to rent one (p.239, 246) or try a desert driving course (p.22), during which a pro will fill you in on all the basics. Once you're ready to go, try the area around Big Red, near Hatta (p.87). These red dunes are an off-roader's dream and great for perfecting your skills before you venture out further into the desert. Also try Fossil Rock (p.26) for the perfect first-timer's off-road trip. Looking for an additional challenge? If you like your desert fun a bit more down and dirty, you'll find plenty of places renting dune buggies, quad bikes and dirt bikes in this area – with more to be found on the E11 near Ajman. If you're a keen mountain biker, be ready for the rains – they may not fall often but, when they do, the sands of Big Red harden enough to become an MTB playground!

THRILL SEEKERS

For a weekend that is bound to set your heart racing, you need barely leave Dubai. What better way to kick-start an adrenaline adventure, for example, than jumping out of a plane (p.221)? While you're freefalling above The Palm, take a good look at Aquaventure (p.169) – the near-vertical Leap of Faith slide should be next on your list. In fact, why not double up on the -waterpark action and head straight to Wild Wadi for plenty more heart-rate increasing slides and rides? What comes down must go back up, so, for more high kicks, try the climbing wall and the cable climb suspended assault course at Adventure HQ (p.240) before coming truly back down to earth at Dubai Autodrome (p.222), where there are high-speed indoor and outdoor karting tracks. From there, it's a short journey down Emirates Road to Sharjah – rope in some friends (or sworn enemies) for all-out war at Sharjah Paintball Park (p.229).

ARE YOU AN ULTIMATE EXPLORER?

ALL OF THE ULTIMATE EXPERIENCES AND EXCITING EXPLORATIONS SHOWCASED IN THIS FANTASTIC GUIDE COULD BE YOURS FOR THE DOING IN ONE WHOLE YEAR...

Launched in early 2011, the Search for the Ultimate Explorer is a UAE-wide hunt for one very special individual who, after proving their worth, gets to spend a year living for free and experiencing all there is on offer in this great nation. The annual campaign is open to anyone over the age of 21 with a valid UAE resident visa and offers the final champion not only a plethora of weekend activities, from the adrenaline pumping to lavishly indulgent, but also a luxury apartment, car, shopping allowance and international flights – all for free for one whole year!

Entry is simple, just log on to askexplorer.com and register your interest – you will be informed when entry opens at the beginning of the year. However, the race to the finish line does require some commitment – if you're lucky enough to be picked as one of the 100 first round winners you'll be heading off to enjoy a complimentary experience, such as a hot air balloon ride or dinner for two. You will then

write a 100 word review of your experience to test your roving reporter skills and **explorer** will pick the best 20 reviews.

Do not fear if you don't make round one – there is also a chance to win a Golden Ticket which gets you straight into the quarter finals along with those 20 lucky reviewers. Each of the final 30 get their hands on a digital camera to record their short film, giving them the chance to tell us why they should be the Ultimate Explorer. After a vote at **explorer** HQ the final ten advance into the semi-finals, along with two wild cards, and it is up to the public to vote online for their favourites.

After some serious campaigning the final five go head to head in the Ultimate Challenge – battling it out in various tasks around the UAE which test their stamina, cultural knowledge, creativity, determination and sense of adventure. At the end we have our new Ultimate Explorer and their year of fun begins....

Follow the current Ultimate Explorer's adventures at askexplorer.com.

15,000 TO ONE
From over 15,000 entries the journey to the big prize is as follows:
First round winners: 100
Quarter finalists & golden tickets: 30
Semi-finalists: 12
Finalists: Five
Ultimate Explorer: ONE!

WINNERS

THE 2012 WINNER OF THE SEARCH FOR THE ULTIMATE EXPLORER WAS 35-YEAR-OLD TEACHER, TIM JOHANSEN WHO WAS AWARDED A LUXURY APARTMENT AT THE ASCOTT PARK PLACE, AN FJ CRUISER, DHS.50,000 AT ADVENTURE HQ AND VIRGIN ATLANTIC FLIGHTS! IN THE INAUGURAL SEARCH 30-YEAR-OLD ALEC HARDEN TOOK THE TITLE, ADDING ULTMATE EXPLORING TO HIS DAY JOB IN PR.

HOW TO ENTER

Log on to askexplorer.com to register. You will need to be over 21 and have a valid UAE residents' visa. Also keep an eye on explorer's facebook and twitter on additional ways to enter and golden tickets and you could be the next Ultimate Explorer!

'Imagine sleeping in your dream house, driving the best car, enjoying dinners and flights - all without worrying about the cost. It is just incredible - more than I ever expected. My year as the Ultimate Explorer was packed with so many new experiences and adventures, it was simply out of this world. The competition was a rollercoaster in itself and so much fun, especially meeting so many great people along the way. The whole year is one that I will never forget.'

Alec Harden
2011 Ultimate Explorer

LIVE THE RIDING EXPERIENCE

OFF-ROADING

OFF-ROADING

WHEN IT COMES TO THE GREAT OUTDOORS, THE GCC DESERT IS A TRULY UNIQUE ADVENTURE PLAYGROUND.

With vast areas of rarely-visited wilderness to explore, dune and wadi bashing are popular pastimes in the UAE.

Desert driving is a tough challenge that asks a lot of both car and driver but, once you've mastered the skill, it opens up the vast deserts and can also be amazing fun. From sandboarding to camping under the stars, learning to drive on sand reveals a whole new side to life in the UAE and the good news is it only takes a day of training.

While off-road driving is exciting and adventurous, it does require skill. To ensure that most of your off-roading memories are good, you'll find a few pointers listed in this section to help you get on your way.

The key elements are simple: be prepared and use your common sense. Leave any macho fantasies of invincibility you may have at home – the good off-roader is careful and cautious, with a high regard for safety and the environment.

GEAR AND EQUIPMENT

It is key to always be prepared and the right gear and equipment (see box below) can be sourced through the Directory on p.244 & p.248 at the back of the book.

Popular providers include Adventure HQ (adventurehq.ae), Ace Hardware (aceuae.com) and even Carrefour (carrefouruae.com).

SAFETY

Off-road driving is fun, but safety should be your top priority. Always be sensible and patient, and follow these guidelines:
• Take your mobile phone.
• Always travel with an experienced off-road driver. That second vehicle or extra pair of hands could literally save a lifesaver.
• Pack a first-aid kit (see p.236 for more details), and know the medical histories of your passengers.
• Always take plenty of drinking water; at least three litres per person per day.
• Wear your seatbelt – it might not be comfortable while bumping over dunes, but

the benefits far outweigh the inconvenience.
• Spread the word – even though you might not be getting that far away from 'civilisation', let someone know where you're going and when you'll be back.

ACCIDENTS & BREAKDOWNS

If you have an accident, having a second vehicle may literally save your life, which is why it is always a good idea to drive in convoy. The first rule of driving in convoy is that each driver is responsible for the car behind. This ensures that everyone returns to civilisation together.

Not too close, however; you don't want crashes out there – especially as, in some emirates, you have to leave your car at the scene for the police to inspect. In reality, unless you have a second car or are very close to civilisation, this may be impossible.

If you are using GPS, mark the coordinates of your abandoned car. If not, try to remember the location as meticulously as possible (especially in the desert, where

everything looks the same). Common sense should prevail, so if driving out in the damaged car is the only sensible solution, then you should do it. Go straight to the police for an accident report and explain the situation. If you have a camera with you, take some pictures of the accident scene.

If your car breaks down, it is advisable to know a few basics of car maintenance, such as how to change a tyre or check the oil.

FINDING YOUR WAY

GPS or compasses are essentials, especially when used in conjunction with a good map. However, if you have neither (or they break during a trip), it is worth knowing how to read the sky.

By day, the sun rises in the east and sets in the west, which can indicate which direction you are heading.

At night, the north is indicated by the Pole Star. The two lowest stars of the Plough or Great Bear point towards the Pole Star, which is about four times the distance between the two stars away.

ESSENTIAL OFF-ROAD CHECKLIST

MUST-HAVES
- Well-maintained, fully-serviced vehicle
- Detailed map of off-road route
- Jack – conventional, airbag or, best of all, highlift
- Plank or block of wood for supporting jack on soft ground
- Tow rope and shackles
- Basic tool kit (including the tools to change a wheel)
- Mobile phone (fully charged)
- Shovel
- Fire extinguisher
- Tyre pressure gauge
- First aid kit (for the full list of what your kit should contain, turn to the First Aid section on p.236)
- Spare tyre in good condition and fully inflated
- Fluid levels checked (water, oil, clutch, steering, coolants, radiator, battery)

OPTIONAL
- Foot pump or compressor
- Tyre repair kit (tubeless)
- Sand mats or trays
- Jump leads
- Spare fuses
- Heavy-duty gloves
- GPS receiver
- Multi-purpose pocket knife
- Torch (and spare batteries)
- Camera
- Binoculars

PAPERWORK
- Insurance papers (copies are fine)
- Vehicle registration card
- UAE driving licence
- Accident report (if you have existing damage to your car, however minor)
- Ensure your passengers have personal ID

INSURANCE

If your trip takes you into Oman, make sure your vehicle is insured for both the UAE and Oman. If it's not, you can extend your cover for the duration of your trip, although this will probably involve an extra charge. You'll need to obtain a certificate to prove that the insurance covers you for driving in Oman. For a list of providers turn to the Directory on p.242 & p.248.

When it comes to hiring a 4WD, ensure that the insurance specifically covers off-road driving. Bizarrely, not all companies will provide off-road cover automatically for 4WDs. There are plenty of car rental agencies that you can use, such as Off-Road Zone (offroad-zone.com). The full list is available on p.239 & p.246.

LEARN TO OFF-ROAD

There's a host of qualified instructors and driving schools to choose from, and the scope of training ranges from comprehensive programmes to customised outings with a group of friends.

If you're new to dune bashing, there are a number of companies and organisations that run beginners' courses. Try Desert Rangers (desertrangers.com), Off-Road Zone (offroad-zone.com) or contact Emirates Driving Institute (edi-uae.com) for details about their one-day training programmes, which give you safety skills as well as a desert driving certificate.

Meanwhile, Sand Trax (04 289 5202) is a self-drive experience, where an instructor leads a convoy of 4WDs along a natural trail set among dramatic dunes.

Following each other in a pre-arranged order, you'll be able to weave in and out of small dunes, along windblown trails and across sweeping sands. The fully automatic 4WDs are easy and safe to drive, and make for an unforgettable desert safari experience.

JOIN A CLUB

Most clubs are extremely welcoming to newbies and organise beginners' drives when more experienced drivers are happy to show first-timers the ropes. There are several clubs and groups based in the UAE that are ideal for getting off-road – some are more active than others, sending out regular email blasts about weekend rides and camping trips, and are ideal for meeting adventurous, like-minded drivers.

All of the clubs take off-roading and safety issues seriously, but for some of them it's just as much about the social element of off-roading.

- Abu Dhabi 4x4 Club (ad4x4.com)
- Almost 4x4 Off-Road Club (almost4x4.com)
- Emarat Club (emarat4x4.com)
- FJ Cruiser Owners Club (fj-uae.com)
- Facebook and Twitter are also excellent resources for clubs

For the full list, turn to p.244.

HOW TO CHOOSE A 4WD

Choosing the right 4WD is an important decision. Most of us have to finance a vehicle, and if you make the wrong choice you will be stuck with it for some time. Peter Gladstone, head of the Jeep Off-road Academy UAE (jeepuae.com), explains some of the main things to consider.

1. Serious off-roading requires a low range option on the transmission – if the vehicle isn't equipped with a transfer case then don't expect to be able use it for rock crawling and heavy recovery.

   You will also need low range to get out of the sand should you get stuck. It's a major advantage if the vehicle has one (or all) of the following installed: diff-lock, traction control and limited slip differential (LSD).

2. If the vehicle is to be used for off-road driving full time, then consider the possibility of a manual transmission. This will give you more options and more control off-road (but will drive you crazy when in traffic on Sheikh Zayed Road!).

3. Safety and security are also very important. Jeep Wranglers, for example, feature standard electronic stability control, electronic roll mitigation, trailer-sway control, hill-start assist and brake traction control (among two dozen available safety and security features).

4. Make sure that the approach, departure and break over angles, as well as the ground clearance, are adequate for the use that you have in mind for your vehicle.

5. If buying a second hand car, it is always best to buy from a reputable dealer. Either way, make sure you test the 4WD system off-road before making any decisions – take it to a sandy area and make sure it engages and that there aren't any nasty grating noises when turning (disengage stability systems before testing).

   Also, check the service history. This should give you a good idea of how the vehicle has been maintained. Finally, get underneath the vehicle where you can check if any damage has occurred due to rough handling.

> **'IF THE VEHICLE ISN'T EQUIPPED WITH A TRANSFER CASE, THEN DON'T EXPECT TO BE ABLE USE IT FOR ROCK CRAWLING AND HEAVY RECOVERY.'**

GO WHERE FEW HAVE GONE,
SEE WHAT FEW HAVE SEEN.

mideast.jeep.com

Jeep Compass   Jeep Patriot   Jeep Grand Cherokee   Jeep Wrangler   Jeep Cherokee

You don't find adventure, it finds you. Atop a cliff; amongst the city's side streets; at the heart of the desert as the warm, humid air brushes across your face. But, it's not about where you find your adventure; it's about who you share your adventure with that makes the difference. Share your adventure with the people that matter the most. Share those moments in a Jeep.

Jeep® is a registered trademark of Chrysler Group LLC.

f Join us at Jeep Middle East

trading enterprises

An *Al-Futtaim group* company

CALL TOLL-FREE 800-4-119

DRIVING A TRUCK

Ford Middle East's (me.ford.com) chief engineer Ziyad 'Z' Dallalah on how to choose the best off-road truck.

Q: What are the advantages of choosing a truck for off-roading?

A: Capability. Trucks are built for the sole reason of out-performing regular cars on tough and extreme terrains, whether that is towing or driving on various terrains, even with heavy loads. Trucks are also built to clear different terrains so the under-carriage will not hit the ground or damage the vehicle in any way.

Q: What are the important features to look out for when choosing a truck?

A: Dimensions, capability, engine and transmission, and safety features. You should make sure that the truck will fulfil your requirements. Our Ford F-Series, for example, is packed with all the essential features, backed up with the right power trains to get the most out of the truck.

Q: Would you advise that a driver learns to off-road before using a truck?

A: It would be beneficial to get familiar with your truck due to the difference in size and weight. Trucks clear the ground much higher, while still providing clear vision all around the vehicle. Dimensions differ from those of a regular vehicle.

Q: Which features would you say are a must for an off-road journey?

A: There are certain features available on trucks that make the off-roading experience safer and comfortable:

1) Hill Start Assist: prevents a vehicle from rolling back by maintaining brake pressure until the engine delivers enough torque to move the vehicle up the hill.

2) Hill Descent Control: allows the driver to control the speed of hill descents without applying the brakes, even in reverse.

3) Electronic Locking Differential: provides additional off-road capability to retain optimal traction and maintain momentum.

4) SelectShift Automatic Transmission: for the driver who wants more control of transmission gear selection. A toggle switch engages the mode, where the transmission doesn't second-guess the driver, giving him or her total control over gear selection and performance feel.

Q: In case of a breakdown, or the vehicle getting stuck, what is the best course of action?

A: Call your local dealer or authorised recovery specialist to schedule a recovery pick-up. Find a shady place, and stay hydrated while waiting for the recovery service.

WHERE TO GO

THE UAE AND NEIGHBOURING OMAN OFFER PLENTY OF EXCITING ROUTES FOR OFF-ROADING ADVENTURES.

Whether going for a day or a whole weekend, you will be spoiled for choice with the number of routes on offer in the region.

In this book, we cover five routes, some of which can be combined with other activities but, to combine them with other off-road routes, discover even more 4WD adventures in explorer's *UAE Off-road* and *Oman Off-road* guide books.

ONE-DAY TRIPS

For a full day out, with some of the best driving in the Emirates, combine the eastern side of the epic Wadi Bih route (p.38) with the shorter Wadi Asimah route (p.44) near the east coast. The Asimah track takes you right through the trees and has off-route diversions for walking and exploring.

Fossil Rock (p.26) offers a great all-round desert experience, and can be tackled by any level of driver (with more challenging dunes off the main track). After lunch at the rock, head through Dhaid to the drive through Wadi Asimah (p.44), which provides completely different scenery and driving – mountains, farms, plantations and villages where life hasn't changed in decades.

WEEKEND TRIPS

A trip to the Liwa Oasis (p.48) is truly unique and, unlike other trips, it can't really be combined with other routes.

With the length of the drive to Liwa, and the vast area of desert to explore once you get there, this route should really be planned over a few days, with at least two nights spent in the desert. A three-day stay would allow you to have a good explore of the Liwa oasis, and then head into the desert for at least two days of intense off-road driving.

If you can budget even more time to allow for long lunches and early camping stops, you will get the full benefit of the amazing surroundings. For most people, a trip to Liwa inspires further visits, so don't try cramming too much in – you'll be back.

| Route Name | Page | Total Distance (km) | Total Unpaved (km) | Terrain | | | Activity | | | | |
				Mtn	Desert	Wadi	Camp	Climb	Hike	Bike	Swim
Fossil Rock	p.26	39.9km	32.2km		✓		✓				
Wadi Bih	p.38	129.6km	101.6km	✓		✓	✓	✓	✓	✓	✓
Wadi Madbah	p.32	39.8km	17.1km	✓		✓	✓	✓	✓		✓
Wadi Asimah	p.44	27.7km	16km	✓		✓	✓		✓		
Liwa Oasis	p.48	252km	150km		✓		✓				

FOSSIL ROCK

A MERE 20 MINUTE DRIVE FROM DUBAI, THIS ENJOYABLE TRIP IS GREAT FOR BOTH BEGINNERS AND EXPERTS ALIKE.

ROUTE INFO

DIFFICULTY RATING	★☆☆☆☆ Easy, tricky at the end
TERRAIN	Desert, rocky outcrops
SUITABLE FOR	Camping, dune driving, fossil hunting, picnics
ALSO KNOWN AS	Jebel Maleihah, Jebel Mileihah

DISTANCES		
	From Dubai to start of route	31km
	Route	8km (paved), 37km (unpaved)
	End of route to Dubai	67.5km
	From Abu Dhabi	Add 300km for the round trip

Officially called Jebel Maleihah, this large outcrop is more widely known as Fossil Rock, after the marine fossils that can be found on its slopes. This is the closest route to Dubai, and a great desert drive for beginners or experts alike. In fact, due to its close proximity to the emirate, the trip can be completed by Dubai residents in just half a day.

Initially heading along a sandy track from Al Awir via camel farms and Wadi Faya, it's an easy introduction to sand driving, which becomes as challenging as you want to make it when you get near Fossil Rock.

As the closest area to Dubai to get off-road, there are a number of places popular with people for a quick foray into the desert. You can follow the route just into the dunes, then branch off and explore the dunes on your own. Alternatively, carry straight along past the palace to the Military Base, where a track off the road to the right takes you up into some easy terrain to practice on with fun drops.

To head there, follow the Dubai-Hatta road. At 31km outside Dubai, just after the interchange with the E611 Dubai bypass, you will reach a smaller roundabout. Take a left (which is the second exit) into Al Awir.

Driving in Al Awir, take the right turn just before the prominent mosque, almost as if you are driving into the petrol station. Head past this and straight on past the shops. At the far corner of the large walled compound, turn right and follow the wall south. Keep going straight along the wall until the road turns into a track. It is here that you should start deflating your types.

After that, follow the track alongside the smaller compound, around the corner to the right (where it gets sandy), and then after 200m, head left up among the dunes in a southerly direction.

On the way to Fossil Rock, the track can get slightly boring (due to lack of scenery); therefore, to liven up this part of the drive, head up onto the ridges following alongside the track. Here you can pick a little more challenging route, while still staying in easy sight of the main track.

On clear days, you will be able to make out the distinctive V-cut shape of Fossil Rock in front of you – bear this in mind if you get lost along the way!

TAKE CARE

The sand quarry here has dangerously steep slopes; don't mistake them for dunes and try to drive down them! Check your route in this area well ahead before tackling anything big, and aim to steer clear of the quarry.

If you do happen to stray from the main track, you can follow any one of the many tracks heading in the same direction to reach it.

As you approach Fossil Rock, the driving starts to get a little more difficult, weaving through the dunes, and the steep and bumpy track up to the base of the rock is quite challenging, but offers splendid views over the desert if you get there.

INITIALLY HEADING ALONG A TRACK FROM AL AWIR, IT IS AN EASY INTRODUCTION TO SAND DRIVING, WHICH BECOMES AS CHALLENGING AS YOU WANT TO MAKE IT WHEN YOU GET NEAR FOSSIL ROCK.

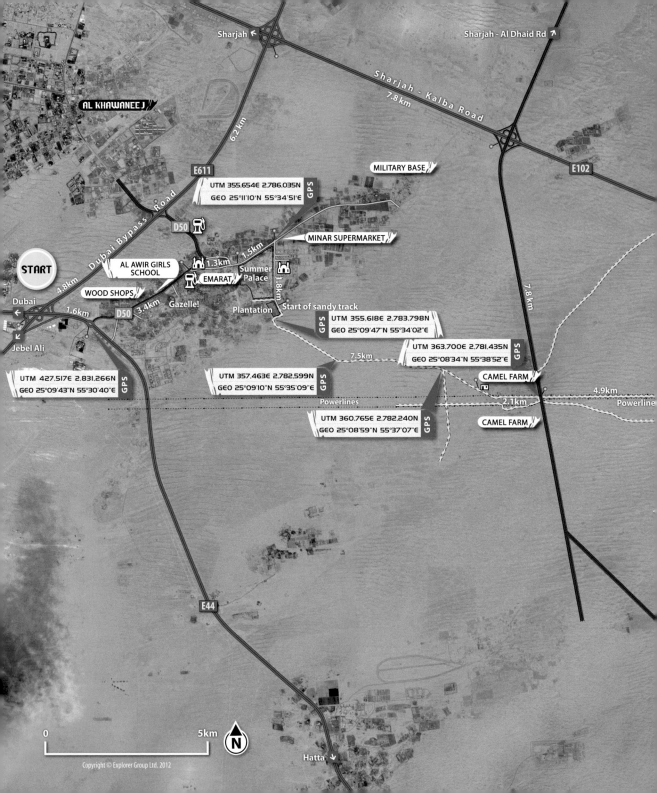

Sharjah ←

Sharjah - Al Dhaid Rd ↗

Sharjah - Kalba Road

7.8 km

AL KHAWANEEJ ↗

E611

E102

6.2 km

UTM 355,654E 2,786,035N
GEO 25°11'10"N 55°34'51"E

GPS

MILITARY BASE ↗

D50

MINAR SUPERMARKET ↗

START

AL AWIR GIRLS SCHOOL

1.3km

1.5km

Summer Palace

1.8km

Dubai Bypass Road

4.8 km

EMARAT

Dubai ←

1.6 km

WOOD SHOPS

D50

3.4 km

Gazelle!

Plantation

Start of sandy track

UTM 355,618E 2,783,798N
GEO 25°09'47"N 55°34'02"E

GPS

Jebel Ali ←

UTM 363,700E 2,781,435N
GEO 25°08'34"N 55°38'52"E

GPS

7.5 km

UTM 427,517E 2,831,266N
GEO 25°09'43"N 55°30'40"E

GPS

UTM 357,463E 2,782,599N
GEO 25°09'10"N 55°35'09"E

GPS

CAMEL FARM ↗

4.9km

2.1km

Powerlines

Powerlines

UTM 360,765E 2,782,240N
GEO 25°08'59"N 55°37'07"E

GPS

CAMEL FARM ↗

7.8 km

E44

0   5km

N

Hatta ↓

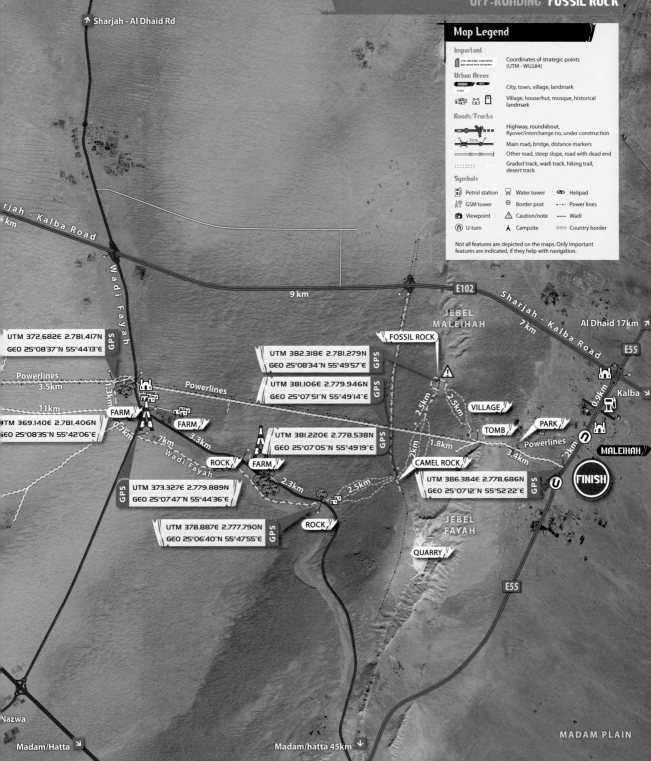

↑ Sharjah - Al Dhaid Rd

rjah - Kalba Road

Wadi Fayah

9 km

E102

JEBEL MALEIHAH

Sharjah - Kalba Road

7 km

Al Dhaid 17km ↗

E55

Kalba

0.9km

MALEIHAH

Map Legend

Important

Coordinates of strategic points
(UTM - WGS84)

Urban Areas

City, town, village, landmark

Village, house/hut, mosque, historical
landmark

Roads/Tracks

Highway, roundabout,
flyover/interchange no, under construction

Main road, bridge, distance markers

Other road, steep slope, road with dead end

Graded track, wadi track, hiking trail,
desert track

Symbols

🚏 Petrol station   🚰 Water tower   👓 Helipad
📡 GSM tower   ⊙ Border post   ·-·-· Power lines
📷 Viewpoint   ⚠ Caution/note   ∿ Wadi
Ⓝ U-turn   ⚑ Campsite   ⌇ Country border

Not all features are depicted on the maps. Only important
features are indicated, if they help with navigation.

UTM 372.682E 2.781.417N
GEO 25°08'37"N 55°44'13"E

Powerlines
3.5km

11km

TM 369.140E 2.781.406N
GEO 25°08'35"N 55°42'06"E

1.3km

Powerlines

FARM

0.7km

FARM

3.3km

7km

Wadi Fayah

ROCK

GPS

UTM 373.327E 2.779.889N
GEO 25°07'47"N 55°44'36"E

FARM

2.3km

UTM 378.887E 2.777.790N
GEO 25°06'40"N 55°47'55"E

GPS

ROCK

2.5km

FOSSIL ROCK

UTM 382.318E 2.781.279N
GEO 25°08'34"N 55°49'57"E

GPS

UTM 381.106E 2.779.946N
GEO 25°07'51"N 55°49'14"E

⚠

2.5km   2.5km

VILLAGE

TOMB

PARK

UTM 381.220E 2.778.538N
GEO 25°07'05"N 55°49'19"E

GPS

2km   1.8km

Powerlines

3.4km

2km

CAMEL ROCK

UTM 386.384E 2.778.686N
GEO 25°07'12"N 55°52'22"E

GPS

Ⓝ

Ⓤ

FINISH

JEBEL FAYAH

QUARRY

E55

Nazwa

Madam/Hatta

Madam/hatta 45km

MADAM PLAIN

AL AWIR

Al Awir is a small but fertile oasis town, and just the drive along the main road on this route shows how much ground water there is, with the huge amount of established plants and trees. Look a little harder and you'll find many things of interest.

Halfway along the road from the roundabout, on the right hand side, is an estate that is home to many gazelle and deer. You can also often see horses in paddocks beside the road, while there are stables on the sandy tracks weaving through the farms, and you can sometimes see the horses out on training runs on or close to this route.

The large walled compound you drive around just before getting to the desert is the summer house of the Maktoum family, where they traditionally escaped from the high summer temperatures for less humidity and slightly cooler nights inland. You'll only catch a glimpse inside the gates, but there's a truly royal amount of greenery and landscaping, and a huge lake.

WILDLIFE

The dunes between Al Awir and Fossil Rock are full of a broom-like bush, and you'll see no end of tracks in the desert made by insects, reptiles and mammals.

Look for those made by beetles, such as the Unicorn Beetle, while animals you should look out for are the Cape Hare and the Yellow-spotted Sand Lizard (recognised by the elliptical shaped cream spots on its flanks). If you're lucky, you may see a blue-headed agame.

FOSSIL ROCK

This area is rich with the fossils of shells and small sea creatures that were on the ocean floor millions of years ago when water covered much of Arabia. It's great fun to explore and search for the fossils, which are quite easy to find.

The presence of iron oxide gives the sand in this area a lovely rich, orange-red colour. The dunes around Fossil Rock are especially spectacular in the late afternoon and at sunset. If you have the revs and skill, the track continues up the back of Fossil Rock, and then down a steep rocky section and a 200-metre sand slope to the base.

DO NOT DISTURB...

When off-roading, do not disturb the natural habitat of animals. Avoid driving over rocks or stones that could be home to many creatures. The same goes for camping. Most creatures found on this route tend to be harmless, and won't bother you if you don't bother them.

OFF-ROAD TUTORIAL

The key to driving on sand is maintaining controlled momentum by using higher than normal revs. Make sure that you are in 4WD mode and stick to the lower gears (not low range yet). Selecting the correct gear and engine revs will come with experience, but try not to over or under accelerate when tackling soft sand. The more you practise, the more you'll be able to anticipate where your vehicle is going to struggle, and change down a gear before you hit the tricky patches. It is all too easy to grind to a halt in sand, so practise flipping the clutch down and changing gear with lightening speed.

Sand driving should be seen as 'surfing' the dunes, not ploughing through them. Look at the shape and form of the dune. It is usually better to travel with the direction of the dunes (the direction of the wind). But be careful, because while you may find it easy going with the flow on the way up, it gets a bit tricky if you find yourself going back against it once you have turned around.

Existing tracks normally define the best route to take. If there are no tracks, plan a route that seems the easiest and limits damage to flora and fauna. You should only be using the accelerator, and barely touching the brakes or clutch. The general aim is to pick up enough momentum going down to allow you to coast over the top of the next dune smoothly.

The sand's consistency changes during the day and also seasonally. When it is very hot, dry conditions render the surface soft and loose. Blowing sand collects in hidden hollows and can catch out an unwary driver.

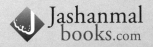

WADI MADBAH

A SIMPLE DRIVE INTO THE MOUNTAINS, WITH POOLS AND WATERFALLS, THIS IS A PLEASANT ROUTE IN AL AIN.

This route makes for a lovely beginner adventure or family trip into a relatively unspoilt area, and the tracks off both sides of the road leading to Madbah provide short routes to points of interest, such as the small village of Madbah. Most distinctively, there are pools here that have water in all year round, and this is also where you'll find the UAE's highest waterfall – Victoria Falls it may not be, but the interestingly coloured stream and pools on the way in make it a very picturesque place to explore and discover.

One of the real advantages of this route is that all the main attractions are easily accessible, which makes it great for families with younger children. It's just a short stroll up the wadi to the first pool and just around the next corner is where you'll find the main pool and a waterfall.

There is a great walk around to the top of the cliff above the falls, where you'll find a fantastic view and even more pools that are worth discovering but, if the kids' legs are getting tired, you can actually drive up too.

Although nowhere near as bad as the more visited sites, like Wadi Wurrayah and Hatta Pools, litter is starting to become

more of an issue, and you should also bear in mind that the water levels in the pools can drop after long spells with no rain.

However, from Madbah it is possible to explore further into the mountains, finding even more remote streams and pools, and, on the other side of the road, a track takes you through a cutting to a large basin completely surrounded by mountains, known to the UAE's climbing community as Wonderwall.

WONDERWALL

As you drive through the cutting in the rocks into a bowl entirely encircled by mountains, it appears as if a whole new world lies before you.

Admire the strange rock formations to the left, while the mountains in front of you are particularly picturesque. Along this face, called Wonderwall, there is some reasonable rock climbing, but the sandy area at the base of the mountains also makes a comfortable spot to picnic or camp.

There are also opportunities for general scrambling and exploring, so be sure to leave plenty of time for these activities, as you will be spoiled for choice with what to do.

TRIP INFO

DIFFICULTY RATING	★★★☆☆ Driving is short, but sometimes rough
TERRAIN	Mountains, wadis
SUITABLE FOR	Camping, hiking, rock climbing, swimming

DISTANCES		
	Dubai to start of route	160km
	Route	22.7km (paved), 17.1km (unpaved)
	End of route to Dubai	160km
	From Abu Dhabi	175km

IRAN

Khasab
MUSANDAM
(OMAN)

Ras Al Khaimah
UAQ

DUBAI   Fujairah

ABU DHABI
UAE   Sohar

Al Ain   Wadi Madbah

OMAN

N

ALL ALONG
THIS ROUTE,
THERE ARE
POSSIBILITIES
FOR WALKING,
MOUNTAIN
BIKING, PICNICS
AND WADI
EXPLORATION.

Map Legend

Important

S UTM 399,832E 2,810,950N
GEO 26°04'43"N 55°52'43"E
Coordinates of strategic points
(UTM - WGS84)

Urban Areas

DUBAI | ISA
City, town, village, landmark

FORT

Village, house/hut, mosque, historical
landmark

Roads/Tracks

E66 Highway, roundabout,
flyover/interchange no, under construction

7km Main road, bridge, distance markers

Other road, steep slope, road with dead end

Graded track, wadi track, hiking trail,
desert track

Symbols

⛽ Petrol station   🏢 Water tower   🚁 Helipad

📡 GSM tower   ⊙ Border post   ••• Power lines

📷 Viewpoint   ⚠ Caution/note   ～ Wadi

↻ U-turn   ⛺ Campsite   ～ Country border

Not all features are depicted on the maps. Only important
features are indicated, if they help with navigation.

QUARRY

GPS UTM 400,125E 2,675,038N
GEO 24°05'37"N 56°01'03"E

← 2.3km

**Al Ain/Buraimi 27km
V-cutting 8.2km**

Truck Road

1.3km

4.3km

START

QUARRY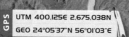

1.3km

1.3km

Truck Road

GPS UTM 401,620E 2,670,487N
GEO 24°08'37"N 56°11'54"E

QUARRY

0   2km

N

WADI & WATERFALL

Park the car and wander up the wadi, and you'll come across numerous small pools and rivulets. There is even a falaj-like canal carved out of the bedrock, which effectively channels the water down the wide riverbed. It's an attractive view from here back down the valley. The first big pool and its waterfall are reached after 200m. The easiest way around the pool is to scramble up and over the rocks on the right. Continue up the dry and stony riverbed for an even bigger surprise – a large, deep pool and an impressive waterfall (by UAE standards). It's worth the scramble

to take a refreshing dip and splash around under the falls with the toads, or just to bask in the sun with your feet in the pool being nibbled by the little fish.

PLATEAU

Prepare yourself for a breathtaking view from the plateau overlooking the waterfall – from here, you can peer over the edge of the wadi, with the river and pools surprisingly far below, but do watch out for loose ground when approaching the edge. This large, flat area is ideal for camping, as long as you don't have wandering toddlers or sleepwalkers in your group!

POOLS

Where the track ends at the 'mini roundabout', there is a path going down into the wadi. It's a quick and easy walk down and at the bottom there is a stream running through the narrow wadi with several pools, some deep enough to swim in. There's scope for further exploration downstream, towards the top of the waterfall, where you'll find bigger pools and sections where you'll need to climb up or down (the shady side of the wadi has some climbing routes with holes drilled, but currently no bolts in place). Watch out for the hot rocks if you're climbing in summer. Upstream, the stream fades away, sinking underground as the wadi bed gradually rises to the head of the valley.

FURTHER OFF ROAD

For an alternative, quieter area to explore and camp, head south through Madbah village towards the wide gap in the mountains. The track winds across a gravelly plateau and a small wadi. There's not much shade, but there are some small clean pools in canyons cut into the rock, and plenty of peace and quiet for remote mountain camping. Previously, it was possible to keep on going south on a poorly maintained track in and out of the wadi, through the gap in the mountains, and then left onto the graded track heading east up Wadi Ajran in Oman; however, with the tightening of the border between the UAE and Oman, this track is now blocked off.

TAKE ONLY PHOTOGRAPHS, LEAVE ONLY FOOTPRINTS

Although both the UAE and Oman governments are taking strides in cleaning up and protecting some of the countries' areas of outstanding beauty, many of the most popular sites still see a lot of rubbish and a large amount of graffiti. Make sure you're not part of the problem. 'Leave it cleaner than you found it' is a great rule for all explorers to live by.

WADI BIH

THIS ROUTE CONSISTS OF TWO WADIS, WADI BIH AND WADI KHAB AL SHAMIS, WHICH BOTH HAVE A DISTINCT FEEL.

TRIP INFO

DIFFICULTY RATING	★★☆☆☆ 2WD possible
TERRAIN	Coastal, mountains, wadis
SUITABLE FOR	Camping, climbing, mountain biking, hiking
ALSO KNOWN AS	Wadi Beh/Byh, Wadi Khab Al Shamis, Wadi Khab Shamsi

DISTANCES		
	Dubai to start of route	147km
	Route	27.4km (paved), 101.2km (unpaved)
	End of route to Dubai	147km
	From Abu Dhabi	Add 300km for the round trip

Cutting and twisting through and over the mountains of the east coast near Dibba into the central section of Musandam, this route offers some of the most dramatic yet accessible mountain scenery in the country.

Unfortunately, in 2008, the UAE border post in Wadi Bih was closed to all expatriates for unreleased reasons. While this has shut off the way in and out from the RAK side, it is still possible to access the entire off-road part of the route from the Dibba side. As you now have to backtrack out the way you go in, this may restrict the distance you drive in before turning around. But if you allow a weekend for the trip, you will be able to see and do everything.

At the Dolphin roundabout, take the second exit left towards Dibba, and once you reach the Fort roundabout, take the second exit, heading straight across. Just after the mini roundabout, drive through the UAE Border Post and head straight. Make sure you bring your passport in case your papers need to be checked.

From Dibba, the road ascends through a narrow, twisting gorge called Wadi Khab Al Shamis. The carved, smooth faces of the rock provide welcome shade, accompanied by a surprising amount of greenery, which gives this wadi a different, refreshing feel compared with the stony sparseness of Wadi Bih on the west side.

After a steady climb up through the wadi, the road then gets a lot steeper for the final ascent to the summit, which is at almost 1,000 metres and where you will find some of the most beautiful views in the country, along with some great places to camp.

The track down to Wadi Bih is a lot more open, with the views stretching out over the mountain tops in all directions, including central Musandam to the north. The descent is quite lengthy, with the good quality, graded track dropping around 700 metres in just over seven kilometres – a blast on a mountain bike.

Climbers and hikers will find an awful lot to do in this area as it has really become one of the region's adventure sport hotspots, yet it is also a nice place to camp in amongst the silence of the sheer cliffs, especially now there is a lot less traffic passing through the wadis from coast to coast.

HIKERS WILL FIND A LOT TO DO IN WADI BIH. IT IS ALSO A NICE PLACE TO CAMP IN AMONGST THE SILENCE OF THE CLIFFS.

OMANI CHECKPOINT

Where the track drops down into Wadi Bih, you will come to the Oman border checkpoint. Previously, you could pass through, turn left and head west into the wadi as border guards waved you through or quickly checked documents. However, it is now required that you have your passport with you in order to pass through border post 3 (please refer to the map on the next page).

As always in this part of the world, however, the rules could change without notice.

WARNING

Cars have been the object of some 'curiosity' in this area, so it is best to park out of sight of the main village (but in open view of the road for security purposes).

In order to avoid security problems, the best option is to take your valuables with you on your hike. Also, do not forget to lower your radio aerial (if you have one), and make sure you lock all doors at all times.

UAE

Jebel Qihwi
▲
1,792m

UTM 420,716E 2,847,515N
GEO 25°44'36"N 56°12'34"E
GPS

PARK
DAM
1.4km

UTM 425,386E 2,837,010N
GEO 25°38'56"N 56°15'23"E
GPS

1.3km

3.3km

DABA HOSPITAL

QUROON A' SAYD

EAST COAST HIKE

Masafi 40km

BORDER POST 1

1.5km

PARK

1.8km

1.7km

4.3km

Wadi Khab Al Shamis

E89

UTM 427,517E 2,831,266N
GEO 25°35'49"N 56°16'41"E
GPS

DABA

GLOBE R/A

ABSOLUTE ADVENTURE

ZIGHY

DIBBA

PORT

START

PORT

BORDER POST 2

PORT

GOLDEN TULIP RESORT

SIX SENSES ZIGHY BAY

GULF OF OMAN

KARSHA

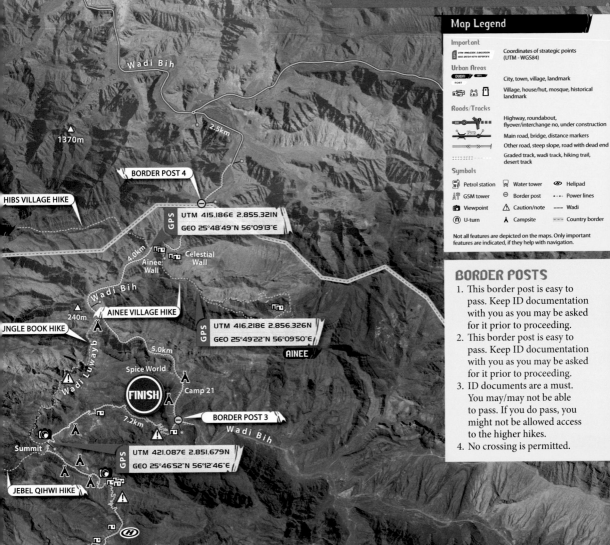

Map Legend

Important

Coordinates of strategic points (UTM - WGS84)

Urban Areas

City, town, village, landmark

Village, house/hut, mosque, historical landmark

Roads/Tracks

Highway, roundabout, flyover/interchange no, under construction

Main road, bridge, distance markers

Other road, steep slope, road with dead end

Graded track, wadi track, hiking trail, desert track

Symbols

Petrol station	Water tower	Helipad
GSM tower	Border post	Power lines
Viewpoint	Caution/note	Wadi
U-turn	Campsite	Country border

Not all features are depicted on the maps. Only important features are indicated, if they help with navigation.

BORDER POSTS

1. This border post is easy to pass. Keep ID documentation with you as you may be asked for it prior to proceeding.
2. This border post is easy to pass. Keep ID documentation with you as you may be asked for it prior to proceeding.
3. ID documents are a must. You may/may not be able to pass. If you do pass, you might not be allowed access to the higher hikes.
4. No crossing is permitted.

Wadi Bih

2.5km

1370m

BORDER POST 4

HIBS VILLAGE HIKE

GPS UTM 415.186E 2.855.32IN
GEO 25°48'49"N 56°09'13"E

4.0km

Ainee Wall

Celestial Wall

Wadi Bih

AINEE VILLAGE HIKE

240m

JNGLE BOOK HIKE

GPS UTM 416.218E 2.856.326N
GEO 25°49'22"N 56°09'50"E

AINEE

5.0km

Wadi Luwayb

Spice World

FINISH

Camp 21

7.2km

BORDER POST 3

Wadi Bih

Summit

GPS UTM 421.087E 2.851.679N
GEO 25°46'52"N 56°12'46"E

JEBEL QIHWI HIKE

26.8km

OMAN

GPS UTM 426.419E 2.850.000N
GEO 25°45'58"N 56°15'58"E

QUICK HIKE TO PLATEAU

0   5km

DIBBA BEACH

One of the most popular beaches on the east coast of the UAE, this is a great place for a relaxing dip in the ocean and quiet seaside picnic to take on some sustenance before heading up into the mountains.

DHOW CHARTERS

As Dibba is a fishing village with two ports, it's easy to hire a dhow or speedboat to take you along the coast towards the Musandam.

SIX SENSES ZIGHY BAY

Located over the steep mountains in a lovely, secluded bay, the Six Senses Hideaway offers an exclusive getaway with poolside villas, its own spa and a range of dining options, including a restaurant set on top of the hills overlooking the bay.

EAST COAST HIKE

For a hike on the east side of the country, from the village in the bottom of Wadi Khab Al Shamis, just north of the Zighy turnoff, a trail takes you up to a plateau which is home to the locals' summer houses and some amazing views down over the east coast and Dibba. It is best to park your cars just south of the trailhead, to the northern edge of the houses, then look

for the beginning of the track on which to start your ascent up the steep, rocky hillside. The route can be difficult to find, but get into the spirit of exploring and blaze your own trail – for the first part of the hike, just gaining height is the aim.

Then when you reach the top, you can take as much time as you want walking on the gently sloping plateau to the highest point, or admiring the views from the edge. Allow yourself enough daylight to make the return trip, as the descent is quite tricky.

QUICK HIKE TO PLATEAU

This is a good introductory hike, as the vast majority of it is across flat terrain and following a clearly marked track. Don't be dissuaded by the steep ascent at the start, as this only lasts for 25 minutes before flattening out. The hike shouldn't take more than five hours in mid-May, allowing for numerous stops. However, it could be done a lot quicker in cooler weather. See p.89 for a more detailed rundown on this hike and others in the area.

TERRACED FIELDS

The houses and terraced fields in this area of the mountains date from the 13th and 14th centuries and were built

AS DIBBA IS A FISHING VILLAGE WITH TWO PORTS, IT'S EASY TO HIRE A DHOW TO TAKE YOU ALONG THE COAST TOWARDS THE MUSANDAM.

during the Julfar period (1200 –1600). Julfar was a successful trading town located north of Ras Al Khaimah.

JEBEL QIHWI HIKE

From the high point of the track you can see Jebel Qihwi, clearly visible as twin peaks in a south-westerly direction. A straightforward hike to the summit takes about three hours each way. See p.43 for more on this hike.

CAMPING

Once at the top, in the dip between the two peaks, you'll find the remains of one of many old farming villages. Terraced fields frame scattered ruins of small stone dwellings – look for petroglyphs on the walls of some of these.

As with camping anywhere in the UAE, if a settlement still looks inhabited, or the fields look as if they are still used for crops or animals, the farmers (and the goats) would appreciate it if you find somewhere else to camp. However, this particular area is a pretty safe bet, and a popular place at the weekends.

MOUNTAIN BIKING

If you want to test yourself on one of the UAE's toughest climbs, the track from Wadi Bih up to the summit is a great and challenging climb, with a fast descent the reward. Leave your car at the top (a good, cool place for camping if you're staying overnight) and do the downhill first to get the blood racing; then you have no choice but to turn around and head back up the climb.

SUMMIT CLIMB

If you can talk your way through the Oman border checkpoint, another great biking route heads into Musandam on Wadi Bih, then climbs up to the summit beneath Jebel As Sayh (2087m). It is one of the toughest challenges you'll experience in the UAE, gaining over 1,500 metres of vertical height in 25 kilometres.

BRANDT'S HEDGEHOG

This is prime real estate for the very cute Brandt's hedgehog. They are nocturnal animals, so watch out for them on the roads when driving here after sundown.

WEST COAST HIKES

If you choose instead to enter this route from the Ras Al Khaimah side on the west coast (remember, you can no longer access the full coast-to-coast route) you'll be rewarded with a couple of nice hikes in the form of the Hibs Village hike and the Ainee Village hike.

Hibs Village is a great trek to a deserted village high up above Wadi Bih. The Ainee Village hike is a relatively straightforward loop following a well-established path (once out of the wadi), taking you initially along the wadi floor, then up and out of the wadi, before winding your way up to a deserted village of about 30 houses nestled at the base of the cliffs.

GRAB A DIBBA DHOW

Jumping on a dhow trip from Dibba is one of the great Middle East experiences. There are a couple of excellent operators (see p.238 & p.246 for more on boat trips and p.182 for details of tour operators) that do single or multi-day cruises up along the dramatic and spectacular coastline on the Musandam. Some provide scuba stops, while others are focused more on snorkelling and soaking up the sun on deck, with food and drinks served up.

WADI ASIMAH

THIS ROUTE TAKES IN SECLUDED VILLAGES, SMALL POOLS, QUIET STROLLS AND PLENTIFUL GREENERY.

TRIP INFO

DIFFICULTY RATING	★★★☆☆ A little tricky in parts
TERRAIN	Wadi, oasis
WATER	Pools, streams
SUITABLE FOR	Camping, hiking
ALSO KNOWN AS	Assimah, Asymah, Wadi Mawrid

DISTANCES		
	Dubai to start of route	107km
	Route	11.7 (paved), 16km (unpaved)
	End of route to Dubai	119km
	From Abu Dhabi	Add 300km for the round trip

For many years, this was actually part of the main route from the east coast to the west, continuing on through Wadi Tayyibah.

The highlights of this trip include some wonderful opportunities for camping near Al Ghail and a lovely short walk down Wadi Al Fara with its stream, seasonal pools and waterfall.

Further along, Wadi Al Mawrid has some slightly more challenging driving through lush oasis scenery, with an old falaj (irrigation system) built into the wadi walls. Even the village of Asimah is quaint and picturesque. This is a truly historic, if a little bumpy, trip down memory lane.

CAMPING

Rather unusually, this attractive area features sand dunes directly between stark rocky outcrops. It is an ideal place to stop for a photo, a picnic or just a break from driving, and peaceful spots are easy to find just a short distance from the road – head into the desert at any point you fancy, but keep away from people's property.

Further into the dunes there are plenty of places suitable for camping, good for the day before or the evening after driving this route.

DIVERSION

From the hilltop graveyard, a small winding track takes you five minutes down the wadi to where you have to leave your car and explore on foot (depending on the time of year, you may have to stop earlier due to the condition of the track).

In the wet season, the stream spills over the rocks and suckerfish wriggle their way up under a waterfall. Follow the stream past palm trees and greenery and enjoy a swim or some bouldering (climbing) above the small quiet pools.

OASIS

Full of greenery, the length of the stream, this hidden wadi is a true oasis.

The old falaj, which supplies the small palm groves and cultivated areas with water, is cut into the side of the wadi and often hidden behind vegetation.

As the track weaves its way through the wadi, you will pass several dams which catch water during the rainy season.

NAVIGATION

Keep following the meandering Wadi Al Mawrid, sticking to the main track in the wadi, and you can drive all the way to Asimah. The minor tracks that branch off to the sides all end at small villages, single houses, or farms and plantations.

In some places, the track traverses rocky slabs, but stick with it and you'll get there.

ASIMAH

The village of Asimah is strikingly pleasant, clean and peaceful. There is still a very laid-back way of life evident here.

Friendly children run around the street and wave as you pass by, while in the afternoons, people sit in shady courtyards or just outside their gates under the trees, chatting and generally relaxing in the slow pace of village life. Absolutely beautiful.

On this route, the driving gets a little interesting in a couple of places as the track meanders between falaj, dams and plantations. It's fun but requires concentration and a few skills.

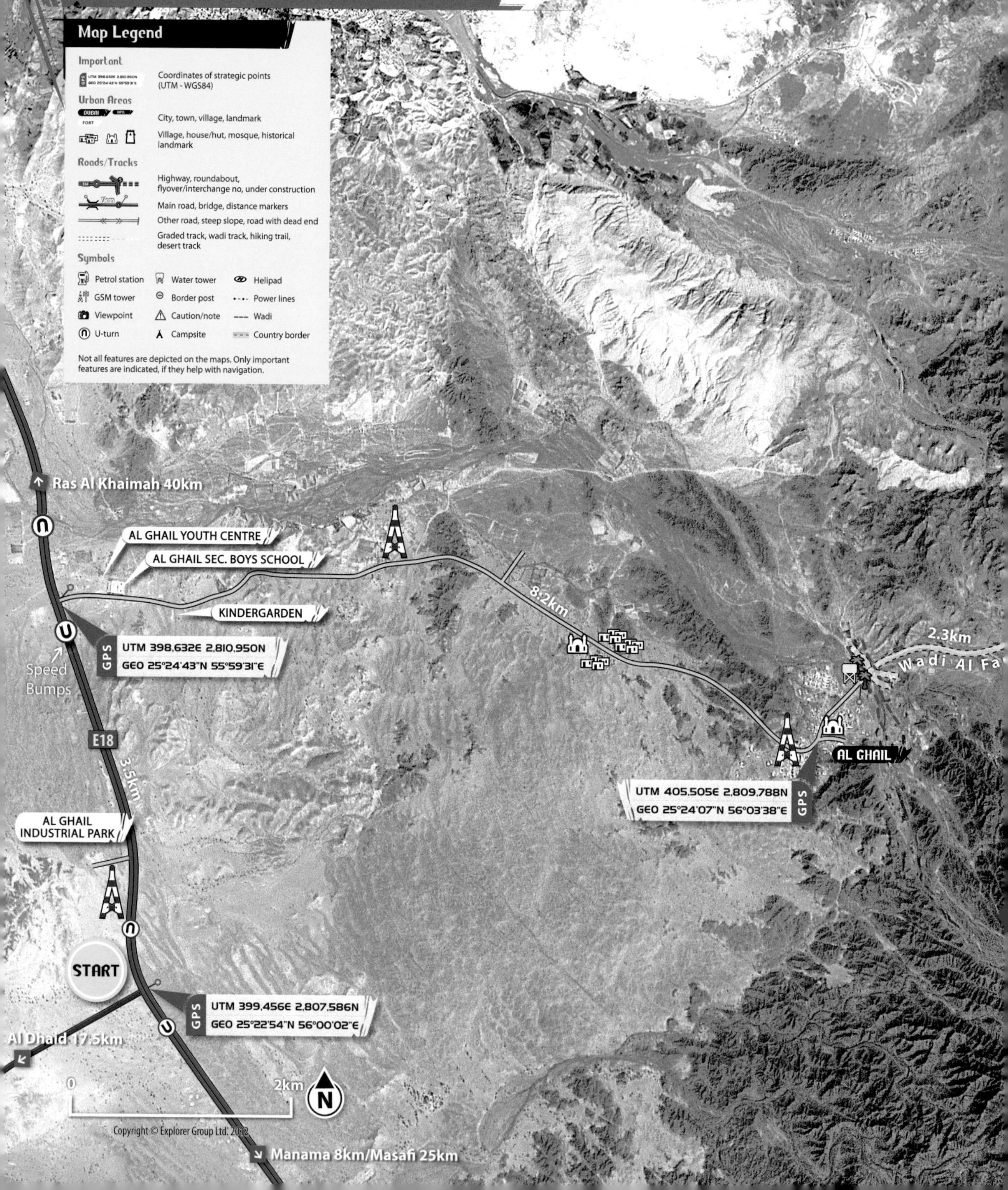

Map Legend

Important

UTM 398.632N 2.810.950N
GEO 25°24'43"N 55°59'31"E

Coordinates of strategic points
(UTM - WGS84)

Urban Areas

DUBAI | town — City, town, village, landmark

FORT

Village, house/hut, mosque, historical
landmark

Roads/Tracks

7mm — Highway, roundabout,
flyover/interchange no, under construction

Main road, bridge, distance markers

Other road, steep slope, road with dead end

Graded track, wadi track, hiking trail,
desert track

Symbols

Petrol station | Water tower | Helipad
GSM tower | Border post | Power lines
Viewpoint | Caution/note | Wadi
U-turn | Campsite | Country border

Not all features are depicted on the maps. Only important
features are indicated, if they help with navigation.

↑ Ras Al Khaimah 40km

AL GHAIL YOUTH CENTRE
AL GHAIL SEC. BOYS SCHOOL
KINDERGARDEN

8.2km

2.3km

Wadi Al Fa

GPS UTM 398.632E 2.810.950N
GEO 25°24'43"N 55°59'31"E

Speed
Bumps

E18

3.5km

AL GHAIL
INDUSTRIAL PARK

AL GHAIL

GPS UTM 405.505E 2.809.788N
GEO 25°24'07"N 56°03'38"E

START

Al Dhaid 17.5km

GPS UTM 399.456E 2.807.586N
GEO 25°22'54"N 56°00'02"E

0 | 2km | N

↓ Manama 8km/Masafi 25km

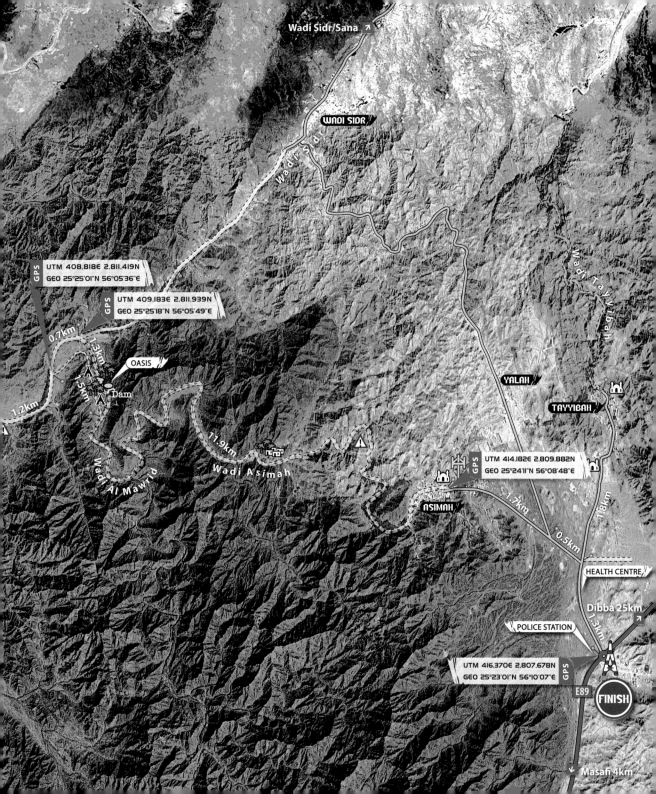

Wadi Sidr/Sana ↗

WADI SIDR

Wadi Sidr

Wadi Tayyibah

GPS **UTM 408,818E 2,811,419N**
GEO 25°25'01"N 56°05'36"E

GPS **UTM 409,183E 2,811,939N**
GEO 25°25'18"N 56°05'49"E

0.7km

1.3km

OASIS

1.5km

Dam

1.2km

YALAH

TAYYIBAH

Wadi Al Mawrid

Wadi Asimah

11.9km

GPS **UTM 414,182E 2,809,882N**
GEO 25°24'11"N 56°08'48"E

1.7km

ASIMAH

0.5km

1.8km

HEALTH CENTRE

Dibba 25km

1.3km

POLICE STATION

GPS **UTM 416,370E 2,807,678N**
GEO 25°23'01"N 56°10'07"E

E89

FINISH

↓ Masafi 4km

LIWA OASIS

A TRIP TO THE EMPTY QUARTER IS A MUST FOR ANY OFF-ROADER DURING THEIR TIME IN THE MIDDLE EAST.

TRIP INFO

DIFFICULTY RATING	★★★★☆ Varied, spectacular
TERRAIN	Desert, oasis, sabkha
SUITABLE FOR	Dune driving, sandboarding, camping, picnics
ALSO KNOWN AS	Empty Quarter, Rub al Khali

DISTANCES	Dubai to start of route	322km
	Route (Round trip)	8km (paved), Endless (unpaved)
	End of route to Dubai	395km

A trip to Liwa in the Empty Quarter (or Rub Al Khali) is a must for any off-roader during their time in the Middle East. It's the biggest sand desert on the planet, and the sheer scale of the scenery and the size of the dunes has to be seen to be believed. This epic route is more of an expedition than just a spot of dune-bashing, so go prepared for the experience of a lifetime.

Covering parts of Oman, Yemen, the southern UAE and almost all of southern Saudi Arabia, the Rub Al Khali was historically regarded as the edge of civilisation by people in the region. The Liwa area, on the edge of the Rub Al Khali, is one of the largest oases on the Arabian Peninsula. Home to the Bani Yas tribe, ancestors of the current ruling family of Abu Dhabi, the fertile Liwa 'crescent' stretches over 150km and is dotted with small villages.

The main feature of this route is, of course, the desert, with its dramatic dunes rising more than 300m, but there are also several other attractions along the way, including a surprising amount of greenery, a fish farm and a number of palaces visible from the roadside. The majesty of the red and gold dunes and the scale of the vast desert scenery were vividly captured in the writings of adventurer Wilfred Thesiger.

Before exploring this region, it's worth getting your hands on a copy of Thesiger's *Arabian Sands* which can enhance your understanding and enjoyment of the area, and make you appreciate the harsh conditions and the fragility of life in the days before air-conditioned 4WDS. Just outside Mezaira'a, and along the crescent, are a few forts that have recently been renovated and are interesting to poke around in.

MEZAIRA·A

If you're heading into the desert, the shops and the petrol station at Mezaira'a will be your last chance to buy provisions and fuel, so it's important to stock up here. Extra jerry cans of petrol are essential and it's always better to take too much food and water than too little.

LIWA HOTEL

With a raised location giving spectacular views across the Rub Al Khali, the green oasis and the palace on the hilltop

opposite, Liwa Hotel is a good place to stay if you're not camping. It has good facilities, spacious rooms and green, landscaped grounds – in-keeping with Liwa's reputation as an oasis – with a nice pool.

LIWA RESTHOUSE

Liwa Resthouse is a little past its prime but its (mainly Arab) clientele includes visiting business travellers, government officials and families on holiday.

Accommodation and facilities are pretty basic, but it is clean and functional, and, for the cheapest alternative to camping, it might be worth a look.

CAMPING

An essential part of any Liwa adventure, camping in the desert is the most popular way to spend the night, and can be a truly unforgettable experience. This area provides some of the best desert views in the UAE.

MOREEB HILL

Moreeb Hill is a huge dune which tops out at nearly 300 metres, and is the site of several hill-climb races through the year as well as several stages of the UAE Desert Challenge.

The competition is hot and heavy, with a course record of just under 12 seconds, but the emphasis is on opening the event up for anyone. Spectators are a particularly important and welcome part of the whole event. Keep your eyes out for events.

FISH FARM

Perhaps the most unusual place to visit in the Liwa area is the fish farm near Khanur, with the water coming from underground sources. There are many pools and breeding tanks, with the types of fish farmed including tilapia, bulti and catfish. There are even some carp in the falaj feeding water into the larger pools, which aren't grown to eat. The farm was set up by a Liwa resident for personal use, but it now sells fish locally.

MORE DESERT

From umm hisin, at the
westernmost end of the crescent,
take the e15 towards ruwais to
experience even more desert.
Although not filled with the epic
dunes that characterise Liwa, this
immense area of sand stretches as
far as the eye can see, offering peace,
isolation and the rare absence of any
signs of man. It gives a true sense of
the impressive scale of the Rub Al
Khali, the world's largest sand
desert. just don't get lost.

QASR AL SARAB DESERT RESORT

Qasr Al Sarab offers five-star Arabian opulence near Hamim. It has 150 rooms, some villas and a tented village, as well as a sensational pool with a swim-up bar, and it also arranges all manner of desert excursions for guests. The spa, featuring hammam baths, sits amid a peaceful courtyard, fountains, plants and flowers.

To get to the fish farm, head towards Arada and take the right turn after the petrol station (GPS 39Q 2,555,483N 766,660E) onto the road signposted for Khanur. At the roundabout turn left, go straight at the next roundabout, then take the next left (GPS 39Q 2,557,390N 765,178E).

Just before the mosque and watchtower, turn left towards Al Id. After about three kilometres (GPS 39Q 2,555,176N 762,386E), by the small mosque, turn right onto the small road leading to a villa with a red roof, where you will immediately see the fish pools, and park up. For a tour of the farm and more information on the fish, ask for Ahmed in the buildings on the left – but it's best to know some Arabic to get the most out of his tour.

DUNE DRIVE

Once you're out here you can blaze your own trail, making your route as adventurous and exciting as you want. The epic Liwa dunes, between the areas of sabkha, provide fun and challenge enough for any level of dune-basher. Some are hard going, so straight lines may not be possible, but instead will need quite a lot of zig-zagging.

As a GPS is essential equipment for any Liwa desert trip, try working out GPS points from the map on the various areas of sabkha (using the UTM grid), and picking your own way through the desert from checkpoint to checkpoint. You can tackle as much, or as little, as you wish,

either heading across the dunes between sabkha flats, or staying in the sand and keeping high in the dunes all the way. You can change the route as you like, or get back to the road, at any point.

HAMIM TO AL AIN

For a completely different way back to civilisation, the track from Hamim to Al Ain is now tarmac all the way, heading east, then north, arriving near Jebel Hafeet. In the past, a certain amount of luck used to be needed to get past the border patrols but there should be no problems with access now.

FARMS

This is a good way to see the cultivation underway in the oasis. The tracks in between the fields lead into an area of dunes, which is great for a play around and some more dramatic views of the expansive desert.

EASY RIDERS

If you have elderly passengers or young children with you, or if you just prefer sedate over severe, the tracks across and around the salt flats provide easy routes through the dunes and plenty of spectacular desert views, without having to leave the horizontal – so no motion sickness. Just be careful when crossing the sabkha after rains, as the surface can look hard but can get dangerously soft and very difficult to get out of if your car gets stuck. If in doubt, keep to the edges where the ground should be firmest.

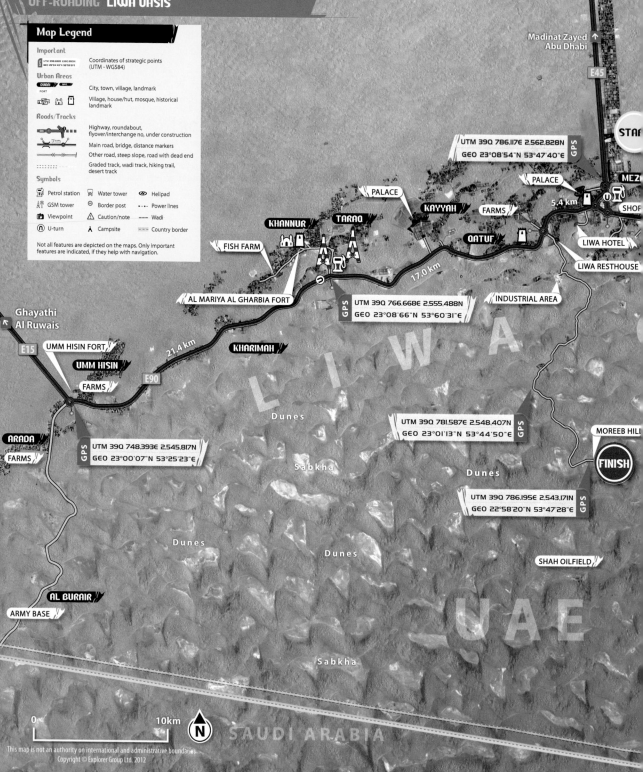

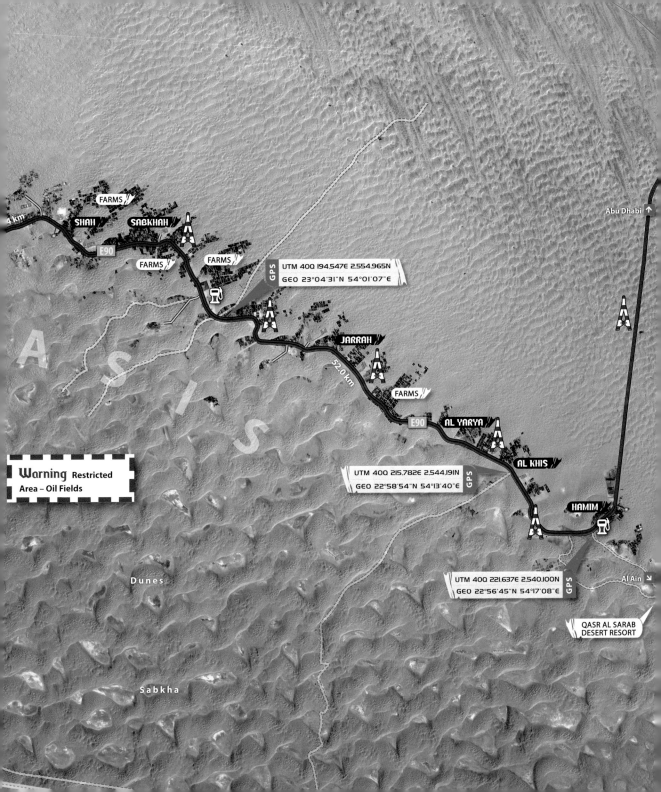

DESERT ACTIVITIES

FROM OFF-ROAD BIKING TO SANDBOARDING, YOU'LL NEVER RUN OUT OF HIGH-ENERGY ACTIVITIES TO DO IN THE DESERT.

Off-road sports and activities are exciting and enjoyable, and many of the off-road routes mentioned earlier on in this book will take you places not easily accessible in a 4WD.

Riding in desert sand is a lot different to riding on a conventional track, and it will take a while before you can 'read' the desert and become familiar with the reaction of your equipment or vehicle in various sand types. Your first experience of riding in the sand is a little scary as the sand grabs the tyres, which can feel very unstable, especially at low speeds. If you do come to a stop, be careful when pulling away as you could bog down, especially in soft sand.

Not all sand will give the same ride, but you will learn to know the difference between hard sand and soft, powdery sand, which is sometimes hard to spot and can be quite dangerous if you are not expecting it.

You'll be able to identify hard-packed sand by ridges or grooves on either side of the dunes. Another clue to the texture of the sand is the colour.

One of the most important rules to remember when riding in the desert is never to ride hell-for-leather over a dune without knowing what is on the other side. There may be something unexpected, like a sudden

drop, a quarry or a happy family enjoying a nice Friday picnic, and by the time you've shot over the top of the dune, there's little you can do about it.

If you don't like hospital food, dunes should always be approached by going up at an angle, so that you can check what lies ahead and choose your descent based on any obstacles in your path.

Another hazard to watch out for is 'camel grass' – these are hard mounds of sand with bunches of grass growing through them – and while they should be dodged by inexperienced riders they are good fun to jump over once mastered.

ESSENTIALS

The basic kit needed for off-road biking really varies on the safety needs of each rider and the amount of money they are prepared to spend to avoid a spell in hospital should concentration be lost.

However, the following items are highly recommended, and should be seen as necessary items for beginners: a good helmet, goggles, a chest protector (preferably with built-in elbow protection and back support), a CamelBak and a pair of boots.

DUNE BUGGYING

This activity offers a new dimension to off-road exploring. Each buggy is usually an 840cc single-seater, allowing you to set off on an adventure like no other.

If part of a group, your team leader/instructor should guide you around a natural trail of the dunes, picking up speed as your confidence increases.

Even though each dune buggy comes equipped with a full roll cage, bucket seats and a full safety harness, it is recommended that you start off slowly in areas that are not too tricky.

QUAD BIKING

A quad biking adventure makes for an excellent desert safari excursion in and around the UAE, and is popular with both children and adults.

It is especially exciting in the evening as the ride gets more challenging over and around the dunes.

There are plenty of operators that provide tours or quad bike hire. Turn to p.245 & p.248 for more information on where to go. And remember – make sure you listen to the instructions of the professionals accompanying you. Although fun, quads can be dangerous if misused.

QUAD BIKES AND SAFETY

The experts at POLARIS UAE offers their top tips on operating all-terrain vehicles (ATV) and staying safe in the region.

1. Never operate an ATV without wearing an approved helmet that fits well. Also wear eye protection, gloves, boots, long-sleeved shirt or jacket, and long pants.

2. Always inspect your ATV each time you use it to make sure it is in safe operating condition.

3. Always keep both hands on the handlebars and both feet on the footrests of the ATV during operation.

4. Allow greater distance for braking.

5. Always go slowly and be extra careful when operating on unfamiliar terrain. Always be alert to changing terrain conditions when operating the ATV.

6. Never operate at excessive speeds. Always travel at a speed which is proper for the terrain, visibility and operating conditions, and your experience.

7. Never operate on excessively rough, slippery or loose terrain.

8. Avoid operating the ATV in deep or fast flowing water. If you cannot avoid water which exceeds the recommended maximum depth, go slowly, balance your weight carefully, avoiding sudden movements, maintain a slow and steady forward motion, do not make sudden turns or stops, and do not make sudden throttle changes.

9. Wet brakes may reduce stopping ability. Test your brakes after leaving water. If necessary apply them lightly several times to let friction dry out the pads.

10. Never attempt wheelies, jumps or other stunts.

11. Always follow the inspection and maintenance procedures and schedules described in the manual.

12. Always use the size and type of tyres specified in your ATV's manual, and always maintain proper tyre pressure.

13. Never modify an ATV through improper installation or use of accessories.

14. Never exceed the stated load capacity for an ATV. Cargo should be properly distributed and securely attached. Reduce speed and follow instructions in the ATV manual when carrying cargo.

15. Always remove the ignition key when the vehicle is not in use to prevent unauthorised use or accidental starting.

IF YOU JUST CAN'T AGREE ON ONE DESERT ACTIVITY, JOINING UP WITH A DESERT TOUR IS GREAT FUN AND REPRESENTS REAL VALUE FOR MONEY.

ABU DHABI DESERT CHALLENGE

This professional level rally is an important fixture for top riders and drivers competing for the championship, but it is one of the only rallies in the world where amateurs are allowed to compete in the same event as the pros. However, not just anybody can do it: it is a gruelling challenge of 2,500km over some of the region's harshest terrain.

You'll need a lot of preparation and to put in some hard training just to complete the race, not to mention an experienced team of seconds and mechanics. The five-day event attracts participants from around the world, and is held in the last week in October. abudhabidesertchallenge.com.

SANDBOARDING

Sandboarding is a sport of its own and requires balance, strength and no small amount of tenacity. Once you climb your way to the top of the dune, it's best to wax the bottom of the board to reduce friction between the board and the sand. Strap your feet onto the board, bending your back knee slightly and slide on down, using your heels and toes to turn.

All major tour companies (p.245 & p.248) offer sandboarding experiences with instruction.

GET STARTED & GROUPS

If you'd like to try your hand at motocross, you can either try a tour (see below) or, alternatively, contact mx-academty.ae or head down to the Dubai Motocross Club near Jebel Ali Hotel – both provide courses and can advise you on bikes and gear. Alternatively, there are loads of motocross, dirt bike and quadding groups on Facebook, such as Dubai Motocross, UAE Professionals Club, Gulf Petrolheads and Oman Auto.

JUST GO FOR IT

If you just can't agree on one desert activity – or you're in search of a complete wilderness experience and want to try them all – joining up with a desert tour is great

Off-roading in Shuaib.

fun and represents real value for money. There are countless options when it comes to safaris, but, generally speaking, each tour follows a similar itinerary.

You'll be picked up from town in a 4WD and driven straight to a desert meeting point. You'll then travel in convoy deep into the desert. The professional drivers take pride in their skills, cranking up the music, while racing up and down sand dunes, flying over mountains and hitting angles that make the car almost topple over. After a

turbulent ride, drivers navigate their way to a prime spot in the desert to allow travellers time to savour a breathtaking Arabian sunset. Finally, it's a small journey on to the central camp in the heart of the desert, where everyone can relax, unwind and enjoy a sumptuous spread. While you're waiting for the shawarmas to cook, activities abound both outside and inside the Bedouin camp.

A list of tour operators can be found in the Directory (p.245 & p.248).

To discover more off-road routes and activities across the UAE and Oman, pick up a copy of explorer's *UAE Off-road* or *Oman Off-road*, out now in bookstores across the region. Alternatively, visit our e-shop at askexplorer.com.

THE PERFECT COMPANION ON EVERY ADVENTURE

Born in the USA, loved all over the world. Ever since George Stephen invented the game-changing kettle barbecues in 1952, Weber barbecues have been crafted with passion and precision in the heart of America. The same goes for Weber's range of portable charcoal and gas barbecues which are ideal for cooking delicious tasting food in the great outdoors. www.webergrill.ae

WEBER® SOLD ACROSS THE MIDDLE EAST

CAMPING

CAMPING

WHEN YOU'RE IN THE THICK OF THE CITY, IT'S EASY TO FORGET THAT JUST BEYOND THE SKYSCRAPERS LIES A VAST WILDERNESS WAITING TO BE EXPLORED.

Camping near Wadi Rayy

To really appreciate the surroundings that the UAE has to offer, you need to venture out and experience the natural wonders of the Arabian countryside for at least a night or two.

Choose from the huge expanses of the desert or the enchanting rocky mountains and breathtaking coastlines and get ready for an unforgettable experience. Throughout this section, we'll pick a few popular camping locations, give you a clear description of the general equipment you'll need, and where to get it from. If you're partial to a more luxurious outdoor experience, we've also got a few 'glamping' spots to make your stay in the wild a little bit more comfortable.

BE PREPARED

Warm temperatures and little rain means you can camp with less equipment and preparation than in most other countries. But, despite camping in the UAE and Oman being generally pretty safe, there are several safety aspects to consider before you venture off.

First of all, you need to make sure that the car you're taking is in very good condition before you leave, and that it is capable of tackling all the roads, tracks and dunes that you plan to drive on. Check the tyre pressure, fluid levels and ensure that you have tow ropes and shackles, a fire extinguisher, tyre pressure gauge, jack, shovel and a basic tool kit. Always have a fully charged mobile and let people know where you're planning to camp too.

EQUIPMENT

While the weather is rarely bad in the UAE, the ideal time for a camping trip is between October and April. During these winter months, it can get cold at night, so it is important to pack more rather than less, especially if you are in a 4WD and have no space issues.

Luckily, in the UAE there's a great selection of stores that offer a huge variety of camping equipment whatever your budget, including the usual sports stores and supermarkets such as Go Sports, Intersports and Carrefour, where you can find the essentials such as tents, chairs, sleeping bags and cool boxes at very affordable rates. Hardcore explorers should also try Jashanmal & Co, Decathlon, Picnico and Adventure HQ (see p.244 for a full directory of outdoor and sports stores) which stock niche items that expert campers might be in the market for, including Swiss army knives, fold-up tables, and larger tents.

CAMPING RULES

Generally speaking, there are no restrictions on where you can camp, with the exception of some private beaches, but obviously people's privacy and property need to be respected. While the people you encounter in the countryside are generally friendly, curious and helpful, this doesn't mean that they want you sleeping on their crops.

If you do end up camping near habitation, try to be considerate with the amount of noise and light you make. Should you be camping in the desert, remember that while it feels as if you're completely alone, chances are there are others looking for camping spots too. Don't pitch your tents directly at the base of dunes where oncoming off-roaders could plough over your camp. Shift a little further out.

For campfires, try to take firewood from a building site (do ask first) or rubbish tip beforehand. Sometimes, wood can be found in the wild, but never knock down a tree unless they are dead first – live trees don't burn well in any case. Alternatively, purchase some from roadside stalls (Dhs.5-10 a bundle). Remember that, while campfires are an essential addition to any camping trip, make sure that yours is properly maintained at all times (and properly buried when you leave) and keep in mind that small fires are easier to control, especially during windy conditions.

As the evening draws on, make sure everyone stays together or you at least know when people are heading off to answer the call of nature, and make sure you keep your shoes on at all times, or you might find yourself stepping on a few nasty creepy crawlies such as spiders, scorpions or snakes. If you do get stung by a scorpion or bitten by a snake, bandage the affected limb, do not apply ice, and seek medical attention.

EQUIPMENT CHECKLIST

- ☐ Tent (to avoid creepy crawlies, heavy dew, rare rain showers, wind and goats)
- ☐ Lightweight sleeping bag
- ☐ Air bed
- ☐ Torches and spare batteries
- ☐ Maps or a GPS system
- ☐ Cool box
- ☐ Water (for drinking and washing)
- ☐ Food and drink
- ☐ Camping stove, firewood or BBQ and charcoal
- ☐ Newspaper to light the fire
- ☐ Matches or lighters
- ☐ Insect repellent and antihistamine cream
- ☐ First aid kit (including any personal medication)
- ☐ Sun protection (hats, sunglasses, sun cream)
- ☐ Warm clothing for cooler evenings
- ☐ Toilet rolls
- ☐ Rubbish bags

BEACH TIME

THE UAE BOASTS SOME BEAUTIFUL COASTLINES THAT JET OFF INTO THE ARABIAN GULF AND THE GULF OF OMAN, MAKING FOR A NUMBER OF GORGEOUS CAMPING OPPORTUNITIES.

Snoopy Island off the coast of Fujairah

Close to the cities in Dubai and Abu Dhabi, it is generally forbidden to camp on the public beaches (or, at least, camping permits from local municipalities are required), but that isn't the case in most of the northern emirates or away from the urban centres.

FUJAIRAH

From the E88, take a left at the Masafi roundabout onto the E89 and this will lead you on to the main coastal road to Fujairah. Head straight at the Dolphin roundabout in Dibba and you'll start passing a set of coastal hotels before eventually reaching the booming tourist region of Al Aqah where the Fujairah Rotana Resort & Spa – Al Aqah Beach, Le Meridien Al Aqah Beach Resort and Sandy Beach Hotel & Resort are located. Pitching options around here are plentiful; park along the roadside and head towards the beaches on foot as the sand here is known to be pretty soft so you might get stuck.

DIBBA

The Hajars on the Musandam side, which rise to over 1,800m in places, are a wonderful backdrop to the village of Dibba (or Daba, as the Omanis call it). At the Dolphin Roundabout (mentioned above) take a left

and you'll reach the small border crossing into Oman, so don't forget to bring your passport. As you drive through, follow signs for the Golden Tulip Resort. This will lead you towards the end of the bay where there's a great sandy beach sheltered by mountains and a perfect spot to relax and camp at.

AL GHARBIA

About 140km west of Abu Dhabi, Mirfa is a small, quiet town located on the coast. While there are not a lot of attractions, the long stretch of beach is a kitesurfer's paradise and many choose to pitch tents here, especially during the popular Al Gharbia Watersports Festival which takes place in March each year.

GOOD FOR...

- People who don't own a 4WD. Most beaches are almost always easy to access from main roads.
- Adventure seekers. There are plenty of activities to enjoy, both water and land based.

BAD FOR...

- Pollution, due to littering.
- High-tide flooding. Before you pitch, check where the high tide reaches so you don't wake up wet.
- Solitude. Beaches can be noisy and very popular in some locations.

RAS KHUMAIS

Turning off the main road 15km after Sila (6km before the Saudi Arabia boarder), this small road takes you up to the headland of Ras Khumais. Before you hit the military post, there are a few areas where you can drive onto the beach and camp right beside the sea while watching pink flamingos as they bob around in the turquoise sea.

WADI WAY TO STAY

WITH DEEP COOL POOLS AND LUSH PLANTATIONS, WADIS CAN MAKE FOR UNIQUE SPOTS TO CAMP NEAR.

WADI MADBAH

Follow the winding river bed of the UAE's Wadi Madhah (p.32) and, after a few kilometres, you'll come to an interesting well and a cave-dwelling on your right. Turn out of the wadi after around 7km and over the undulating, rocky plains to the top of a plateau, which has some amazingly peaceful and remote sites for camping.

WADI BANI AWF (SNAKE CANYON)

This is a perennial favourite and one of the most spectacular wadis in Oman; indeed, a weekend in Wadi Bani Awf is on many explorers' 'must-do' lists. A mere 500m before At Tikhah, just 50m from the road, is

a lovely camp spot, complete with large trees and rustic shelters. Turn left from the graded track and cross a stream to some small pools and a large flat area. There's lots of room, so even if you have to share the campsite with others, you'll have plenty of space. This is

a great option before taking the plunge (literally) into Snake Canyon (see p.98).

WADI BIH

Famous for hikes, rock climbing and mountain biking, Wadi Bih offers a plethora of activities for the keen explorer and camping spots abound in the area too. Once over the top of the mountain, you'll find the remains of one of many old farming villages. Terraced fields frame scattered ruins of small stone dwellings. As a rule, many of these fields grow animal feed, so don't camp right on top of them. Try the good, gravelly area, left of the road, just before you reach these particular fields.

> ### WARNING
> While the UAE boasts low rainfall, flash floods can and do occur. Should you spot any signs of bad weather brewing, pack up and move away. Never set up camp within a wadi bed.

Wadi Bani Awf (Snake Canyon)

GOOD FOR...
- Spectacular views and scenery.
- Water-based fun. There are many secluded pools and waterfalls around wadis.
- Hikers have many routes to choose around here.

BAD FOR...
- Flash floods. If you are camping near a wadi, be mindful that these can and, occasionally, do flood very quickly. Always camp above the wadi – never in the wadi itself.

IN THE MOUNTAINS

AS THE TEMPERATURES BEGIN TO SOAR, HEAD TO THE MOUNTAINS FOR A COOLER CAMPING EXPERIENCE.

If you are planning on a hiking trip up in the mountains (see p.75) then mountain camping can make a good addition to your adventure, and there are some stand-out spots that are superb for pitching up; these sites are particularly suited to the hotter months as temperatures remain bearable up high. Jebel Yibir is the UAE's highest (named) peak and the best option in the UAE. Otherwise, the Hajar Mountains in Oman offer stunning scenery at higher altitudes.

JEBEL YIBIR

While the summit is actually off limits due to a military installation, you can drive up to 1,350 metres. If you're not looking to escape the heat, though, the plateau at 400m altitude has several easy spots to pitch up to. Drive north on the E18 until you reach the roundabout that meets the E87 and head towards Tawain. Pass two schools and drive straight for 7km until you reach the plateau.

JABAL SHAMS

Whether you're coming from the UAE or Muscat, the drive to Jabal Shams is a long but rewarding one.

The region boasts seemingly endless, towering mountain terrain, and is home to Oman's deepest canyon. In fact, Wadi an Nakhur is known as the 'Grand Canyon' of Oman thanks to the thrilling terrain, and camping at the rim of the canyon offers spectacular views of the sultanate.

MUSANDAM

Dramatic and unspoilt, with breathtaking natural scenery, this trip will take you all the way from the 'fjords' up to nearly 2,000m at the top. Head for Khasab and then follow signs to Daba (i.e. Dibba in the UAE). Jebal as Sayh is the highest point in the Musandam and is approximately 30km from this point. Around it are wonderful areas to camp in, especially during the hotter months.

Khab Al Shamis in Musandam

Jabal Shams

GOOD FOR...
• Spectacular views and scenery.
• Camping in the hotter months as it remains relatively cool at these higher altitudes.
• Hikers have many routes to choose from around here.

BAD FOR...
• Pitching tents. Secure corners of the tent with rocks.
• Restless sleepers. You might find yourself sleeping on rocks so choose your spot carefully.
• Rainy days.
• Goat invasions – it's best to keep food hidden away!

DEEP IN THE DESERT

WHEN IT COMES TO THE UAE AND OMAN, THERE'S ONE PLACE THAT DEMANDS OUR ATTENTION MORE THAN ALL OTHERS... THE DESERT.

It makes up more than 90% of the UAE and it's the biggest outdoor adventure playground you could possibly dream of. Off-roading adventures (see p.19) should be at the top of any Ultimate Explorer's must-do list. And of course, with no skyscrapers in sight, a night camping in the desert holds the key to ultimate solitude and adventure.

LIWA OASIS

The consummate desert camping experience is found in the sea of sand dunes at Liwa, where you can go to sleep beneath a perfect starry sky and then wake up completely surrounded by one of the world's most mesmerising dunescapes.

To get to the perfect camping spots, follow the E11 and take the slip road signposted Madinat Zayed and Mezaira'a. Once you reach Mezaira'a, stock up on provisions and fuel as this is the last stop before the wilderness. From there, follow signs for Liwa Resthouse and an industrial area and turn left at the roundabout signposted Tal Mireb (Moreeb Hill). Along the way you'll pass the stunning Sabkha flats before eventually reaching Moreeb Hill. With the giant Moreeb Hill on your left, camp just over one of these dunes and you'll feel secluded but know that a solid path isn't too far away.

FOSSIL ROCK

This is a fun camping spot, especially for kids who can explore the marine fossils that can be found on the rock's slopes. The presence of iron oxide gives the sand in this area a lovely rich, orange-red colour. Camp near the peak and wait for the stunning sunsets to take hold.

BIG RED

Less than an hour's drive away from Dubai, Big Red still creates the feeling of being a million miles away from city. Be wary that this place is a popular off-roading and quad biking haunt and, as such, you need to consider your camp spot carefully. As you pass Big Red, you'll see a few farms dotted along the road; head out around here for good pitching spots.

GOOD FOR...

• Dune bashing adventures.
• Stunning sunsets.
• Peace and quiet.

BAD FOR...

• Inexperienced off-roaders. Your vehicle will get stuck so be prepared to get digging.
• Pitching tents. Secure corners of the tent with rocks.
• Shamals. Should this north-westerly wind blow so strongly that your tents can't stay grounded, it's best to retreat to your car.

DESERT PARTIES

IF YOU PREFER THE COMFORT OF SOMEONE ELSE'S ORGANISATIONAL SKILLS, THEN A DESERT PARTY COULD BE THE IDEAL WAY TO ENJOY THE SANDS.

Desert parties are a perfect escape from everyday life and there are a number of options to choose from.

One easy way to get in the tribal party spirit is with Dubai Drums (dubaidrums. com), which organises monthly Full Moon drumming parties at the Gulf Ventures camp (gulfventures.ae). Either sit back and listen to the music, grab one of the drums provided or take along your own percussion instrument – it's a completely inclusive party where the aim is to create unison amongst everyone. A barbecue is included with the ticket price and, if you're a little shy about your bongo skills, there's a licensed bar where you can 'drum up' some Dutch courage.

Gulf Ventures hosts a number of desert parties but their biggest is the Deck the Dunes event – when the desert (and a tree)

are transformed into Santa's north pole grotto with Santa visiting on camelback. Held each December, families can take part in sand sledging and camel riding, all the while signing Christmas carols.

Dadabhai (dadabhaitravel.ae) does similar parties at its Arabian Village camp near Al Aweer, where shisha, and a barbecue are also on offer.

Most of these camps can provide for those wishing to stay the night.

Of course, you don't have to go along the pre-arranged route; if you've an idea for a particular kind of desert party, there are companies that can help you make it happen. Flying Elephant (flyingelephantuae. com), for example, has organised everything from corporate teambuilding gigs in the dunes to Arabian-themed desert weddings and kids' birthday parties.

CAMPING IN THE DESERT IS A PERFECT WAY TO SPEND QUALITY TIME WITH FAMILY AND FRIENDS.

Full Moon Desert Drumming

Come and join the amazing combined energy of drumming together under the full moon with friendly people and the earthy feel of the desert.

Join Dubai's Drumming crowd, connect with your inner rhythms and de-stress and "chillax!"

Corporate Team Building Events
Community Events
Staff Parties & Celebrations
Full Moon Desert Drumming
New Year Desert Drumming
Kidz Birthday Parties & Adult Parties
School & University Workshops
African Djembe Drum Classes
Summer Camp For Kids

Anchor your company's vision create synergy improve communications.

Leave a positive, lasting impression that people will talk about for months to come.

Corporate Team Building

UAE's first and foremost company for uniting teams and communities through rhythm based events for the past 10 years'

Contact: Dubai Drums 056 744 2129
Dubai Drums, Office 97, Bldg. 8
P.O. Box 73102, Dubai Media City, Dubai
Email: info@dubaidrums.com
Website: www.dubaidrums.com

CAMPING WITH KIDS

THE UAE IS THE PERFECT PLACE TO INTRODUCE THE UNINITIATED TO THE WORLD OF CAMPING.

There are many comfortable and safe camping spots ideal for families or camping novices, all a short distance from the main roads, so a 4WD isn't even necessary. For newbies, it's best to stick to camping spots that are fairly close to services. Organised camp amenities don't exist in the UAE, and venturing into the wilderness may well be a shade too daunting for some young families, so it's best to have back-up facilities nearby; choose somewhere within easy reach of shops or toilets.

Preparation and planning are key to any camping trip with young children in tow. Pack plenty of toys and games: cards, a bat and ball, a Frisbee. Also, ensure you set up a few ground rules (see box); there are likely to be fewer upsets and more happy memories. If you are camping with very young infants, you should bring mosquito nets to protect them from night bites. With proper preparation and the right location, it's the perfect way to spend quality family time.

CHILD'S PLAY

The long stretch of beach in Fujairah is ideal for those travelling with kids. Hotels line some of these beaches and, so, if your attempt at a beach BBQ goes awry, you can always head to a restaurant to fill empty bellies. Toilets in the hotels can also be a sight for sore eyes for those with kids too. Other good locations include Jebel Ali, Dibba and Hatta as they all have hotels nearby. See Beaches (p.62) for more child-friendly camping spots.

CAMPING RULES FOR KIDS

- Stay in sight of the tent at all times
- Stay in pairs while exploring
- Wear a head light if exploring in the evening so mum and dad can see you
- Drink lots
- Avoid lifting up rocks or sticking your fingers into holes
- Keep your shoes on when wandering around
- Do not put your hands underneath your tent (scorpions love dark, cool places)

THE BRILLIANT BARBECUE KIT

A barbecue is an essential item for the great outdoors. Barbecue expert Weber (webergrill.ae) gives us the rundown on exactly what you should pack to make sure your trip is a culinary success.

- Charcoal – sounds obvious, yet it's often forgotten. For the original BBQ taste and the satisfaction of glowing coals, don't forget it.
- Chimney starter and lighter cubes – this is the easiest way to get the fire started.
- BBQ tool set – to ensure easy and safe handling of food on the BBQ.
- Cleaning brush – once you've finished grilling, give the grates a good 30 second scrub while the BBQ is still warm to ensure your BBQ remains in good order and insect free.
- Cleaning supplies – kitchen paper, kitchen foil and waste bags are all essential items.
- Ice box – load up on ice and cold drinks to keep your food cold and fresh at all times.
- Cooking oil – always season your grate before grilling so your food won't stick.
- Small cuts of meat or fish – smaller pieces cook quicker and are easier to handle.
- Marinated vegetables– prepare at home using tasty oils, herbs and spices.
- Plums, peaches and bananas – use the last remnants of heat from the grill to make yummy desserts or roast marshmallows on a stick for the kids.
- Extra spice – add wood chips to your BBQ for an extra smokey flavour; alternatively, you can season using BBQ sauces, lemon pepper, oils, chillies, fresh herbs and spices.

CARRY ON GLAMPING

LOVE CAMPING BUT HATE PITCHING? IN THESE PARTS, YOU CAN ALWAYS TAKE TO THE GREAT OUTDOORS WITH A FEW EXTRA LUXURIES.

Dreamland Aquapark

There are several tour companies that organise desert camping trips which make for a completely hassle-free experience all round. These firms usually offer a full desert safari, complete with dune bashing, camel riding, belly dancers and a BBQ dinner, as well as an overnight stay; but usually tourists choose to skip the staying over part. Check the Directory (p.245 & p.248) for a list of tour companies.

Sheesa Beach Travel and Tourism's permanent campsite (sheesabeach. com) in Dibba comes with showers, BBQ dinners, and an on-site bar – not to mention the all-important comfy bunks in permanent Bedouin-style tents.

Another fabulously fun camping trip with a difference can be enjoyed at Dreamland Aqua Park (dreamlanduae. com) where waterbabies can enjoy the slides before camping overnight in the grounds. You can choose to bring your own tent or sleep in the park's own cosy A-framed cabins complete with air-conditioning and inflatable mattresses. There's even a private barbecue set available for each group.

In Oman, the ultimate chic camping experience can be found around two hours away from Muscat in the Wahiba Sands; head here for a taste of Bedouin life and a slice of luxury. Desert Nights Camp (desertnightscamp.com) comprises 30 tents boasting en-suite bathrooms, aircon and mini bars, as well as traditional camp fire entertainment.

Luxury suite in Banyan Tree Al Wadi

INDULGE!

For those who want to try the very best in glamping experiences try Banyan Tree Al Wadi (banyantree. com), where tented luxury awaits. Expect four-poster beds, tent-service and unrivalled extravagance.

Bedouin life at the
Desert Nights Camp

HIKING, TREKKING & CLIMBING

HIKING, TREKKING & CLIMBING

THE UAE AND OMAN ARE ADVENTURE PLAYGROUNDS FOR 4WD OFF-ROADERS, BUT WHAT DOES IT OFFER FOR PEOPLE WHO PREFER TO EXPLORE THE GREAT OUTDOORS BY FOOT?

Ainee Village, Musandam

The UAE's cities may not be ideal for walking but, for those who really want to stretch their legs, there are some great hiking options just a short drive from town.

To the north, for example, the Ru'us Al Jibal Mountains (the northernmost section of the Hajars) contain the highest peaks in the UAE, standing proud at over 2,000 metres. To the east, the impressive central section of the Hajars forms the border between the UAE and Oman, stretching from the Musandam peninsula to the Empty Quarter Desert, hundreds of kilometres to the south. Most of the terrain is heavily eroded, due to the harsh climate, but there are still places where you can walk through shady palm plantations and lush oases. Routes range from short, easy walks to spectacular viewpoints, to all-day treks over difficult terrain, and can include some fairly major mountaineering. Some hikes follow centuries-old Bedouin and Shihuh mountain paths, a few of which are still being used.

An easy introduction to Gulf hiking is the foothills of the Hajar Mountains just off the Hatta Road, near the Oman border. After the flat desert, rugged outcrops transform the landscape completely. Explore any turning you like, or take the road to Mahdah, along which you'll find several options.

Other great areas for hiking and exploring include Al Ain and Buraimi, Wadi Bih, the mountains near the East Coast and much of northern Oman. The mountains in the region don't generally disappoint and the further off the beaten track you get, the more likely you are to find interesting villages where residents live much the same way as they did centuries ago.

Hiking here is completely different to what most people expect or are used to. There are few established tracks, apart from goat trails, and there is often little shade or relief from the sun. Rocks and boulders are sharp and often unstable, the general terrain often shattered due to the harsh climate, so much of the time is spent watching where you are walking. No signposts in the UAE (in Oman, major hikes are actually well marked) combined with a lack of distinguishable features, can make it difficult to orientate yourself. However, once you become more experienced and accustomed to the local environment, your perceptions change, and you will find it easier to recognise different rocks and trees, and simpler to navigate.

But all hikers are strongly advised to purchase, and learn how to use, a GPS. You can then confidently plot the position of your starting point every time you are out. You should then have no difficulty wandering all day and finding a route back to your car.

HIKING SAFETY

HIKING HERE CAN BE HARD, HOT AND ISOLATED SO SAFETY SHOULD ALWAYS BE THE TOP CONSIDERATION.

As is the case when hiking anywhere in the world, embarking on a local trek is not an activity that should be undertaken lightly, no matter how short or easy you think the route will be, or how experienced a hiker you consider yourself to be.

Always tell someone where you are going and when you expect to be back and don't forget to take a map, compass, GPS equipment and robust hiking boots.

Do not ever underestimate the strength of the sun here, no matter what time of year it is – take sunscreen, and most importantly, loads of water (a CamelBak rucksack is ideal). For most people, the cooler and less humid winter months are the best season for serious mountain hiking. Be particularly careful in wadis (dry riverbeds) during the wet season as flash floods can immerse a wadi in seconds.

Also note that there are no mountain rescue services in the UAE, so anyone venturing out into the mountains should be reasonably experienced or accompanied by someone who knows the area. Don't forget to fully charge your phone and take it with you.

GET A GROUP

There are no official hiking clubs in the UAE, but you can meet like-minded people to hike with through the various Facebook groups that have been set up: Dubai Trekking, Abu Dhabi Hikers, Abu Dhabi Adventurers and Abu Dhabi Alpine Club are some of the most active groups.

Ainee Village, Musandam

CHECKLIST FOR HEALTHY, HAPPY HIKING

Before the trek do your homework. Don't kid yourself; hiking in wadis and mountain terrain is not a walk in Safa Park. Having the perfect body fat to weight ratio means nothing if you don't have the stamina or hiking experience to back it up; you need to know your physical limits – as well as the abilities of others in your group – and to choose your trail accordingly.

The UAE has routes that range from beginner to advanced; start easy and work your way up. And always remember to let friends and family know where you'll be going and when you're expected back, just in case you run into trouble.

Make sure you pack lightly but efficiently. The basic items you should carry with you are: water (at least three litres per person); sports drinks (such as Isostar); sun screen; food, including some salted snacks (salt helps prevent muscle cramps); a torch; and a first aid kit. Other non-essential items that you may consider packing are GPS devices, a compass, a trekking stick, maps and a camera.

It's important to wear light, protective and functional clothing, keeping bulk and weight down. Rain is rare in the UAE mountains, although when it does fall it can be heavy. Skip the haute couture and opt for sports t-shirts and bottoms with breathable fabrics that wick sweat from the body. Resist the urge to wear cottons as sweat tends to get absorbed quickly and will weigh you down. A good rule of thumb is if it looks out of place in a gym then you shouldn't be wearing it – hiking is physical exercise.

You will also need to invest in good hiking footwear (p.81). Standard trainers will be ripped apart by the unforgiving wadi rocks. A wide brim hat will help protect your head and face from the scorching heat.

During long treks make sure you stretch; it reduces muscle tension and allows better, more flexible movement. Take some time to work your lower back, legs, torso and neck – it will help prevent soreness and injury, both during and after the trek.

Know when to quit - there's no shame in turning back when the going gets tough or if external factors come into play (such as rain, exhaustion and lack of rations). Follow your instincts and, when in doubt, stop and reassess the situation.

Rest and refuel regularly to replace the fluids that are gushing out of your body and to maintain your energy levels. Don't wait for dehydration to set in or you'll be past the point of help. A steady supply of nutrition, with snacks and meals, will help keep you going.

Additionally, if you feel your muscles start to cramp up it's because you've lost salt content in your body, so stop immediately and have a bite of something savoury. Another useful maxim is that, if your mood changes for the worse, it's a good sign that you need nutrition.

Pace yourself as not everyone has the same pace. To deviate from your own pace can be uncomfortable and push your limits too far. Remember you're not out there to impress anyone.

Stay on route. Most trails can easily be identified through worn out paths and key marker stones for a reason – they generally guide you along the path of least resistance. GPS and maps can come in quite handy when navigating unmarked trails. If lost, don't panic; try to get to the highest point on the trail and look for visual cues on how to get back.

Keep track of friends. If you're in a group, never lose sight of the person in front and behind you. It's important that everyone practises this rule so that no one gets left behind or lost.

After the trek rest, rest and rest some more. Hopefully, if you didn't overexert yourself, a good night's rest should be enough to do away with any pains.

In severe cases, if the pain doesn't subside over one/two days it's best that you get checked over by your physician and get as much rest as possible to heal your muscles. But as mentioned before, if you are a beginner, take things easy at first.

WALK THIS WAY

HAVING THE RIGHT GEAR IS THE KEY TO A SUCCESSFUL HIKING TRIP. THANKFULLY, A NUMBER OF STORES ACROSS THE COUNTRY CAN HELP GET YOU STARTED.

The UAE and Oman have been fairly quick to catch on to their new-found statuses as hiking paradises, as have a number of stores and big outdoor brands, so you can now pick up all the equipment you need, whether you're looking to escape the city and hit the foothills or are planning a week-long adventure.

The absolute essentials are shorts or trousers and t-shirts – these should be sporty and made from a light, wicking material. If you're likely to camp out, or make an early start to your day's hike, a fleece could also be a good option.

Sun & Sand Sports (sunandsand sports.com) has branches in Abu Dhabi, Dubai, Sharjah, Ajman and Ras Al Khaimah, and whether through its multi-brand superstores, or through the individual stores, it sells Timberland, Colombia and North Face, all of which should fit the bill. Trespass and Jack Wolfskin (both orlandosportsuae. com), in Dubai, can kit you out with the necessities, as can Adventure HQ (adventurehq.ae), which stocks Sherpa and Berghaus outdoor clothing.

In reality, however, any comfortable sports clothing will do the trick and you may find some good deals to be had at the likes of Go Sport (in most the big malls) and Sports Direct. There are also plenty of outlet shops in the UAE that offer good quality, discounted items.

There are a few things you should definitely buy from proper outdoor clothing brands, such as a hat (or maybe even a pair of hats – a warm one for nights around the camp, and a wide-brimmed hat with SPF protection for once the sun comes up), a backpack and hiking boots.

See the Directory on p.244 & p.248 for full store listings.

Jungle Book hike

A TOOL FOR ALL TREKS

You never know what unforeseen circumstances may pop up during a day or two of hiking, and carrying a tool for all eventualities would mean a 100 litre backpack and plenty of jangling. It's this thinking, of course, that led to the invention of the Swiss Army Knife in the late 1800s.

If you'd like one of these iconic bits of kit, Jashanmal (jashanmalgroup. com) stocks Swiss Army Knives by the original manufacturer, Victorinox, as well as other pocket knife gadgets, rescue tools and activity-specific timepieces.

To discover more amazing treks in Oman, pick up a copy of explorer's *Oman Trekking* guide book, out now in bookstores across the region. Alternatively, visit our e-shop at askexplorer.com.

Wadi Bih hike

BOOTS

Choosing the right footwear is key to how much you enjoy your hiking experience. The footwear experts at Adventure HQ give some pointers:

• It's good to do some research but try also to go in with an open mind. The shoes you want are often not the ones you need.

• Even if know your size, the assistant should measure your feet precisely and look at the shape of your foot. Certain brands have characteristics that suit particular foot shapes.

• Do you pronate, supinate or have a neutral stride? Do you need some stability in your sole?

• Height is a factor. If you have a weak ankle or are likely to tackle some steeper, more technical terrain, a full height boot could be required. If you enjoy trail running, or just like to take on easier hikes, then a super light endurance trainer might do the trick.

• There's no point getting the perfect shoes if you then put on the wrong pair of socks. Get some hiking specific socks, which feature a stocking-like liner. They wick sweat away from your feet and feature a double layer that reduces friction, reducing the likelihood of blisters. Here in the UAE, thermolite socks are ideal.

HOW TO CHOOSE A BACKPACK

• What size do you need? This depends on how long, on average, you're likely to be hiking and the type of hikes you'll be tackling. If you tend to head out for a few hours, then a 20L pack will be enough for water, a couple of snacks and your mobile phone. If you do long weekend hikes that require tents and significant supplies, then you'll need at least an 80L pack.

• Get a pack that fits. It sounds obvious, but all packs are different sizes and, although straps can be adjusted, some will mould perfectly with your back. Equally, different packs have different points for adjusting or internal structures to add rigidity. Remember, a backpack should not be worn high up on the shoulders but the weight should be taken through the hips and pelvis.

• What access do you need? Do you want a pack that incorporates a water bladder, so that you can drink on the go? Should there be some pockets on the waist strap for easy access? Do you want everything to fit snugly into the pack, or do you prefer a pack with plenty of straps and bands for attaching equipment to the outside. Lots of pockets or few pockets?

HIKING ROUTES

A FEW OF THE BEST HIKING, TREKKING AND SCRAMBLING ROUTES TO GET YOUR ADVENTURE STARTED.

The UAE and, to an even greater extent, Oman are both packed with some amazing and fascinating hiking routes that will be quite unlike anything that you've experienced anywhere else. There are literally hundreds of places that you can hike – check out the areas covered in the off-roading (p.19), mountain biking (p.106) and camping (p.59) chapters for starters – however, there are certain routes and areas that are especially worth trying. And remember, if you're not going with an experienced guide, you should always carry a GPS with your starting point firmly logged; trails are rarely marked clearly and, although a route may seem obvious on the way out, as weather conditions alter and the angle of shadows change, it can be easy to misread the land and get lost.

NORTHERN EMIRATES

LOOK NORTH AND YOU'LL FIND THE BIGGEST PEAKS THAT THE UAE HAS TO OFFER. AND THAT MEANS PLENTY OF VALLEYS, WADIS AND TREKKING ROUTES TOO.

WADI WURRAYAH

The open, green area and waterfall that, for many, mark the end of the Wadi Wurrayah off-roading adventure, are where the hiking fun begins.

If you scramble your way up and above the wadi (it's really not too tough a climb),you're in for quite a treat as, above the waterfall, the stream runs along a small tributary of Wadi Wurrayah. Walk for one or two hours and you'll eventually arrive at a quiet and secluded second pool, which also has a waterfall. Thanks to the wadi walls here being extremely steep, this hike is cool and predominantly shaded, making it possible to tackle this route almost all year round.

Alternatively, you can hike up the main wadi, following the course of a stream that flows all year round.

The first hour is the most interesting, but you can really continue exploring as far as you like, as the wadi takes you in and out of shallow water, forcing you to wade through pools and climb up or slide down the small waterfalls.

Look out for a small cave which is home to small brown bats. When the stream peters out, you can keep on climbing higher, over the watershed, then hike down a small similar wadi that winds its way to the Masafi-Dibba road. As always, keep an eye on the weather and get out of the wadi at the first sign of rain.

ACTIVITIES
Hiking, swimming

Other Names
Wurayyah Waterfall

GPS
Hikes begin from:
25'23'44"N 56'16'10"E

TRIP INFO

GOOD FOR
Beginners and young families.

GET THERE
From the E99 coast road, just south of Bidiyah in the emirate of Fujairah, an easy 13km drive up Wadi Wurrayah leads to a green open area and waterfall, from where a couple of relatively easy hikes depart.

JEBEL YIBIR

Jebel Yibir provides a huge variety of routes, not just for hikers but mountain bikers and campers too. Drive up the initial climb (around 2.3km long) and the road plateaus a little. The area on the left here is flat, cool and excellent for camping. Keep climbing and, another 4km up on the left, you'll find two sections of man-made paths; although these may appeal more to mountain bikers, for hikers, they offer an easy way into the local mountains, with some great remote campsite potential.

Drive to the very end of the road near the top of Jebel Yibir (around 7km from the foot of the mountain) and, just before the road stops, with the military base denying you access to the very summit, you'll find a flattened parking area on the left. Immediately below, a well-marked trail takes you down to a small village, and up the other side by a telecommunications tower. Further on, these trails lead to small villages and old farming areas.

One great route is the Tala and Baqal hike. From the trail head described above (GPS 25°39'0.10"N 56° 7'6.42"E), the hike descends into the gully where you can either turn right, into the small village (Mahra), or carry straight on up the other side of the gully. Carry on and, after 30 minutes or so, you'll come to a large flat area (GPS 25°39'28.41"N 56° 6'25.82"E). From here, the track carries on for another 1.7km to the small village of Tala (GPS 25°40'22.67"N 56° 6'18.80"E).

To the right, you will see a large radio mast in the distance. If you leave the

track and go to the left, you get a good view of Baqal village below. From Tala, you can either turn around and retrace your route, or you can go to the next village, Baqal (GPS 25°41'24.12"N 56° 5'22.33"E), which is clearly visible to the north-west. There is no visible track between the two villages, but the route is marked with three large cairns – just don't be tempted to try to take a short cut through the gully or you'll soon be lost.

From Tala, it takes about two hours to get to Baqal, but allow more time for the return, as it is all uphill. There is very little shade to Tala and none from Tala to Baqal, so it's definitely one for the cooler months. Bring plenty of water.

TRIP INFO

GOOD FOR
Finding variety.

GET THERE
From the E87, which runs east to Dibba, follow the signs to Al Tawian and then follow the route along Wadi Khabb. Finally, you'll see the climb up to Jebel Yibir ahead.

ACTIVITIES
Hiking, mountain biking, camping, climbing, picnics

GPS
Road climb starts: 25°37'42"N 56°07'19"E
New trails start: 25°37'42"N 56°07'19"E
Main peak hikes start: 25°38'58"N 56°07'07"E

WADI NAQAB

Located close to Jebel Yibir, Wadi Nakab is a hike that is suitable for beginners, thanks to its relatively easy route, which can be completed in just under two hours. It is also perfect for families that want to take their child on their very first hiking adventure. However, be warned, it can get tiring in the end for little legs.

Getting there is easy; from Dubai's Emirates Road, follow the signs leading to Ras Al Khaimah, then continue following the signs to the emirate's airport. At the first two roundabouts, keep on driving straight.

Upon arriving at the third roundabout, take the second exit (left), and drive straight, before taking the second right.

Drive for a further 4km before making a right turn, then continue driving for 2.5km. Then take the first left.

You should be now seeing a number of rocks and quarries that lead up to the road where the tarmac ends. This is the wadi road (the front quarry entrance), where you can park and begin your hike.

WARNING

Regular hikers will tell you that driving up to the Wadi Naqab hike can sometimes be tricky due to the rocky/uneven surface, so make sure you are in a strong 4WD. Also, avoid going on this hike when it is raining.

TRIP INFO

GOOD FOR

Beginners, as well as families with young children. There is some beautiful scenery during this two-hour hike. Just look out for the bat caves!

GET THERE

Located near Ras Al Khaimah, this hike is about an hour's drive away from Dubai.

ACTIVITIES

Hiking

OTHER NAMES

Wadi Nakab, Wadi Al Nakab

GPS

Start of the hike:
25°42'53"N 56°06'47"E
End of the hike:
25°42'07"N 56°07'16"E

INLAND

AWAY FROM THE COAST, BOTH HATTA AND BURAIMI (THE OMANI SIDE OF AL AIN) OFFER INSPIRING SCENERY.

BURAIMI

The most popular hike in this area is known, intriguingly, as Hanging Gardens. From Buraimi, follow the road to Mahdah for around 15km, before turning right and following the track towards Jebel Qatar. You'll reach a small hill brow and the trail descends to the left to a large rock and a lone tree – a good place to park up and start hiking.

Set your sights on the escarpment of Jebel Qatar and walk straight up the steep scree slope on your right, heading directly away from the stream bed and the lone tree. You should find a small path that zigzags up from the bottom. This route gets the hardest part of the climb over right at the beginning. As you near the top of the rocky slope, head into the cave (taking care not to disturb the bats) where you will find an amazing panorama over the tracks across the gravelly plains and the red desert, stretching as far as the eye can see. Once rested, walk down to the right and follow the base of the cliff along to the north-east, eventually coming to a steep slope descending to the 'gardens' – this unusually verdant area has a rarely visited air about it. For the descent from the gardens there are several options depending on time and adventure. The easiest route is along the top edge of the wadi, which gently makes its way down to the starting point. For a wilder descent, follow the wadi bed.

An alternative hike starts from the left and lower side of an escarpment way before the first car parking spot. After passing an old, ramshackle farm, head into the corner of the L-shaped rock escarpment and park your car. You can then follow the rocky side ridge up to where it joins the main escarpment. From there, walk up to the highest point and all the way along the top of Jebel Qatar. If you choose to go all the way along the top of the escarpment, the route crosses many wadis, some shallow and inconsequential, but some serious propositions, with walls of up to 20m to scale down and then up the other side. A good head for heights and a good leader are required for this route, especially the last descent off the southern end of the jebel, as it can be hard to find a route down.

For a more sedate option, from Mahdah, follow the road to Khutwa, passing through the settlement of Khutwa and into 'Old' Khutwa village where you'll find lovely gorges and plantations. Park in the old village and head for the mosque – next to it you'll find a falaj (the water channel used to irrigate plantations and fields). You can follow this falaj all the way through the plantation. Once you are out in the open, you will see the next oasis village further up the wadi. You can follow the falaj system which runs next to the narrow, tortured gorge all the way there.

ACTIVITIES
Climbing, hiking

GPS
Hanging Gardens starts: 24°19'29"N 55°53'58"E
Khutwa starts: 24°19'00"N 56°07'21"E

TRIP INFO

GOOD FOR
Variety – both in terms of the hiking and the terrain.

GET THERE
Head to Al Ain, where you'll need to cross over the border into Buraimi, on the Omani side. Therefore, you'll need to make sure you have Oman car insurance, as well as passports.

HATTA

There are a handful of hikes in this area and, thanks to the range of challenges as well as relative accessibility of them, this can be a great place for newer hikers to build up some strength.

On the Dubai-Hatta Road, while still in Omani territory and between the two border posts, you'll come to a road on the left that climbs to Jebel Rawdah – more of a big hill than a mountain, the base can even be accessed in a two-wheel drive vehicle. At the end of the valley, park up and follow any of the trails – the middle is the easiest but they all take around two hours and the views are spectacular.

The nearby Jebel Sumayni Hike is a good introduction to some of the longer walks in the UAE. To get to the trailhead, turn right off the Dubai-Hatta Road (E44) at the roundabout next to the Shell petrol station, following the road signposted Mahdah. After

15km, turn right off the road at a group of palm trees and a farm on the right-hand side. Jebel Sumayni should now be clearly visible, about two kilometres away, as a rounded summit in a group of peaks, with the actual summit just behind the skyline ridge. After turning at the small white house with the large veranda, follow a track past the small settlement that usually has lots of goats outside. Drive into the wadi as far as a large tree that provides good shade. The hike starts from here: head straight towards the mountain and, when the ground rises more steeply, turn to the left behind a ridge. Follow the gully left up to a col (30 minutes) and then go diagonally up to the left for about 300m to a gully that leads directly up to the skyline. Parts are quite steep and offer some scrambling. It's one hour to the top of the gully. From here, walk diagonally to your left across the saddle between the mountains and continue curving your way to the right

around the face of the next mountain. Once you reach the opposite ridge (20 minutes), there is one more gentle descent of about 100m before ascending the final summit. The view from here is magnificent.

TRIP INFO

GOOD FOR
Building your hiking stamina.

GET THERE
Simply follow the E44 in the direction of Hatta. You'll need Omani car insurance, as well as passports or Emirates IDs.

ACTIVITIES
Swimming, hiking, picnics, sandboarding

GPS
Jebel Rawdah starts: 24˚54'28"N 55˚54'42"E
Jebel Sumayni starts: 24˚44'00"N 55˚56'32"E

WARNING
Oman car insurance, ID required.

MUSANDAM

KNOWN AS 'THE FJORDS OF ARABIA', HERE YOU GET DRAMATIC CLIMBS, SWEEPING VALLEYS AND STUNNING TERRAIN. PERFECT FOR SOME HARD HIKING.

WADI BIH

You can't really miss Wadi Bih as, from Dibba, it's about the only route running north. Leaving the town, it starts out as tarmac but quickly becomes a graded track. Some 12km along that track, you come to a water tank on the side of the road, often marked by local farmers' vehicles parked next to it. The large sign in Arabic asks you not to park your cars next to the tank as it blocks access for the water tankers. Please make sure you observe this request. There is a small clearing about 100 metres further along the road on the right-hand side (away from Dibba) where you can park and start the 'quick plateau hike' – a good introductory hike as the majority is on flat terrain and follows a clearly marked track (thanks to the local inhabitants). Starting above the water tank, head straight up the steep slope towards the left. There is a well-worn track and it is just a matter of picking your way around some of the larger rocks near the top. After 25 minutes, you come to a large plateau (550m). A lone tree stands beside a drum, providing a good resting spot and some shade. The track crosses the plateau and rises through a gully. After 15 minutes it opens onto a valley dotted with trees and you have your first view of the village. Continue through the village to the far end of the valley and up a small rise for an interesting view over a large basin surrounded by mountains.

For a couple of more challenging routes, keep on driving to the summit where you'll find room for parking on the left-hand side – the starting point for both.

The Jebel Qihwi hike heads south-west towards the clearly visible twin peaks. A straightforward hike to the summit takes about three hours each way. Facing Jebel Qihwi, take the used path that runs to the left of the parking area and follow the donkey track across the hillside to a quaint settlement overlooking the east coast (about 45 minutes). Once at the settlement, pass through it, keeping to the right and maintaining your height. Keeping roughly the same height as the settlement, follow the contours around and out of the steep hillside to an exposed area. The slope levels off slightly before the final, steep section leading to the northern summit (the right-hand peak). Directly in front there is an obvious chimney and this is ascended by climbing over a wedged block and then scrambling up to emerge through a hole close to the summit. The southern summit is probably a metre or two higher than the northern, and the two are separated by a gap that's too far to jump.

The other route is known as the Jungle Book hike. It was previously tackled from the west coast but now has to be done in reverse due to the closure of Wadi Bih from that direction. It also heads out from the car park, but in a north-westerly direction, and begins with a fairly steep and loose descent before hooking around to the right and following Wadi Luwayb all the way to the bottom of the pass. The complete walk takes about six hours and involves some basic climbing in three places, plus lots of scrambling up, over and around large boulders, but the atmosphere is

extraordinary. You used to be able to do the hike in one direction and then complete the loop along the graded track but now you have no option but to turn around and head back the way you came. Be aware that the journey back is far more testing, with some hairy sections combined with a good deal of elevation to producing a challenging hike.

ACTIVITIES

Camping, climbing, mountain biking, hiking, snorkelling

GPS

Plateau hike starts: 25°45'58"N 56°15'58"E
Jebel Qihwi and Jungle Book start: 25°46'52"N 56°12'46"E

WARNING

Oman & UAE car insurance, valid visas and passports required.

TRIP INFO

GOOD FOR
Strong hikers seeking steeper terrain.

GET THERE
Wadi Bih is no longer accessible from RAK, so the best bet is through Dibba on the east coast. Passports or Emirates ID required.

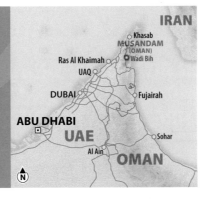

IRAN
Khasab
MUSANDAM
(OMAN)
Wadi Bih
Ras Al Khaimah
UAQ
DUBAI
Fujairah
ABU DHABI
UAE
Sohar
Al Ain
OMAN
N

OMAN

A COUNTRY MADE FOR OUTDOOR PURSUITS, OMAN HAS SOME GREAT TREKKING AND, BETTER STILL, ALMOST ALL OF THE MAIN TRAILS ARE WELL MARKED THROUGHOUT.

RIYAM-MUTRAH

If you're only going to do one walk in the capital, make it this one. It's easy going and the views are superb. Follow the coloured markers from the parking area at the start in Riyam – a rusty, old diesel pipeline is a reminder of a time when Riyah was home to Oman's only power station. Well-placed stone slabs, used by generations of travellers, lead up the hill and up to the highest parts of the walk – ideal for turning around and enjoying the coastal view. Take care descending towards the abandoned settlement and you may even have to scramble down to pass the wadi leading to Mutrah. Be sure to turn left just before Mutrah, or you may end up in a graveyard.

TRIP INFO

REFERENCE
Oman Ministry of Tourism Trek C38

GOOD FOR
A gentle hike if you don't have time to head too far out of the city.

GET THERE
Drive along the Old Muscat Road until you see the C38 sign in Riyam.

ACTIVITIES
Camping, mountain biking, hiking

GPS
23°37'12.74"N 58°34'35.55"E

WARNING
Oman car insurance, valid visas and passports required.

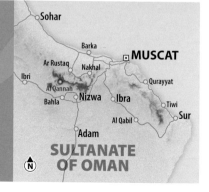

AL QANNAH

A great trek that takes a full day but is actually relatively easy going, the ancient donkey path takes in the west flank of the An Nakhur Gorge (the 'Grand Canyon of Oman'), connecting Wadi Ghul with Al Khitaym, passing through two abandoned villages. From the old village in Wadi Ghul, follow the 'W6a' signs along a spectacular route that climbs up to Al Khitaym, before continuing south-west until close to the rim, when the path follows the edge of the canyon most of the way down until you cross a small wadi. Climb upwards to reach the crest of the hill, which leads to the older of the two abandoned villages. From there, proceed along the old city wall down through the second abandoned village to the bottom of Wadi Ghul and Wadi An Nakhur.

If you're looking for more of a challenge, you could combine this route with hike W4 – get *Oman Trekking Guide* from askexplorer.com/shop for more routes.

ACTIVITIES

Camping, climbing, mountain biking, hiking, snorkelling

GPS

23° 9'0.88"N 57°12'21.46"E

WARNING

Oman & UAE car insurance, valid visas and passports required.

TRIP INFO

REFERENCE
Oman Ministry of Tourism Trek W6a

GOOD FOR
Keen photographers.

GET THERE
From Nizwa, follow the road to Al Hamra and then on to Wadi Ghul – the W6a path starts at the lower abandoned village.

Sohar
Barka
Ar Rustaq Nakhal ▣ **MUSCAT**
Ibri
Qurayyat
Al Qannah
Bahla Nizwa Ibra
Tiwi
Al Qabil Sur
Adam
Ⓝ **SULTANATE OF OMAN**

WADI MISTALL

Combining routes W25 and W24a, this is a challenging mountain trek along an old and once very important donkey path, which could take as long as 10 hours to complete. The marked path starts down in Wukan village and then winds its way through gardens and along the traditional falaj irrigation system.

Ignore the W24b signs and follow W25 to the small mosque above the gardens and continue along to the two exposed areas of the path where less experienced hikers may want to take a rope (5-10m). The path climbs way up to the top of Jabal Akhdar (at 2,000m) where the trail levels and, 2.5km further along, you'll arrive at the Al Manakir/Hadash junction.

From there, follow the W24a to the north to Hadash where you can follow the wadi back down before looping back around to get back to your car in Wukan.

ACTIVITIES
Climbing, hiking

GPS
23° 8'36.48"N 57°44'6.10"E

TRIP INFO

REFERENCE
Oman Ministry of Tourism Trek W25 and W24a

GOOD FOR
Experienced trekkers wanting a full- day challenge.

GET THERE
From the coast road west of Muscat, pass through Nakhal and to Wukan.

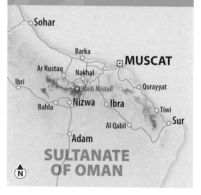

WADI TIWI/ WADI BANI KHALID

This is a classic traverse of the Eastern Hajars, much of which is along an ancient trail, through the green oasis of Wadi Bani Khalid, along dramatic canyons and up to high points that offer amazing views. It is a two-day hike (14-18 hours depending on weight of pack) and you'll need to arrange transport back (doing it in two groups and starting at opposite ends with duplicate car keys is an option). Of course, you can also drive a lot of the route in a 4WD and start the hike further up. The final option is to make it a three-day adventure and hike the return trip too. Although the trek is a long one, the hiking is relatively easy.

The starting point is the village of Al Aqur and it could be a good idea to camp on one of the beaches or cliffs near Tiwi the night before. Follow the painted E25 markers and cairns. From Al Aqur to Sooee is easy and interesting but, after that, the landscape becomes barren and plenty of water is essential – there's nowhere to get water until you reach the villages at the

foot of Wadi Bani Khalid, which could be a full day away. For this reason, most will need to arrange donkey transport (can be done in any of the nearby villages – be prepared to negotiate) or go through a tour operator (see p.248). The route takes you up and over some 2,000m peaks before passing caves and plantations (there are plenty of camping spots where you can pitch for the night) and dropping into the lush, green Wadi Bani Khalid.

ACTIVITIES

Swimming, hiking, camping, cave exploring

GPS

Wadi Tiwi: 22°47'28.52"N 59°13'44.49"E
Wadi Bani: 22°36'51.49"N 59° 5'38.57"E

TRIP INFO

REFERENCE
Oman Ministry of Tourism Trek E35

GOOD FOR
Anyone up for a full weekend of walking.

GET THERE
Really easy – simply follow the coast road from Muscat to Sur, and stop in the coastal town of Tiwi.

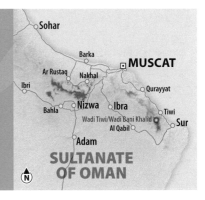

CLIMBS, CANYONS & CAVES

FOR SOME, THE CHALLENGE OF HIKING THROUGH THE UAE AND OMAN'S MOUNTAINS IS NOT QUITE ENOUGH.

CLIMBING

There are a surprising number of climbing walls in the UAE (p.98), which are the ideal places for getting started, improving your ability or practising techniques. They are also where you'll meet likeminded individuals, learn about excursions to Oman and the northern emirates, and pick up pointers from experienced climbers.

Once you're ready to take the leap away from the wall and try your hand at some real rock climbing, the region has plenty of challenging verticals and overhangs, with more than 600 climbs.

CLIMB TOGETHER

There are a number of groups worth contacting or tracking, such as Facebook's 'Real UAE Rock Climbers' and Oman Adventure Sports (omanclimbing. com), as well as international sites such as mountainproject. com and ukbouldering.com.

Ras Al Khaimah is the local climbing capital and where you'll find the majority of good ascents, although the area near Dibba is also excellent with Wadi Bih in particular a popular climbing destination. Elsewhere in Musandam, a number of climbs have been recorded near Khasab. Looking inland a little more, there are a handful of climbs near Al Ain and, if you head through to the Omani side of the Al Ain border, Wadi Madbah offers some reasonable climbing in the form of the wonderfully-named Wonderwall.

The climbs in the UAE and Oman vary from short outcrop routes to difficult mountain routes of alpine proportions. Most range from (using British classifications) Very Severe, up to extreme grades (E5). However, there are some easier routes for newer climbers, especially in Wadi Bih and Wadi Khab Al Shamis.

By and large, you're looking at limestone rock, but it's a brittle variety that can come away easily leaving sharp points – and it also produces quite a lot of loose surface rock. As such, you should take all the usual precautions, from practising a little healthy distrust – even on climbs and bolts you've used before – to always wearing a helmet to protect from loose falling rocks. Popular routes are kept fairly clean (do your part to help) and, although an adventurous can-do attitude is part and parcel of rock climbing's appeal – the topography of the UAE and Oman might not provide the ideal places to push yourself too far out of your comfort zone.

Of course, all outdoor and adventure activities have inherent risks and dangers, but, for most, a little common sense goes a long way. Rock climbing, however, is an exception in that small mistakes can be tragic. Therefore, you'd be highly recommended to do the first (or maybe the majority) of your rock climbs with an activity organiser (see p.7). The likes of Desert Rangers (desertrangers.com) arrange rock climbing trips to well-established locations, catering to everyone from absolute beginners to experienced climbers. Trips include instruction, all necessary safety equipment and lunch. All excursions depart from Dubai and a day of scaling the peaks will cost Dhs.400 per person. Like many other outdoor sports,

Al Hoota Cave

Swimming in Snake Canyon

you can actually climb throughout the whole year, as long as you're sensible with your summer choices. This generally means going a bit higher, which you can do in Wadi Bih and Khasab, or up on Jabal Misht and Jabal Shams – down in Oman, you'll find temperatures may be a little lower (plenty lower at the top of the big mountains) but humidity also tends to plummet, making conditions far more pleasant for climbing.

If you've not already met plenty of other climbers at the nation's climbing walls, then head to Wadi Bih at the weekend and you're sure to find others to climb with.

Alternatively, there are a number of resources available to you. UAE Climbing (uaeclimbing.com), for example, is a mine of information, with an excellent forum and blog (uaeclimbing.blogspot. com) where you can meet other climbers and get details of specific climbs. For a more detailed look at the numerous recorded climbs, including precise routes and photographs, pick up a copy of Toby Foord-Kelcey's excellent book *UAE Rock Climbing* which is available through Amazon and Cordee, and you may find copies in local sports shops and book shops.

BOULDERING

For the hardcore climber, bouldering is a form of 'free' climbing, without ropes or harnesses, and there's a spin-off branch of bouldering known as DWS, or 'deep-water soloing'. For those in the know, the coastline near Dibba and up into Musandam is one of the best places in the world to practise DWS. Basically, hire a boat for the day and find a dramatic cliff with overhangs to climb. The idea is that, when you fall, you'll drop into the deep sea below. Of course, it's more dangerous than that and you should always go out with someone who has done some DWS before. You should also learn how to fall; pushing away from the wall and entering the water safely will minimise the risk of cuts, scrapes and broken bones. And always make sure that the water beneath the climb is as deep and rock free as you think it is.

Adventure HQ

VIA FERRATA

If you're in search of some proper 'boys' own' style adventures, then the via ferrata of Oman are just what the adrenaline-doctor ordered. Literally meaning 'road of iron', via ferrata are lengthy, set climbing paths with fixed ropes, ladders and cables embedded deep into the rock to help you along otherwise impossible routes. Offering up a mix of via ferrata that have been there for decades (most likely installed by British military based in the country) and newer routes that have been placed to encourage Oman's reputation as an adventure wonderland, the sultanate has numerous routes that provide a mix between hiking, scrambling, wading through pools and via ferrata – like nature's very own assault course.

Grand Canyon: Take a look at the Al Qannah route in Hiking (p.92) and, if this spectacular hike alone isn't enough, continue along the W6 route until the abandoned village of Sab, where an uphill walk leads to a tough via ferrata (VF1) climb that takes around an hour. Up on the plateau, there's a cave and large pool to be explored.

Snake Canyon: Lying in Wadi Bani Awf,

CLIMBING WALLS

Adventure HQ, Times Square: Climbing rates for the state-of-the-art wall (and cable obstacle course) start at Dhs.50 and, as the store is one of the biggest regional stockists of all manner of climbing gear, you can even try out potential purchases. adventurehq.ae

Climbing Dubai, World Trade Centre: The Middle East's tallest outdoor climbing wall at 16m. Introductory lessons cost Dhs.85 with courses of five classes costing Dhs.350 for adults and Dhs.250 for kids. A day pass costs Dhs.60. climbingdubai.com

Pavilion Climbing Wall, Jumeirah Beach Hotel: This one is only open to members of the hotel's sports club, but if you are lucky enough to be a member, this six metre wall has plenty to offer, from learning areas to technical sections, with instructors on hand to offer training and advice. 04 406 8800

Pharaoh Club, Wafi: Dubai's first climbing wall, the indoor wall within Wafi offers a range of courses for beginners as well as public sessions for experienced

climbers, with routes of varying difficulty and crash mats for bouldering. Lessons cost Dhs.62 per hour. wafi.com

Playnation, Mirdif City Centre: The wall is one for younger family members and a good introduction to the sport of climbing. For Dhs.90, children aged 10 and over get to try their hand at the climbing wall and also take on the daring sky trail. theplaymania.com

The Club, Abu Dhabi: Another one for members only, The Club (the-club. com) has a five metre outdoor climbing wall for adults and children from the age of 4, with full safety gear provided. There is also another excellent climbing wall at Sorbonne University on Reem Island, but public access is still patchy at best, though this may improve.

Wadi Adventure, Al Ain: Park entry costs Dhs.100 (adult) or Dhs.50 (children) with 20 minutes of climbing, including instruction. Hiring equipment costs an extra Dhs.40. There's also an airpark and zip line to try. wadiadventure.ae

SAFETY FIRST

Climbing a via ferrata should be taken every bit as seriously as traditional mountain climbing or abseiling, with safety always the first consideration. Make sure you take, and wear, all relevant safety equipment (including helmets), that equipment is fully checked beforehand and that you treat the VF with a healthy dose of scepticism – it's not impossible for something to come away from the crumbly sandstone. Climbing a via ferrata can also be extremely physically demanding and many of these routes take several hours. Therefore, it's important to make sure you're up to the challenge.

between the towns of Al Hamra and Ar Rustaq, Snake Canyon is a must-visit for adventurous hikers. Both Little and Big Snake Canyon offer wading and scrambling, with the bigger hike involving some daring jumps into pools and swimming up through ravines. The via ferrata route (VF2) has traverses and zip crossings.

Bandar Khayran: VF3 is a coastal, rather than mountain, via ferrata. It is located on the western island of the beautiful Bandar Khayran area (around 30 minutes south of Muscat) and is best accessed by boat or, for an action adventure, kayak. Across the island, the two hour traverse climbs some 40m above the sea, offering incredible views.

The Chains: Not an actual VF, rather something of a natural obstacle course. Follow Highway 9, which runs from the Muscat-Dibba Road, and continue up Wadi ad Dil and through the town of A'Naamah. Park where the road ends, and start hiking upstream along the concrete falaj. The hike – an hour or so each way – involves rambling, scrambling and wading, as well as climbing some chains. At the end of the climb, you'll be rewarded with one of Oman's most beautiful, emerald pools.

CAVING

Where there are mountains, there are usually caves and the region boasts plenty of opportunities for intrepid types to discover what lies beneath our feet.

The Hajar Mountains boast extensive cave networks but due to the remoteness and difficult access, the majority of these are yet to be explored or recorded. So, for UAE cavers, head for the area around Al Ain: a complicated network weaves under Jebel Hafeet while, just past Buraimi on the Oman side of the border, there are many more underground passages and caves with spectacular displays of curtains, stalagmites and stalactites, as well as gypsum flowers.

For plenty more caving, carry on further into Oman. Al Kittan – nicknamed the marble cave thanks to the beautiful and luminous rock formations – is located just outside of Ibri. Continue south-east towards Nizwa and you come to the Jebel Akhdar range which offers some good

caving. Perhaps the best caving is to be had on the Selma Plateau, however. This is where you'll find the Majlis Al Jinn which is one of the world's largest cave systems and has the planet's second largest discovered underground chamber which is reputed to be so large that the Great Pyramids of Giza would fit inside! Like many of the biggest caves (see Al Hoota, right), the Ministry of Tourism is developing Majlis Al Jinn to open it up to tourism but there are many other equally thrilling caves nearby, such as the popular 7th Hole.

Within the region, caving ranges from fairly safe to extremely dangerous and, as no mountain rescue services exist, anyone venturing out into the mountains should always be well-equipped and accompanied by an experienced leader. To arrange caving trips, contact a local tour operator such as Gulf Leisure or Muscat Diving and Adventure Centre (see p.246 for details of tour operators) or try Mountain High (mountainhighme. com), a Dubai-based company that specialises in caving in Al Ain and Oman.

It's also worth checking out Abu Dhabi Alpine Club (adalpine. wordpress.com) to find more information and other keen cavers.

GEARING UP

From camming and belay devices, carabiners, harnesses and ropes, to climbing shoes and general outdoor clothing, the range of what is available in the UAE has grown exponentially in the past few years; whereas climbers and cavers used to have to buy from abroad or order online and pay expensive shipping costs, you can now find almost all you need in several stores across the UAE.

Global Climbing is the original and biggest exporter of brands including Petzl, Wild Country, Boreal, Fixe and LYON; however you'll find a fantastic range at Picnico and plenty of the main necessities at Go Sports too. The two latest sports superstores to open – Adventure HQ and Decathlon – also stock climbing equipment, with the former having a huge range and the latter offering real value-for-money basics. See p.244 & p.248) for full details.

AL HOOTA CAVE

Found at the foot of Jabal Shams in Tanuf Valley, at over five kilometres long Al Hoota (alhootacave.com) was previously one of the most challenging caves in Oman, with its one entrance being strictly for experienced cavers equipped with ropes, safety equipment, and a guide familiar with the cave. However, the Oman Ministry of Tourism completely overhauled the caves, making them safer and transforming them into a fascinating ecotourism attraction. The first entrance to the cave can be found near the village of Al Hotta (about 1,000m above sea level), and the other is near the town of Al Hamra (about 800m above sea level). Inside, you can see an amazing collection of crystals, stalactites and stalagmites, but perhaps the most interesting sight is the underground lake in the main cave. The lake is inhabited by thousands of blind, transparent fish, who rely on floods to carry in nourishment from the outside world.

EXPLORE FOR A CAUSE

HUNGRY FOR MORE ADVENTURE? JOIN UAE-BASED CHARITY GULF FOR GOOD ON AN EPIC FIVE-DAY ADVENTURE AND RAISE MONEY WHILE YOU'RE AT IT.

If this book has given you a taste for more adventure, then why not try some of the world's biggest challenges while doing some good in the process? Local charity superstars Gulf for Good encourage those based in this region to put their fitness and stamina to the ultimate test by taking part in one of their impressive ventures. Whether it's a trek through Machu Picchu, a hike along the Great Wall, riding along the Caribbean coastline in Cuba or reaching Everest Base Camp, the Gulf for Good challenges will push you through and past your limits.

Now in its 11th year, the organisation has gone from strength to strength, with participants completing 39 challenges so far. The funds raised by each participant go to charities in the country where the challenge takes place.

'Our policy is not simply to hand out money, but to identify important projects that will use the funds wisely,' says Gulf for Good's Patricia Anderson. 'Where necessary, we work closely with other charities to ensure that money is properly allocated and spent'.

Of Gulf for Good's achievements, Patricia says one of their proudest moments came in 2002. 'The Everest Base Camp Challenge raised enough funds to build an entire regional hospital! This was in the Ilam province, in the far eastern part of Nepal on the border with India. Funds raised by later Everest base camp challenges continued to support the hospital to buy vital equipment and to build a maternity wing'.

Sounds like your kind of adventure? Well, Gulf for Good organises around four challenges each year, so if you've missed the next one, there are several more coming up that are bound to excite. Be warned; they are not for the faint-hearted, but, of course, they are incredibly rewarding.

'They are all tough, but no-one would sponsor us if it wasn't going to be tough,' Patricia points out. 'We do have different levels of difficulty each year so that people can choose a challenge with which they are comfortable. But doing the challenge with a group makes all the difference; we work together, encourage each other and make sure that no-one is left behind. This builds an incredible sense of camaraderie, and groups remain friends well beyond their return to their normal lives'.

CHALLENGE YOURSELF

IF YOU'VE BEEN INSPIRED TO PUSH YOUR OWN BOUNDARIES AND CHANGE YOUR LIFE, AS WELL AS THE LIVES OF PEOPLE LESS FORTUNATE, WHY NOT TAKE ON ONE OF THE FOLLOWING CHALLENGES:

TRANSYLVANIAN TREK
Hike through plateaus, gorges, forests and valleys via Dracula's famous Bran castle.

THE ROAD TO MANDALAY
Hike and cycle through the Chin hills, including Mount Victoria, and along the Irawaddy river.

ROOF OF AFRICA
Climb Africa's highest peak – the 5,895m Kilimanjaro.

WILDS OF BORNEO
Ultimate kayaking, cycling and rafting adventure up peaks, and through national parks.

GULF FOR GOOD

Founded: 2001
Participants: More than 750 in 10+ years.
When: Varies. There are regular training days, information evenings and social gatherings, with, on average, four challenges a year.
Registration Fee: Usually Dhs.2,200 per challenge.
Sponsorship Requirement: varies from challenge to challenge, starting at around From Dhs.15,000 (Gulf For Good offers fundraising suggestions).
Contact: 04 368 0222
Website: gulf4good.org

'One of my recent challenges with Gulf for Good was Borneo, which was really tough as it was extremely physically demanding: we sea kayaked 9km between two islands and the mainland, cycled through a tea plantation, trekked up Mount Kinabalu and then headed back down, and, on the last day, went white water rafting! It was fantastic though, as we were supporting two different local charities, and we got to spend time with the children from both. We even got to help out and paint a few walls at the orphanage we visited.'

KAMELIA BIN ZAAL
Landscape Director

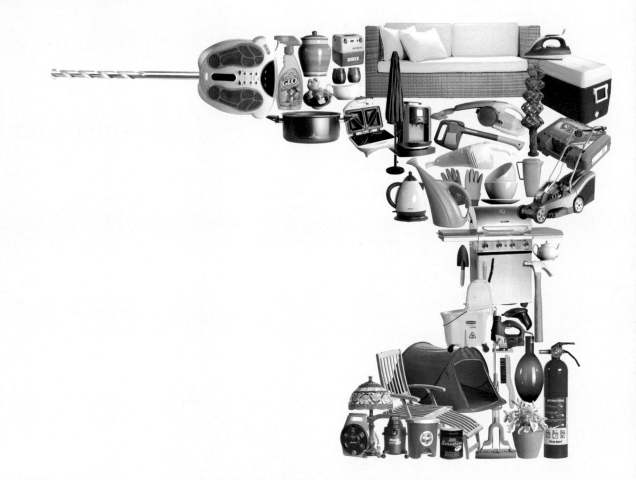

Thinking hardware? Think again.

There's certainly more to ACE than just a hardware store. From automotive accessories to kitchen appliances, camping gear to barbeques, outdoor furniture to paints and plants, gardening items to pet accessories. There's so much to choose from all under one roof. **ACE. One Store. Many Lifestyles.**

Dubai: Dubai Festival City, Tel: 800 ASK ACE (800 275 223), Sheikh Zayed Road, Tel: (04) 341 1906, Fax: (04) 341 7610 **Sharjah:** Tel: (06) 537 1556, Fax: (06) 537 1575 **Abu Dhabi:** Mina Road, Tel: (02) 673 166 Fax (02) 673 0415 **Al Ain:** Sultan Bin Zayed Road, Bawadi Mall (03) 784 0561   e-mail: ace@alfuttaim.ae or www.al-futtaim.ae

CYCLING

CYCLING

TAKE TO TWO WHEELS AND YOU CAN SEE SOME OF THE VERY BEST LANDSCAPES THAT THE UAE HAS TO OFFER; GET IN SHAPE AND DISCOVER HIDDEN CORNERS OF THE CITY.

On the way to Wadi Sumayni

MOUNTAIN BIKING

SINCE ITS BEGINNINGS IN THE 1970s, MOUNTAIN BIKING HAS BECOME AN INCREASINGLY POPULAR SPORT THAT IS TODAY PRACTISED BY MILLIONS ALL AROUND THE WORLD.

In North America and Europe, dedicated bike centres and regions cater for all cyclists´ needs, with places like Moab (Utah), Whistler (Canada) and Lake Garda (Italy) attracting hundreds of thousands of bike enthusiasts each year in what has become a multi-million dollar tourism, retail and sports business. Along with this, there is also a diverse competition scene, with World Cup events having evolved into a range of different disciplines, including cross-country, downhill, trial and dirt jump. This, in turn, has led to the development of discipline-orientated bike designs, which differ significantly in frame geometry, material and suspension technology.

Here in the UAE, increasing numbers of bikers who rode elsewhere and are keen to keep up with their favourite pastime have resulted in several groups being formed as riders head together.

Apart from the vast Rub Al Khali sand desert, the UAE is also geographically defined by the Hajar Mountains which run parallel to the east coast of the UAE. At their highest point up in the Musandam Peninsula, the Hajars reach a height of 2,000 metres and it's in these peaks and valleys that you'll find many graded tracks used initially by 4WDs which also offer the perfect terrain for cross-country MTB. Tracks are typically the width of a car and provide enough space for two cyclists to ride next to each other. Technically, they do not provide too many difficulties but they can become very steep at times. Also, when frequently used by cars, especially in steep zones, there can be a lot of loose gravel which makes cycling a bit slippery and dangerous as those spots are difficult to judge.

On some routes, the track crosses the wadi which makes it more strenuous to ride and harder to follow the trail. In those wadis, the tracks are from time to time covered with fresh gravel after rare but heavy rainfalls that occur mainly during the winter season. In less-used wadis, rains can alter the way of the track, so you might need to search out a new way to go on. Over the past few years, many new tracks have been built to serve larger infrastructure projects; although they may be not picturesque, they are often quite challenging to ride and it's fun to access new areas. Occasionally, sand from the nearby desert can be blown over a track, which makes cycling more difficult.

Other than these, the remains of old donkey routes and walking paths can be transformed into popular single trails after some cleaning and trail building. In the area south of Shawka, in southern Ras Al Khaimah, for example, a group of MTB enthusiasts have put a lot of effort into the building of such a loop.

WHERE TO MTB

Generally speaking, there are four areas that are best for mountain biking and, if you're feeling adventurous and don't want to follow one of our suggested routes (p.110), these are the areas where you might find some less-ridden paths:

- Ras al Khaimah and Musandam – mountains reaching up to 2,000m in height and huge, wide wadis to explore.
- The area to the west of the Masafi-Dibba road –smaller wadis, mountain villages, oases, desert and medium-high mountains.
- The east coast – several shorter dead-end valleys.
- The area south of Shawka close to the Omani border – built single trails in smaller hills.

Descending down Jebel Yibir

GETTING STARTED

If you are completely new to off-road cycling, then your first step should definitely be to get in contact with one or several of the MTB groups in the UAE (for a full list, see Directory p.238). Mainly based in Dubai, most of these groups organise weekly rides in safe, easily-accessible locations, such as near Nad Al Sheba, to help newbies get the feeling for riding without asphalt under their tyres. If you're not yet completely certain that mountain biking is the sport for you, you can rent an MTB (see Getting the gear, p.118) and try a couple of these beginner rides first to see if you take to it. Later, you can join a group on one of their various routes in the Hajars – all groups offer rides of various difficulties to encourage newer riders, as well as routes that challenge the country's more experienced bikers.

Dubai Mountain Bikers (find on Facebook) is a newly-organised group which has the goal of connecting MTBers in Dubai with other bikers who love to share their exciting experiences of off-road riding. Aimed at all levels, it is a good first port of call. The Roost Tah group (again on Facebook) is equally welcoming to different levels, with training sessions taking place on easy terrain. UAE Mountainbiking and Mountain Biking UAE are a pair of informal groups of like-minded riders – drop them a line or check out their Facebook sites for upcoming rides.

The best-established group within the UAE is HOT-COG Mountain Bike Club (hot-cog.com), which runs regular weekly rides and even occasional races but it is definitely aimed at more advanced level riders and isn't for first-timers.

An alternative – and a nice way to get started – would be to combine your first off-road bike experience with a weekend break with family or friends, and take advantage of the organised guided tours that operators offer (see p.245 & p.248 for a full listing of tour operators). This approach gives you the advantage of not having to buy or rent a bike and you can simply follow the guide on a safe trip.

For riders who do have some previous MTB experience elsewhere but want to get started on their UAE riding adventures,

it's best to tackle an easy route, such as those in the area to the northwest of Masafi or the Dadna Circuit (p.110) to get some experience on the terrain.

The dry and rocky landscape here can be quite different to what most riders will be used to and will require fine-tuning your skill set before taking on the more challenging rides. Before you head out, of course, head to a reputable bike shop to stock up on spares, safety gear and to make sure your bike is ready to tackle the Emirates.

GET THE GEAR

So, what do you need to become a mountain biker and where can you buy it from? Although lots of bikes look like proper mountain bikes, their strength and durability of frame, suspension, shifting and braking are simply not up to the abuse of an off-road trip. The simple rule 'You get what you pay for' can almost always be applied to purchasing a bike. Suitable bikes start from Dhs.2,750 while more frequent riders find good value for money from Dhs.10,000 onwards; that price bracket will buy you strong, reliable components which can sustain off road use over a longer time and feature front and rear suspension with adjustable damping and travel adjustment.

Beginners should visit one of the bikes shops in Dubai (they're all in Dubai, see p.118 for bike stores) and ask for an entry-level 24-speed hard tail leisure MTB with front suspension. This is the basic bike to get you up and running on most terrains. The bike should be equipped with a pump and a saddle bag. Inside the saddle bag, you should carry a spare inner tube, tyre levers and a patch kit; if you do not know how to fix a flat tyre yourself, ask the shop or a friendly member of your group to show you how to do it before you venture out on some remote trail.

For cycling comfort and safety you are going to need a pair of cycling shorts, cycling shirt, padded gloves, sunglasses and a good helmet. Don't forget to pick up some good front and rear lights if there's any chance you'll be riding in anything less than full daylight. A special backpack with a water bladder with pipe

to drink from (such as a CamelBak) is a good idea for staying hydrated during rides in the warmer, drier UAE weather.

More experienced riders who ride more frequently and in more difficult terrain should look to upgrade to a full suspension MTB, which makes riding much more comfortable and safe, although full suspension is obviously more expensive than just front suspension. At this stage, riders will probably want to opt for MTB shoes with clipless pedals too. Other desirable gadgets include a bike computer with GPS to measure time, parameters, speed and distance, as well as to stay orientated.

If you already have most of this gear from riding before you arrived in the UAE, you might want to consider switching over to tubeless tyres with special sealant liquids; with sharp rocks and thorny plants prevalent on UAE tracks, these are highly recommended to avoid punctures.

MOUNTAIN BIKE TOURS

The main tour operators (p.245, 248) team up with local activities providers to offer MTB tours across the UAE, although these are often more scenic than challenging. For a special experience, contact Absolute Adventure (adventure.ae) which has been offering mountain biking tours from its Dibba camp since 2005. Guests are briefed,

RENT-A-BIKE

All the main bike stores (see p.118) offer bike rentals but be warned that they have a limited number so, to ensure you get a bike in your size, you're advised to reserve well in advance. Although not the same as riding a bike that has been tailored to your body and riding style, renting is a cost-effective and common sense option if you're just testing the water or are only likely to ride a couple of times per year for special events.

geared up and fitted with bikes before venturing out into the wadis for routes of various difficulty levels. Tours are available from Dhs.350 to Dhs.495, including equipment, transfers to and from camp, a guide, drinking water and packed lunch. You can stay at the camp for a night or two if you'd like to make a weekend of it.

For the most exotic off-road rides in the UAE, check out Abu Dhabi's Anantara resorts (anantara.com) which offer bikers amazing adventures across the dunes of the Liwa desert or the terrain of Sir Bani Yas Island, where you'll come across some amazing wildlife as the island is, in fact, a protected wildlife reserve. Contact Anantara directly for the latest prices and timing.

For a truly special local cycling escape, spend a couple of days down in Oman at The View – an eco retreat located 1,400m up, and overlooking, the incredible Jebel Shams (mountain of the sun) which is the highest peak in the Hajar range. Routes wind through all the valleys and The View has some experienced and knowledgeable guides to lead groups of all levels.

CYCLING SAFELY

Mountain biking is, of course, a high octane sport at times and, like all activities that provide plenty of thrills, there can be the occasional spill. Make sure that, as well as having the correct gear (see p.118), you take extra caution when cycling in the UAE and Oman:

Water: drink a minimum of a litre per hour, and also carry some energy bars and isotonic solution. You will appreciate having some extra water to refresh yourself and clean your hands after a toilet break or doing some puncture repairs.
Heat: avoid riding when temperatures exceed 38°C, which can happen anytime between May and September, as it may result in heat exhaustion or heat stroke.
Light: it gets dark very quickly here, maybe earlier than you are used to. Good lighting on the bike is advisable

for longer trips, as you never know what might delay your plans.
Weather: the weather in the UAE is pretty stable most of the time but look at the weather forecast ahead of each trip. A sudden sand storm might not only affect your speed, but also leave you with sore eyes for days. Even a small rain shower can be very dangerous in the mountains, as you can easily get caught by flood waters in narrow wadis.
Orientation: as little thorough mapping of the mountains exists, you should use a portable GPS to find your way and not get lost. Make use of Google Earth or download some of the GPS tracks available from Explorer (askexplorer. com) to find the best rides.
Wilderness: out there, it is pretty much an outback where no mountain rescue exists, so it is advisable to always ride in groups and carry a first aid kit with you.

DADNA CIRCUIT

THIS ROUTE HAS EVERYTHING THAT A BIG ROUTE HAS BUT IN SMALLER DIMENSIONS, MAKING IT IDEAL FOR BEGINNERS. PAIR IT WITH A HOTEL FOR A WEEKEND AWAY.

The tour starts with some easy riding on asphalt through a quiet residential area with local villas, before winding its way between some nice farms. You can also do a loop inside Fujairah Farm's surprisingly green plantations. Make sure you stop by the farm shop on the main road to pick up some of the refreshing produce for a tasty stop en route.

After crossing the main road, the off-road experience begins on rocky tracks and the occasional small patch of tarmac as you pass a social housing complex and a palace; you'll cycle slowly, climbing through the coastal plains towards the mountains till you reach the lower, smaller dam and the wilderness really begins.

Stop for a moment here; you will be embraced by the total silence of the mountains as you face the wide track ahead. Once in the wadi bed, stay on the right side of the valley and cycle up to the to the great Owais dam and on to its 18m high wall. Enjoy the amazing view; sometimes, you may even spot some water behind this huge retention dam which can hold 3.5 million cubic metres of water.

Continue the track along the wide retention area of Wadi Zikt until a steep climb to your left takes you up to a mountain pass. Climb up to enjoy the fresh air that constantly blows through the rocky gap at the top of the small pass.

After a last break, you can enjoy the downhill back to civilisation, passing the ruins of the old abandoned village to reach the new village houses along with some wonderful oases. The modern tarmac road leads you straight back to the starting point, passing a number of farms en route.

AL AQAH BEACH

This stretch of beach, near the Dadna Circuit, lies between Dibba and Fujairah city. It has become something of a resort for both international guests and the UAE's city dwellers looking to escape for the weekend. Rotana, Ibertotel and Le Meridien all have nice resort hotels here, complete with sprawling pools and watersports centres, although camping here is a popular option. The venerable Sandy Beach Hotel is especially popular with divers. See p.242 in the Directory for a full list of hotels along with their contact details.

110

TRIP INFO

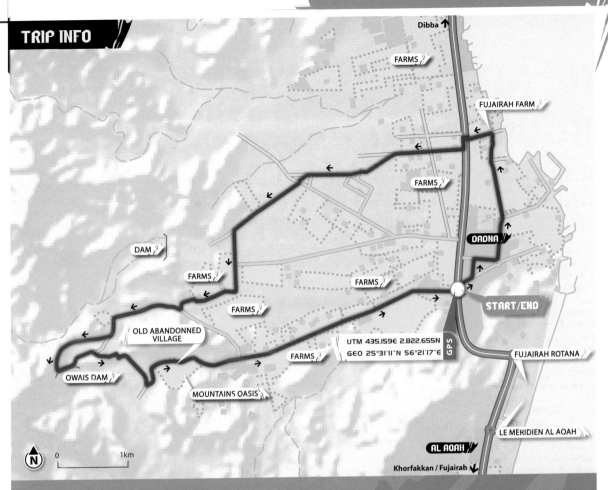

Dibba ↑

FARMS

FUJAIRAH FARM

FARMS

DAM

FARMS

FARMS

DADNA

FARMS

FARMS

OLD ABANDONNED VILLAGE

START/END

FARMS

UTM 435,159E 2,822,655N
GEO 25°31'11"N 56°21'17"E
GPS

FUJAIRAH ROTANA

OWAIS DAM

MOUNTAINS OASIS

LE MERIDIEN AL AQAH

AL AQAH

Khorfakkan / Fujairah ↓

N

0   1km

RATING	Easy
STATS	18km, 150m of elevation, 2-3 hours to complete
TERRAIN	Tarmac, graded track
SCENERY	Coastal plains with green plantations, mountains and wadis

MAIN CHALLENGE

A few small but steep ascents and a fast final downhill

ELEVATION

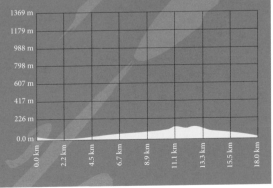

1369 m
1179 m
988 m
798 m
607 m
417 m
226 m
0.0 m

0.0 km 2.2 km 4.5 km 6.7 km 8.9 km 11.1 km 13.3 km 15.5 km 18.0 km

AL HALA ROUND TOUR

AMAZING MOUNTAINTOP VIEWS WITH A GREAT DOWNHILL AT THE END. SCATTERED WITH RUINS, CANYONS, ABANDONED VILLAGES, PLANTATIONS AND EVEN SOME POOLS.

The village of Al Hala lies just off the Masafi-Dibba road (E89) and is easily accessible from all directions. Your best bet is to park up right next to the small strip of shops, where there's plenty of space for leaving your vehicle. The cycling starts with a gentle climb of just 200m as you cruise along on tarmac until you reach the entrance to the beautiful, narrow Wadi Tayyibah.

After 11km of riding (and 308m of climbing) you reach the village of Tayyibah, where you turn right to enjoy some nice tarmac riding – it makes for a relaxing break from the previous uphill, while still delving you deeper and deeper into the mountains until you reach Wadi Sidr.

Take a break in the next small mountain village, which has a small grocery store that is ideal for topping up fluids, before the cycling continues right up Wadi Sidr (still on tarmac), passing the upper retention dam.

The enjoyable ride through the mountains continues until the tarmac comes to an end and the off-road terrain winds up the very narrow valley. It climbs significantly here and soon becomes fairly steep as you rise out of the valley and emerge at the top of the mountains, with some great views of the mighty Jebel Yibir far away on the left. This section will require some low gearing and a decent level of fitness.

You should rest at the summit (on the right side of the track) to enjoy the fabulous views – you're actually only 594m above sea level, although you'll feel like you're on the top of the world as no vegetation obstructs the view. If the weather is good, you can see all the way to Dibba and the Indian Ocean.

Just a bit further down, you reach a mountain plateau where you can choose between two routes; both are dazzling 3.5km downhills and end up at the same spot in the valley. The one on the right is more demanding due to greater steepness and the condition of the track but both are great fun.

Once in the valley, you can enjoy a bit of tarmac until you turn right to cross back over to the start point in Al Hala.

WADI TAYYIBAH

This wadi remains surprisingly green, making it a lovely respite from the concrete cities adn sandy deserts. However, on the flip side, after an admittedly rare downpour, it can become blocked and flooded.

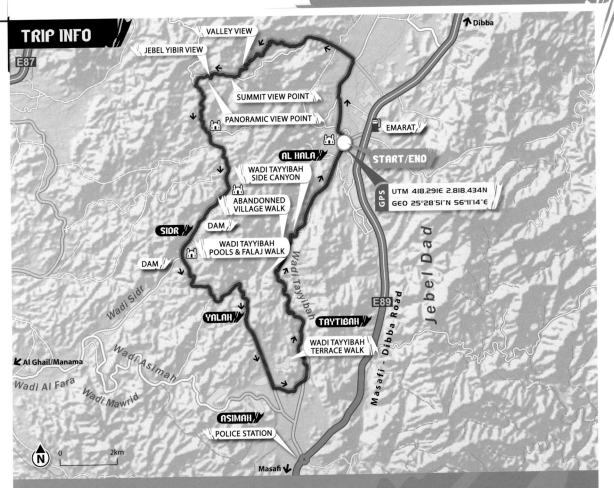

TRIP INFO

E87

- Dibba
- VALLEY VIEW
- JEBEL YIBIR VIEW
- SUMMIT VIEW POINT
- PANORAMIC VIEW POINT
- AL HALA
- EMARAT
- START/END
- WADI TAYYIBAH SIDE CANYON

GPS UTM 418,291E 2,818,434N
GEO 25°28'51"N 56°11'14"E

- ABANDONNED VILLAGE WALK
- SIDR
- DAM
- WADI TAYYIBAH POOLS & FALAJ WALK
- DAM
- YALAH
- TAYTIBAH
- WADI TAYYIBAH TERRACE WALK
- Wadi Sidr
- Wadi Asimah
- Al Ghail/Manama
- Wadi Al Fara
- Wadi Mawrid
- ASIMAH
- POLICE STATION
- Masafi
- Wadi Tayyibah
- E89
- Masafi - Dibba Road
- Jebel Dad

N 0 2km

RATING	Intermediate
STATS	39km, 785m of elevation, half a day to complete
TERRAIN	Tarmac, graded track
SCENERY	Narrows wadis with plantations, mountain villages and summit areas with views

MAIN CHALLENGE

Long ascents with a steep, long downhill at the end

ELEVATION

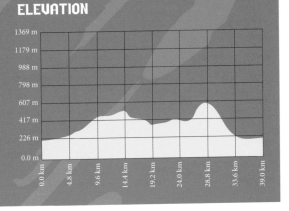

1369 m
1179 m
988 m
798 m
607 m
417 m
226 m
0.0 m

0.0 km 4.8 km 9.6 km 14.4 km 19.2 km 24.0 km 28.8 km 33.6 km 39.0 km

JEBEL YIBIR ROUTE

THE TOUGHEST CLIMB YOU'LL FIND FOLLOWED BY THE MOST AMAZING 9.7KM DOWNHILL THAT TWISTS THROUGH SWITCHBACKS. HIGH ALTITUDE FUN WITH AMAZING VIEWS.

The starting point for this is right off the Ras Al Khaimah-Dibba Highway (E87), almost exactly halfway from either side. The exit is signposted Al Mihtaraqah. Once you start cycling, you will soon escape civilisation and experience the remoteness of the UAE mountains, passing small settlements and houses where locals still live the simple life.

Over the first 10km, you will tackle three minor but sporadically steep ascents, which are followed by three descents which take you right back down to your starting altitude. At the top of the third climb, after 6km of riding, you will get your first sight of the mighty Jebel Yibir which, at 1527m, is one of the highest

mountains in the UAE. One last downhill leads you into the mighty Wadi Khab.

Turn right, following the wadi upwards to the last T-junction where a left turn will leave you with an extremely steep ramp up towards Jebel Yibir directly in front of you, deep at the end of the huge wadi. If you are already feeling a little fatigued, best not to think about the fact that you are still at exactly the same altitude as when you started!

Now, you quickly gain 120m altitude on this first steep mountain step. Once you have fought your way up the first few winding bends, the view widens as you reach a 430m high mountain plateau. From here, you

can clearly see the day´s destination, Jebel Yibir, and the steep track that leads up to it.

If you decide to continue, you should be prepared for a very steep and constant uphill climb which gains altitude quickly. You should take your time climbing, stopping to enjoy some of the amazing viewpoints looking back over where you have just come from, as well as over the surrounding mountains. At 875m above sea level, look down to see a huge canyon rising from your right.

In the upper half of the climb, the track heads a bit deeper into the mountains for further remoteness and wilderness. Although the summit area is restricted from access, once you reach the 'no entry' sign, you are already at 1360m – the perfect place to relax on some of the big rocks under the open skies up here and pride yourself in having mastered a total of 1455m of elevation up to this point. What follows is one of the longest downhills the UAE has to offer; you will be virtually dragged down by gravity and can really enjoy each of the many switchbacks that eventually deliver you 9.7km away and 1090m lower, back in Wadi Khab. From here, you still have 10km and 378m of total climbing to go until you reach the car on the same path you followed on the way in.

DARING DOWNHILLS

The most important thing when tackling a crazy downhill such as Jebel Yibir is body position. Try to keep a vertical line between your feet and your core – so, as the downhill gets steeper, your weight is shifted further back behind the saddle.

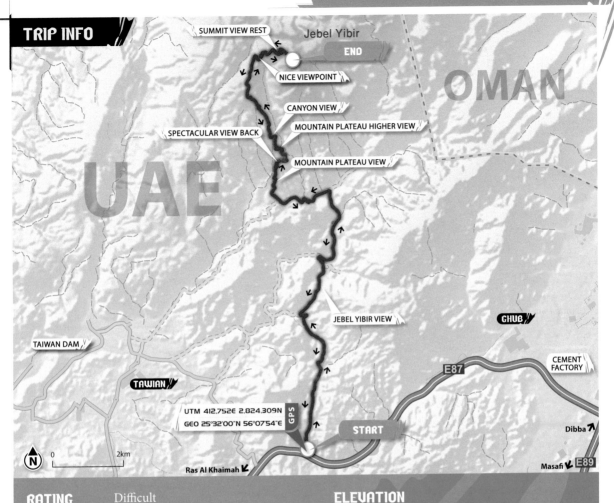

TRIP INFO

SUMMIT VIEW REST

Jebel Yibir

END

NICE VIEWPOINT

CANYON VIEW

MOUNTAIN PLATEAU HIGHER VIEW

SPECTACULAR VIEW BACK

MOUNTAIN PLATEAU VIEW

OMAN

UAE

JEBEL YIBIR VIEW

GHUB

TAIWAN DAM

CEMENT FACTORY

E87

TAWIAN

UTM 412.752E 2.824.309N
GEO 25°32'00"N 56°07'54"E

GPS

START

Dibba

N   0   2km

Ras Al Khaimah

Masafi E89

RATING	Difficult
STATS	42km, 1833m of elevation, full day to complete
TERRAIN	Graded track and compacted dirt
SCENERY	Wide wadis, amazing mountains and some of the very best views over Musandam and the Northern Emirates

MAIN CHALLENGE

Three minor ascents and descends on the 10km approach before a very steep and long ascent up to Jebel Yibir, all of which you repeat in reverse before getting back to the car

ELEVATION

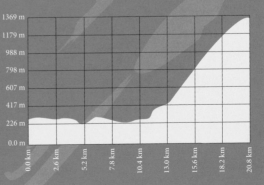

1369 m
1179 m
988 m
798 m
607 m
417 m
226 m
0.0 m

0.0 km   2.6 km   5.2 km   7.8 km   10.4 km   13.0 km   15.6 km   18.2 km   20.8 km

LEISURE RIDING

FOR MANY, CYCLING INVOLVES GENTLY PEDALLING EARLY IN THE MORNING, AFTERNOON OR EVENING TO EXPLORE THE GREAT OUTDOORS AT A MODERATE PACE.

If you have your own bike – or are able to hire one (p.118) and transport it – then try parking up near Creek Park.

Begin with a lap or two of the park first and then head down the creekside, past Dubai Courts and the Rolex Towers and through Bastakiya (map 1), following the Creek past the souks and the abra stations on a mix of roads and pavements, eventually arriving at the Heritage Village in Shindagha. Here, a pedestrian tunnel takes you under the Creek and brings you back up opposite the Gold Souk on the Deira side. You can either explore the front in Deira or head back up the Creek, through Al Ras (with its great views back to the Bur Dubai side) and past the Spice Souk. Follow the long wharf past the abra stations and hundreds of dhows, finally crossing back at the Floating Bridge. This trip is 11.5km long (not including detours in Deira or Creek Park) and, if you do it early on a Friday morning, you can ride right through middle of the souks.

Jumeirah Road (map 2) is another great place for a leisurely ride and, if you don't have your own bike or haven't hired

1-Dubai

PORT RASHID
BUR DUBAI
DEIRA
HOR AL ANZ
KARAMA
OUD METHA
AL RIGGA
AL ITTIHAD RD
UMM HURAIR
AL KHAIL RD
GARHOUD
DUBAI INTL AIRPORT

0   2km

NOTE

The RTA is set on making Dubai a more bike-friendly environment, creating more and more cycle paths, especially on routes leading to and from the various Metro stations. Work has also neared completion on a dedicated cycle path that will run from near Arabian Ranches to the Bab Al Shams resort, creating a 90km total loop. In the years to come, a giant park will be added in the centre of the loop. The old Nad Al Sheba camel track has also recently been converted into the NAS Cycle Park, with lights having been added to the 4km, 6km and 8km loops. There are other facilities there too.

from elsewhere, the Eppco (04 348 1908) near the Burj Al Arab and Umm Suqeim Park rents bikes. From there, it's a 13km ride down to Jumeira Open Beach, Dubai Marine Resort and Jumeirah Mosque.

There are several spots along **Dubai Marina (map 3)** where you can hire pedal-powered karts, such as outside Dubai Marina Mall and on Marina Walk behind the Dorra Bay building, but this is also a fantastic place to ride. Both sides of the marina feature around 4km of smooth, flat pedestrian walkways and, if you cross the bridges at each end, you can easily create an 8km loop that gives you an incredible view of Dubai

Marina throughout. You may have to get off your bike and walk for brief busy sections at the easternmost end of the marina due to the cafes that spill out and many more people strolling along, but the rest is pretty hassle-free. Dubai's parks are great to explore by bicycle (and safe if you've kids riding with you) and the pick of these is arguably Mushrif Park, thanks to the 5km cycle path that loops around the outside of the park. Al Mamzar Park is also a good size and, if you don't have your own bike, you can rent by the hour in both of these locations.

Abu Dhabi Corniche (map 4) is maybe the very best place in the UAE to take a fun

bike ride. Bikes can be rented from outside the Hiltonia Beach Club and, from there, there's a cycle path that follows the Corniche Beach Park for 8km along the Corniche, all the way to the port with its dhow yards and souks. There are, of course, plenty of places to stop and grab a cold drink or ice cream en route too.

In the other direction, you can ride up on to the Breakwater and along to the Heritage Village or Marina Village. If you negotiate your way across the busy roundabout, you can continue your ride past the InterContinental Abu Dhabi and down to the dhow yards and marinas of Al Bateen.

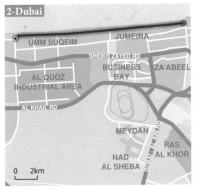

ROAD BIKING

FOR EVERY LEISURE CYCLIST, THERE IS A ROAD BIKER: WHERE IT'S ALL ABOUT RACKING UP SERIOUS KILOMETRES.

Road cycling has exploded in popularity over the past few years and it's not hard to see why. Cycling burns more calories per hour than running, it gets you out into the fresh air, it can be a social or individual pursuit and, in these ecologically-minded and austerity-focused times, a mode of transport that costs nothing to run and produces no fumes makes it the vehicle for the 21st century.

The Middle East clearly isn't its natural home for a variety of reasons. For all but the most committed, cycling during the summer months really isn't an option, and commuting to work on bike is not possible in the way that it is in European cities.

However, for eight months a year, temperatures remain pleasant. Get out of town and you'll find immaculate, wide roads with little traffic and these highways have become like second homes to an increasing number of cyclists.

GETTING THE GEAR

If you're looking for evidence of cycling's explosion in popularity, the number of new bike shops popping up across Dubai should suffice. Like mountain biking (p.106), not everything that looks like a road bike is a road bike and, again, you do get what you pay for. Of course, a top of the range, full carbon bike with low profile carbon wheels and electronic gearing will set you back tens of thousands of dirhams but you can get out on the roads with a decent and reliable new bike for around Dhs.3,500.

As the price increases, the quality and reliability increases and the weight decreases, but it can be fun to start with something fairly basic and add new components as you improve. This also takes some of the sting out of the price tag.

There are a few things that you shouldn't look to save money on, however. A good helmet could save your life, as could some high quality, bright front and rear lights for your bike. Cycling clothing is optional but recommended for comfort, although once you start riding regularly, you'll want to get some specific cycling shoes which make a big difference to the efficiency of your riding.

A good pair of sunglasses not only stop the eyes from streaming, they can save your vision if some debris kicks up from the road. Make sure you always have a spare inner tube, a pump (or CO2 cartridges), tyre levers and a small Allen key set in your saddle bag too.

Finally, always carry plenty of fluid on your bike. Even days that start with a chill in the air tend to end up hot and sticky after a few hours of riding.

Adventure HQ Has a good range of both MTB and road bikes, with Merida a good entry-level brand and BMC representing the high-end roadie choice. There's also some clothing, accessories, components and nutrition.

Decathlon The superstore has a good range of leisure bikes, MTBs and road bikes, and its own brand bikes are some of the most affordable around and are of surprisingly high quality. In terms of components, clothing and accessories, it's a good place to get some cheap basics.

Go Sport The stock is mainly provided by Ride, although there are some extras. A good choice for entry-level gear.

Intersport The regional distributor for Orbea bikes and clothing, which has some excellent entry-level MTBs and road bikes.

Micah's One of the latest additions, Micah's is for the experienced MTB rider only. Stocking beautiful Ellsworth handcrafted frames and wheels, the staff really know their stuff.

Probike Although Probike does sell MTBs, it is mainly a roadie shop with a good selection of triathlon-specific bikes, accessories and clothing. Most of the bikes are from the British Planet X brand, which is renowned for its value for money.

Revolution Cycles A new store in Motor City that stocks a lot of top brands that you'll not find elsewhere, like GT, Cannondale, Trek and Ridley bikes, and accessories like Catlike helmets and Louis Garneau clothing. Ride The new SZR megastore is the Middle East's biggest bike shop. Ride specialises in Giant bikes – the world's biggest bike manufacturer, which offers excellent value for money. Sells both MTB and road bikes. Wolfi's Bike Shop The oldest and most established bike store in Dubai, this is where you'll find some of the more specialist, technical gear you can't find elsewhere, along with bikes, clothing and accessories. Staff are extremely knowledgeable.

GROUPS

Whether you're a beginner or an experienced rider, you'll want to join up with a group; riding with others is the safest way to get out on your bike in the UAE. You'll also be kept up-to-date on everything from newbie training rides to overseas excursions. You'll find plenty of smaller groups organising regular rides on Facebook, but in terms of the main groups to look out for, Abu Dhabi Tri Club is the only option in the capital. The club organises a couple of Friday and Saturday rides of different distances (50 to 130km), with a newbie ride taking place on the first Friday of each month. In Dubai, there are a couple of options. CycleSafe is great for all levels, as the Friday rides range from a beginner's to advanced rides. The group also runs the popular Saturday coffee ride – a 30km ride out to Bab Al Shams for breakfast, before returning to Dubai. Finally, there's the Dubai Roadsters. The Roadsters do training rides at Nad Al Sheba on Sunday and Tuesday evenings, while the main Friday ride (80km and 120km options) is the biggest group ride in the UAE, often hundreds strong, although it moves along at a fair pace and is not recommended for new riders.

THE AMAZING RACE

Local groups are very active in organising MTB race events but without any fixed schedule. They tend to take place during the cooler winter months. Subscribe to the various newsletters and Facebook pages, and keep an eye on premiermarathons.com, from where you can enter most races.

Another event worth checking out is the annual Wadi Bih Adventure Race (wadiadventure.com) which is a multi-discipline (MTB/mountain run) race set in the dramatic and stunning Hajar Mountains near Dibba (Musandam) for individuals and teams of two people. There is also a separate MTB hill climb race held for those who only want to cycle.

For roadies, CycleSafe and Revolution Cycles have been instrumental in creating a number of great races throughout the year, with December's Dubai 92 (a 92km race through Dubai) preceded by a series of time trial style events between September and December. They also organise a number of criterium races (essentially, do the most laps you can in a given time) at Dubai Autodrome.

Probike organises a series of time trials over distances ranging from 10km to 40km (with some team TTs too), at a course in Academic City, while Yas Marina Circuit has recently chipped in with a couple of races.

For information on all bike racing in the UAE, keep your eyes on premiertiming.com, which has a full calendar of events and is also where you can enter.

At the other end of the spectrum, of course, is February's Tour of Oman. Coming early in the European cycling season, many of the top teams in pro cycling send some of their biggest stars over to the Sultanate to gain some early season fitness; for fans of cycling, it's essential viewing.

ROAD BIKING ROUTES

STARTERS

Yas Marina Circuit is open to the public on Tuesday evenings, with Dubai Autodrome following suit on Wednesday evenings. This car-less environment makes the race circuits popular training venues, especially suited to newbies trying to get comfortable on their bikes before hitting the roads. CycleSafe often provides free beginner bike skills classes at the Autodrome too.

TRAINING

If you have the hang of it and are looking to do more than laps of the race courses, there are a few possibilities. In Abu Dhabi, many cyclists head to the west of the island where there's a loop starting at the top of 10th Street in **Al Bateen (map 1)**, and heading down 10th, 8th and 16th Street (going straight across four roundabouts). Turn around and head back, and you'll have a 9km loop that usually sees little traffic.

Between Abu Dhabi and Dubai lies the **Ghantoot (map 2)** area and here you'll find a popular 13km loop that is even quieter than Al Bateen, as the only real traffic is from vehicles heading to the Golden Tulip or Cassells hotels, or one of the palaces.

In Dubai, the roads around **Nad Al Sheba and Meydan** or the new **Nad Al Sheba Cycle Park (map 3)** are the places to head for. There are various routes and combinations available to keep interest levels up. However, certain sections, such as 34th Street, remain unlit at night and, so, are best avoided; other sections have streetlights throughout. Although a relatively quiet area, drivers here have something of a blind spot to all the cyclists. The NAS Cycle Park is, wonderfully, completely and utterly vehicle-free.

BIG RIDES

These are generally the routes followed by the big group rides. They usually involve riding on busier roads and, therefore, are best tackled in a large group and early on a Friday morning when traffic is lightest.

In Abu Dhabi, start at the west of the island and cycle along the corniche and on to the new **Sheikh Khalifa Highway (map 4)**, which leads through Saadiyat and Yas;

you can add loops of Yas Island or head on to the mainland for extra loops around the airport and Masdar before making the return journey back to the Corniche.

In Dubai, the Roadsters route (map 5) heads out from the Lime Tree Cafe in Jumeira, passes Safa Park and then crosses over into the Meydan and Nad Al Sheba area before following Manama Rd out to Academic City. To add distance, extra loops around Mushrif Park and Mirdif, Al Khaawaneej and Al Awir can be done, before heading back to Dubai.

Finally, the traditional CycleSafe route (map 6) starts at the Al Qudra Roundabout (follow Umm Suqeim Rd past Arabian Ranches and Motor City and over the Dubai Bypass Road and you'll come to a roundabout with parking on the right). From there, the journey straight out into the desert covers 18km before meeting a roundabout where you have a few options. You can turn left and follow the road past Dubai Stables and towards Al Lisaili (around 40km out and back). Or, turn right and you'll arrive at Bab Al Shams after 12km; turn there or you can carry on a further 23km until you come to a cattle grid; take a left after the cattle grid and you'll hit some rolling terrain as the road follows the dunes – something of a rarity in Dubai.

You can now do the majority of these routes on the fantastic new cycle-only path which runs to the side of the road. But, either way, remember that you're a long way from civilisation here – if you run out of water, there are no convenient service stations to top up at and you're still a long way from home.

CHALLENGES

Although not weekly occurrences, there are some great rides that take place from time to time that help relieve the tedium of repeating the same laps and loops in Dubai and Abu Dhabi. All the main groups organise trips to Hatta, for example, where one great ride heads out from Hatta Fort Hotel and across the Hajars to Kalba (map 7). It's beautiful but difficult terrain with some serious climbing involved. To Kalba and back is around 105km with

more than 2,000m of climbing; however, you can obviously turn around before Kalba (usually after the first or second tunnel on the S116 Sharjah-Kalba Rd). Dubai Roadsters have recently started running another equally hilly route that tackles part of the new Dubai to Fujairah highway, but the group's best-known (and hardest) challenge is the twice-a-year 220km coast-to-coast ride that crosses the Hajars between Dubai and Fujairah.

Finally, for those who are real gluttons for punishment, there's Jebel Hafeet (map 8) in Al Ain. It may have been named one of the world's greatest driving roads, but it's a painful challenge for cyclists. Park at the top and enjoy the fast descent to Green Mubazzarrah; then you simply don't have the choice but to turn back around. The 12km road climbs more than 1,200m through 21 switchbacks. It's hard work but rewarding.

GPS

The old-fashioned bike computer is a thing of the past. Today, a number of brands – with Polar and Garmin at the forefront – sell advanced bike-mounted GPS units that do everything from using satellites to accurately tell you how fast you're going and how far you've been, to providing full TomTom-style mapping, so you need never get lost again. If you pick up one of the more advanced units, there's no reason to only use it while out riding; remove from the mount and it's just as useful for off-roading, hiking and sailing. All the main bike shops stock cycling GPS units while Adventure HQ has a large range of multi-purpose units.

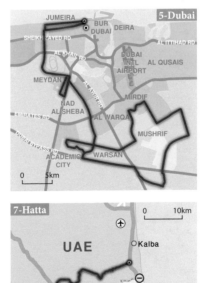

ENDURANCE NATION

AS WELL AS CYCLING, THE WORLD OF ENDURANCE SPORTS IS FULL OF LIFE AND KICKING HARD HERE IN THE UAE.

SWIMMING

Although by no means the most practised sport in the UAE, swimming is increasing in popularity thanks in part to the work done by the UAE Swimming Federation, which has attracted some big, international swimming and diving meets to the state-of-the-art new 50m pool in Dubai Sports City. Open 08:00-20:00, Sat to Thurs, entry

to Sheikh Hamdan Bin Mohammed Al Maktoum Sports Complex costs Dhs.20 per swim (find a map on Facebook). There is also a 50m pool in The Officer's Club, Abu Dhabi (afoc.mil.ae; open 07:30-22:00 with monthly and annual memberships available).

There are plenty of places where you can learn to swim, improve your technique or train with other wannabe water babies.

Most health clubs and hotels (p.242) provide coaching for all ages, while Speedo Swim Squads (speedodubai.net) and Super Sports Dubai (supersportsdubai.com) have dedicated training squads for kids. Older children who are already strong swimmers may like to attend Hamilton Aquatics' (hamiltonaquaticsdubai.com) or Aquaswim's (aquaswim.ae) competitive squads.

For adults in Abu Dhabi, check out training sessions organised by Abu Dhabi Tri Club (abudhabitriclub.org), while Dubai residents are lucky enough to have an excellent masters programme in the form of Dubai Masters Swim Club (see facebook group), which welcomes swimmers and triathletes of all levels.

The competitive swimming calendar isn't packed with events, but there are few races worth attending. Super Sports runs a series of aquathlons (run-swim) as well as a series of the popular Mina Mile open water swim meet, while, several times a year, Aquaswim holds its difficult Lazy River Challenge – a race against the current in the rapids at Wild Wadi. Finally, there's November's Swim Around The Burj, an annual event held to raise money for Medecins Sans Frontieres.

RUNNING

The running calendar is even busier. The big name, big money races that attract superstar runners from around the world are the Dubai Marathon and RAK Half Marathon, but the Dubai Creek Striders Half Marathon and Abu Dhabi Creek Striders Half Marathon are perhaps the more enjoyable races, with great courses and real community atmosphere. Whether tackled as part of a team or as an intrepid (and slightly mad) solo runner, the Wadi Bih run is another completely unique event. Over shorter distances, there are all manner of 5ks and 10ks taking place everywhere from the Sevens Stadium, Yas Marina Circuit and Dubai Autodrome to Jumeirah Beach Hotel, Zayed Sports City and Mushrif Park.

To train for those events, there's just as much choice. In Abu Dhabi, there's Abu Dhabi Striders (abudhabistriders.com) and, inland, Al Ain Road Runners (050 472 1566). In Dubai, choose from Dubai Creek Striders (dubaicreekstriders.org), Dubai Road Runners (dubairoadrunners.com), ABRaS Run Club (abrasac.org) and Mirdif Milers (mirdifmilers.com). All tend to run two or three times a week and all clubs welcome new runners, as well as the more experienced. If you're very new to running, however, Nike Free Run Club (see Facebook) might be the way to go. One part run club, one part running-focused bootcamp, it's a great introduction to running and the

coaches teach you everything from how to warm up and cool down to how to mix up your run training.

TRIATHLON

Add all these sports together and you get the world's fastest-growing mass participation sport – triathlon. Often referred to as 'the new marathon', the relatively young sport (created in the 70s and an Olympic sport since just 2004) is booming globally thanks to the challenge it represents and the fact that the cross-training involved means more interest, less over-use injuries and more complete whole-body fitness than just one sport provides.

Abu Dhabi Tri Club is a one-stop shop for all swim-bike-run training, with Al Ain Multi Sport providing an equally comprehensive programme for triathletes in the Garden City. There is no longer a Dubai Triathlon Club, although there are a number of teams, such as Tri2Aspire (teamt2a.com), Dubai Tri Pirates (tri-pirates.com) and TriBe. For many triathletes – or would-be triathletes – however, it's simply a case of joining a few of the swimming, cycling and running groups available, where you're bound to meet like-minded multisports fans.

The biggest triathlon is without doubt the Abu Dhabi International Triathlon which attracts a stellar pro field thanks to one of the biggest prize purses in the sport as well as almost 2,000 amateurs who compete across the three available distances. Abu Dhabi's other showpiece triathlon is Tri

SIGN UP TO RACE
You can find details of almost every race mentioned on this page – as well as hundreds of other races in these sports and other disciplines – at premiermarathons.com, where you can also register and pay online to enter the events. The notable exceptions are the Dubai Marathon and the Abu Dhabi International Triathlon, which can be entered at dubaimarathon.org and abudhabitriathlon.com respectively.

Yas which offers something closer to more traditional sprint and Olympic distances on its Yas Marina Circuit course. Elsewhere, Emirates Triathlon runs a sprint series that, throughout winter, takes place monthly in Ghantoot, while Super Sports runs a three race series in Al Mamzar which covers both sprint and Olympic distances.

Al Ain Multi Sport has done a great job in bringing something different to the UAE's triathlon scene. With events based around the lakes at Wadi Adventure (p.150), so far it has organised The Beast (a sprint-distance triathlon but with the 20km bike incorporating the 1,200m climb to the summit of Jebel Hafeet and the run taking place at the top of the mountain) and The Sting – three consecutive super sprint triathlons done back-to-back – as well as a more traditional sprint triathlon.

DIVING

Divers are spoiled for choice when it comes to exploring the seas that surround the UAE and Oman. The lower Arabian Gulf and the Gulf of Oman should satisfy all tastes and levels of experience, whether you're a diver, a snorkeller, or enjoy a little of both.

There are more than 30 wrecks to choose from, almost all in relatively shallow waters, with tropical coral reefs and dramatic coastlines that are virtually un-dived just waiting to be discovered and explored.

The water temperatures are ideal too; although the land temperatures can hit the high 40s in the summer months, it is rarely too hot when dipping into the sea, where temperatures range from around 20°C in January to 35°C in July and August.

INTO THE SEA...

THE UAE AND OMAN OFFER SOME REALLY SPECIAL DIVING AND THERE ARE HUNDREDS OF POPULAR DIVE SITES THAT SHOULD SATISFY ALL TASTES AND LEVELS OF EXPERIENCE.

DIVE LOCATIONS

The best dive sites are located in three main areas: the east coast, the west coast and Musandam. These range from shallow reef dives, to wreck diving and the nesting sites of turtles. There are literally hundreds of options and the choice is yours – to get you started on underwater explorations, turn to p.130 for our pick of the best-known and popular sites in each location.

The weather on the east coast can be very different to that in the west. The east coast and Fujairah are typically a few degrees cooler during the summer months and this side of the peninsula also tends to be more protected from the shamal winds which can cause rough seas on the west coast of the UAE. Given that most dive sites are within a couple of hours' drive from the main cities, you can be sure to find a dive spot with favourable weather just about any day of the year.

DIVE CLUBS

There are many excellent diving centres and clubs operating here that will help you enjoy the region's wonderful diving. These centres are your best bet if you're a novice diver, as most have a great selection of equipment for hire and you get to dive with experienced dive masters. See the Directory (p.240 & p.247) for further information and contact details.

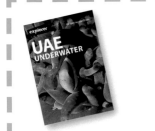

To discover more dives in the UAE and Oman, pick up a copy of explorer's *Underwater Explorer*, written by Carole Harris and Tony Schroder out now in bookstores across the region. Alternatively, visit our e-shop at askexplorer.com.

EQUIPMENT

Dive gear is easy to find and the range is generally good. Entry-level gear is widely available across the country; most hypermarkets stock basic equipment, such as snorkelling kits and fins, while all major sports stores offer specialised dive gear. Go Sport, for example, stocks a range of Mares and Cressi gear from fins and masks to regulators and dive computers. Likewise, Intersport has a good selection of dive gear to serve most divers' needs.

For more specialised equipment, the numerous dive centres and schools are your best bet. In addition to stocking a great selection, you'll also find knowledgeable staff who are able to help with gear maintenance and airfills. Al Boom Marine

(alboommarine.com) and Gulf Marine Sports (gulfmarinesports.com) are just two of these – see p.244 & p.248 of the Directory for full listings.

Many of your dives here will be done as part of a group and you'll go out to the site by boat. Seeing as most dive gear is pretty uniform (black neoprene with possibly a splash of colour), it makes sense to mark your gear so that you'll be able to spot it quickly on a dive boat or in a dive centre when everyone is kitting up.

Rinsing your gear off well in cold, desalinated water after each dive is a must. Also, remember that the climate in this region requires that you need to do gear maintenance checks more frequently than you might elsewhere in the world.

SUITING UP FOR GULF DIVING

While Gulf waters are typically warm, every diver has different tolerance levels for the cold and you'll feel even chillier if you're doing repeat dives, long dives or deep dives. If you plan on diving during the winter months, you'll want to opt for a thicker 5mm suit, while diving in a thin Lycra suit alone is possible during the summer.

GETTING CERTIFIED

TO START EXPLORING MARINE LIFE, YOU MUST GET CERTIFIED BY PADI OR ONE OF THE OTHER ORGANISATIONS.

In order to be able to dive anywhere in the world, you must pass an open water diver course from any one of the reputable training organisations – CMAS, NAUI, PADI, SSI and SDI. Of these, PADI is the largest, and the one you're most likely to encounter. Once you've completed the training, you'll receive a certification card which allows you to go on an 'open water' rated dive of up to 18m in depth. After this, you are allowed to dive anywhere in the world within these guidelines.

If you'd like to take it a step further, you can continue with advanced diver training. This is a good way for you to upgrade your skills and explore aspects of diving that are of particular interest to you. The specialities include underwater photography, wreck diving and night dives – the choice is yours. Learning to dive or advancing your existing qualifications with an internationally recognised organisation is very easy to accomplish in this part of the world. Training and certification can be arranged through one of the many excellent dive centres (listed on p.240 & p.247).

Once you've got advanced diver certification, you'll find there is still plenty more to do and learn. For example, it's a good idea to complete a rescue and first aid course. And then, if this is where your interests lie, you'll be ready to take on the more technical side of diving, such as diving on Nitrox and going to depths of 30 to 40m, which is the generally accepted recreational diving limit.

WHAT ABOUT THE KIDS?

There are various underwater programmes designed for children. These familiarise children with the underwater environment, teach them water skills and prepare them for scuba diving. Certification is possible from 12 years onwards. Contact one of the dive centres listed on p.240 & p.247 of the Directory for further information.

ASK THE EXPERT

Paul Sant
Divers Down UAE
Master Instructor

Why diving?

Diving has always played a part in my adult life, whether for pleasure or work. When the opportunity came in 2000 to turn diving into a career, I seized it and have not looked back since.

Favourite dive spots in the UAE and Oman?

My top five would be Anemone Gardens, Martini Rock, Inchcape 2, Coral Gardens and Shark Island.

What makes the UAE and Oman special as dive destinations?

On any one dive, you get to see more than in most other places in the world. In one dive, you can see turtles, sharks, rays, sea horses, lion fish, barracuda, nudi branches, shoals of snapper and much more... all in 50 minutes. The dive sites change on a daily basis; one day it is 25m visibility, the next 6m; one day there are rays, the next the rays have gone and instead you see Frog Fish – even after 12 years, it never gets boring!

Fantasy dive spot worldwide?

Bikini Atoll, the place to go for big wrecks and great diving. It is remote, which means not too many divers and the wrecks are all yours to explore!

Best underwater moment?

The day I went diving in Anemone Gardens and saw a leopard shark, guitar sharks and a whale shark, all on the same dive! The visibility was great and I had capable divers with me so I managed to also fit in a chance to go sea horse spotting at the part of Anemone Gardens known as Sea Horse Alley.

Top tips for other divers?

Know your dive limits and stay well within them; if you are not confident or otherwise happy about something, speak up and let your buddy or dive operator know immediately.

If you're planning a diving holiday, plan well in advance and do your research: use sites such as Scuba Board or Trip Advisor as they will steer you away from shiny websites and tell you what it's really like to dive there.

Finally, it's important to always keep learning – after more than 20 years of diving, I still take courses; re-breathers will be my next one to allow me to dive bubble free.

> 'THE DIVE SITES HERE CHANGE ON A DAILY BASIS; ONE DAY THERE ARE RAYS, THE NEXT THE RAYS HAVE GONE AND INSTEAD YOU SEE FROG FISH! EVEN AFTER 12 YEARS OF DIVING, IT NEVER GETS BORING.'

ASK THE EXPERT

Kathleen Russell
Al Mahara Diving Center
PADI Course Director

Why diving?

It's my passion to explore the aquatic realms and share these amazing experiences with others.

Favourite UAE dive spot?

I'd name three – west of Abu Dhabi in Marawah MPA, Sir Bani Yas Island and near Ras Baraka.

Best underwater moment?

It's a tie between diving with sea lions in the Sea of Cortez and penetrating a turtle tomb off Sipadan.

Tips for other divers?

Dive with good boat supervision and make sure you assess visibility and temperature before you dive. It's also important to remain environmentally aware when diving; always do your best to protect and conserve our Mother Earth's oceans.

BREAKWATER

THIS 'CITY DIVE' OFFERS PLENTY OF MARINE LIFE A STONE'S THROW FROM ABU DHABI ISLAND.

This beautiful dive site is located just off Abu Dhabi's Al Bateen area. The area is characterised by its combination of sandy seabed and lots of hard corals growing along the side of the Breakwater. There is also a large container box which attracts a plethora of marine life.

DIVING

The short boat journey from Abu Dhabi island makes this an excellent choice for those short on time. For the same reason, this is a popular spot for night diving, especially for first-time night divers. Overall, the shallow depth of around 8m makes the Breakwater site ideal for novice divers. However, there's plenty to see to keep more advanced divers coming back too.

Most divers start by exploring the 20ft container which is located near the corner of the Breakwater. Situated on the north-facing side and lying on the bottom of the ocean at a 45° angle, it is a magnet for varied sea creatures. If you come at night, there's a great opportunity to watch some hammours come out of it. The container is open in the middle and experienced divers can swim through it.

Elsewhere, you'll get to admire stunning hard coral species that include porites, acropora and brain corals, as well as a huge variety of other fish that are attracted to this shallow spot.

MARINE LIFE

Despite the site's close proximity to urban areas, divers can expect to be spoiled with marine life sightings here. Batfish, parrotfish, the orange spotted hammour, juvenile trevallies, schooling snappers, golden trevallies and sweetlips are just some of the aquatic creatures typically seen here.

The other attractions include cuttlefish, squid and anemones with cute clownfish. In addition, a curious family of batfish is often known to be present and following divers around. Occasionally, you may also come across a sea turtle or too, as well as humpback dolphins.

When the water temperature is around 25°C, the site is known to attract plenty of stingrays. These tend to be spotted on the sandy bottom. The types of rays you can expect to see include leopard rays, butterfly rays, torpedo rays, feather tail rays and shovelnose rays.

SNORKELLING

This is an excellent destination for snorkelling. Thanks to the shallow depths and clear waters you can expect to spot a wide range of marine life even without going below the surface. However, if you're willing to duck dive just a few metres below, your chances of spotting the site's colourful habitants are even better.

BREAKWATER

DEPTH	8m
SNORKELLING	Yes
NIGHT DIVE	Yes
GPS	24°28'39"N
	54°17'52"E

DISTANCE FROM HARBOUR
Al Bateen
Marina   3.3nmi

8 m

8 m

Emirates
Palace Hotel

CEMENT BARGE

VARIED MARINE LIFE FROM SQUIRTS TO STINGRAYS MAKES THIS WRECK DIVE A GREAT CHOICE ON THE WEST COAST.

Having sank in 1971 when it ran into heavy weather en route to Dubai, this cement barge sits more or less intact and upright in 12 metres of water. Today, it is a magnet for a variety of fish. Located within easy reach of most of the harbours on the west coast, it is well worth a visit; not only is it an excellent site for most types of training dives, but it also offers some of the best night diving around.

DIVING

Start your dive on the sandy bottom and swim around the wreck. Look under the stern for the hammour and snapper that like to hide in the depression where the sand has been washed away beneath the propeller shaft. On the port side of the stern lie the remains of the funnel. The lower section of the bow has collapsed, leaving an opening right through the wreck. All that remains of the bridge and cabin is the framework, while the separate holds still contain their ship's cargo of cement bags. The bulkheads are now breaking up and, if you use a bright light, you'll often find a variety of large fish resting in the gaps.

MARINE LIFE

There's always an abundance of fish on this wreck, which has several resident clownfish nestling within the anemones. Sponges, thorny oysters, sea squirts, clams, scallops and barnacles cover every available surface, including the cement bags.

The holes and cracks hide a variety of fish, including hammour. Gobies and their symbiotic shrimp can be seen in the sand surrounding the hull. The gobies guard the hole while the shrimp busily clear sand from their homes. You'll have to be very patient to see the shrimp though, as they dart back into the safety of their home at any sign of movement.

Blennies hide in small holes, and there are several species of dottybacks, small, beautifully coloured fish that are always nearby in search of a titbit. Large shoals of yellow snapper surround the wreck and sometimes you'll see schools of juvenile barracuda patrolling the perimeter.

You'll have to keep an attentive eye out for stingrays – they can be difficult to spot as they're usually covered with sand with only their tail visible.

SNORKELLING

One of the few wrecks that's shallow enough to make snorkelling a possibility, the cement barge is easily viewed from the surface. For those with a good lung capacity, the whole of the top section is worth a duck dive down to explore.

CEMENT BARGE

DEPTH	12m
SNORKELLING	Yes
NIGHT DIVE	Yes
GPS	25°10'19"N
	55°12'17"E

DISTANCE FROM HARBOURS

DIMC	5.7nmi
DOSC	0.7nmi
Dubai Creek	7.8nmi

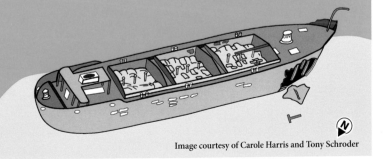

Image courtesy of Carole Harris and Tony Schroder

DIBBA ISLAND

TURTLE SIGHTINGS ARE VIRTUALLY GUARANTEED AT THIS COLOURFUL SITE THAT IS A REAL TREAT FOR DIVERS AND SNORKELLERS ALIKE.

This small rocky island has long sloping sides that are covered by a reef formed by a variety of soft and boulder corals. The side nearest the shore is only 3-4m deep, so it should be dived at high tide. The seaward side has a long sloping rocky reef with many green and purple whip corals that make it a very attractive dive site.

DIVING

If you're in a hurry, it's possible to complete a circuit of the island in one dive, but only at high tide. Regardless of the tide, if you're planning several dives in this area, it's a good idea to explore the wall that runs parallel to the island. The area is prone to both thermoclines and strong currents. At low tide it's best to keep to the north (seaward) side of the island; otherwise you'll be snorkelling, instead of diving, on the south (shore) side.

High tide offers a great opportunity to explore the shallower side of the island that's nearest the mainland. There's a good chance you'll see turtles here, among other things.

Once darkness falls, Dibba Island makes a lovely, easy night dive. It is simple to navigate and there are lots of beautiful, swaying corals that will have their polyps out to feed at night. You'll also find plenty of sleeping fish that have lodged themselves between the rocks, often leaving their tails exposed.

MARINE LIFE

You're virtually guaranteed sightings of turtles on this site and you'll see many fish species here too. Look out for the unusual jawfish (or hole goby), noticeable for their rather ugly features – huge heads and large eyes and mouths. They build lovely 'drainpipe' homes, and line the walls with pretty shells to prevent them from collapsing.

The drainpipe goes down quite a long way and, once the jawfish disappears into it, it takes a long time to reappear. When it is mating season – usually from June to August – they pop out of their holes, exposing and revealing their colourful and beautifully patterned bodies.

SNORKELLING

This is one of the best snorkelling sites around, especially for seeing turtles. The turtles are most prolific on the seaward side of the island where there are lots of coral reefs, and it seems that snorkellers will see turtles, even when divers don't.

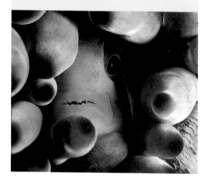

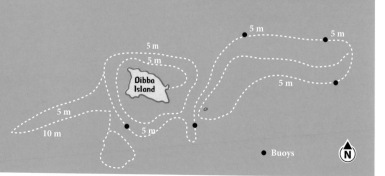

DIBBA ISLAND

DEPTH	16m
SNORKELLING	Yes
NIGHT DIVE	Yes
GPS	25°36'14"N
	56°21'05"E

DISTANCE FROM HARBOURS
Dibba Bayah Harbour 5.2nmi
Khor Fakkan Harbour 15.2nmi
Lulaya Harbour 12.8nmi

Dibba Island

5 m
5 m
5 m
5 m
5 m
5 m
5 m
5 m
5 m
10 m

• Buoys

N

DIBBA ISLAND ISN'T KNOWN AS ONE OF THE REGION'S TOP SITES FOR TURTLE SPOTTING FOR NOTHING - THE TURTLES ARE MOST PROLIFIC ON THE SEAWARD SIDE OF THE ISLAND.

JAZIRAT SIR BU NA·AIR

AN ISLAND SANCTUARY FOR SPOTTING MAGNIFICENT CORALS WHILE MINGLING WITH TURTLES, RAYS AND LARGE PELAGIC FISH.

Jazirat Sir Bu Na'air is a small island that lies 70km off the Emirates' coast. Measuring just over 1km long by 0.5 km wide, it's a UAE military outpost and coastguard station, but also a protected turtle breeding area – a fact that makes it a delight for divers looking to spot these graceful creatures in their natural habitat. The turtles have benefited greatly from the fact that the island has been a protected nature reserve for more than a decade. In 2001, an administrative order banning all activities considered harmful to the environment of Jazirat Sir Bu Na'air was issued. The six article order seeks to halt the deterioration of the island's environment, protect its marine life, and develop its natural resources.

The nature reserve status means that, turtle spotting aside, divers get to admire some fantastic coral formations and a huge variety of fish which are attracted to the area thanks to the absence of fishermen.

Bear in mind that while there are no restrictions on sailing or diving near the island, it is a sensitive military base so landing is not advisable.

DIVING

This site is characterised by coral reefs, a shelving sandy bottom and lots of drop-offs. Towards the northern end of the island there's a large area of table and staghorn coral in magnificent condition. The coral runs north to the 20m mark and then the seabed shelves down to a depth of more than 30m. The north-eastern side has large flat rocks and coral, and there are more extensive areas of coral to the north-west. Off the southern tip of the island, the sandy bottom runs to 20m, ending with a small sea mount. At the entrance to the harbour on the south-east side, you'll find the partially submerged wreck of a barge.

MARINE LIFE

The island is rarely visited by divers or fishermen and the resulting lack of disturbance encourages prolific shoals of fish. There are numerous large pelagic fish, spotted eagle rays, barracuda and large rays. It's a long journey to the island, but the diving and snorkelling at Jazirat Sir Bu Na'air is definitely worth the trip.

SNORKELLING

The island isn't just for divers – snorkellers will have a wonderful time here too. The visibility is good, and as it is one of the protected turtle breeding areas, turtles are frequently seen by snorkellers. Concentrate on the northern coral field, which starts at 5m and runs gently into deeper water.

JAZIRAT SIR BU NA·AIR

DEPTH	36m
SNORKELLING	Yes
NIGHT DIVE	Yes
GPS	25°13'30"N
	54°13'00"E

DISTANCE FROM HARBOURS

Abu Dhabi Club	43.5nmi
DIMC	51.1nmi
Dubai Creek	58.7nmi
Jebel Ali Marina	46.3nmi

Coral Reef · 36m · 36m · Jazirat Sir Bu Na·air · 10m · 10m · 10m · Harbour · N

THE LANDING CRAFT

THIS SHELTERED MUSANDAM SITE OFFERS DIVERS AN EXCELLENT OPPORTUNITY TO PRACTISE THEIR WRECK PENETRATION SKILLS.

This dive spot has formed around the wreckage of a landing craft that specialised in carrying water to the remote Musandam villages that weren't able to receive water by road. As the hull of The Musandam split with age, it was decided that the vessel would be decommissioned and sunk, along with a light aircraft.

This is an ideal site for students as it's on the edge of a protected bay with the rocky shoreline close by. Its proximity to the harbour means that it's also a quick and easy destination for a night dive.

DIVING

The diving here takes place around the small vessel which sits upright and relatively intact on the seabed at just 10m, with its bow facing 20°.

The Musandam has a well-preserved and undamaged wheelhouse, which is surprising given that it's only 3-4m from the surface, and you can swim in and out of it easily. You will be able to see the engine room through gaps in the deck. However, beware that it is a very tight squeeze and

entry is should not to be attempted without adequate training.

Another interesting feature is the aeroplane laid out on the deck with its wings alongside. You can see the propellers and the cockpit area with petrol tanks underneath what's left of the seats. At the front of the vessel is the landing deck which seems to attract a plethora of fish life. After looking for shrimps, crabs and blennies in all the nooks and crannies on the wreck, take a swim over to the edge of the reef and look in the staghorn corals. You're likely to find a citron goby city in every coral you peer into.

MARINE LIFE

As the wreck has been here for over three decades, you'll see many shells and a variety of hard corals on it; primarily brain and staghorn corals encrusted onto the wreck's surfaces.

Musandam is less frequented by divers than most other sites and the fish appear to be quite unconcerned about divers; often, they'll swim almost into your face.

SNORKELLING

Snorkellers will enjoy this site too thanks to the fact that the wreck does not lie in deep waters – the whole site is relatively shallow and it's possible to see the wreckage even from the surface when there is no wind and the water remains calm.

THE LANDING CRAFT

DEPTH	10m
SNORKELLING	Yes
NIGHT DIVE	Yes
GPS	26°12'40"N
	56°17'05"E

DISTANCE FROM HARBOUR	
Khasab Harbour	3.5nmi

Image courtesy of Carole Harris and Tony Schroder

LIMA ROCK

BOULDERS, LIMESTONE CAVERNS, ABUNDANT REEF LIFE AND A NEARBY ISLAND TO CHILL OUT ON - A PERFECT COMBO.

Lying north of Dibba, Lima Rock marks the southern entrance to Lima Bay. This small island is a pinnacle of limestone rock with jagged sides. The waves have undercut the rock in places, leaving shallow caves and deep fissures. Sheer cliffs drop almost vertically to a depth of about 12m to create some very interesting and unique dive spots. The sandy seabed sits at 60m deep.

DIVING

The beauty of Lima Rock is that it can be dived in most weather and tidal conditions. If the sea is rough, or the current is running on one side, the other side is usually calm. However, you should always remain aware of the currents at the eastern and western tips of the island.

On the southern side of the island, there are a couple of relatively deep caves. At the south-eastern end of the island, a massive boulder guards the easternmost tip of the island. If the currents are mild, wait on this monolith and look out into the deep water for tuna, jacks, sharks and manta rays. If you're lucky you may even be rewarded with the sight of a whaleshark or a sunfish.

On the north side, steep walls drop down to the sand at 20m. Note that this side of the island is in the shade from mid-morning onwards.

MARINE LIFE

The marine life is abundant, with large shoals of reef fish. Between 12 and 20m, the boulder field is covered with hard corals (table, staghorn, brain and boulder coral), and patches of soft corals, including orange and pink teddybear coral. At 20m and deeper, abundant yellow and green coloured black coral, and numerous clumps of purple coral appear between the patches of sand, creating a very beautiful site.

Look out for the yellow-mouthed morays that look as if they've just returned from the paint shop with their vivid, colourful markings. Moving deeper towards the shelving sand, white tip sharks and leopard sharks are often seen resting on the bottom. The island is also home to a variety of birds such as ospreys, swifts and sooty falcons that frequent the high ramparts of the rock, making it an interesting location to wait between dives.

SNORKELLING

Although near-surface marine life sightings are more limited here than at some of the more shallow dive sites, snorkellers will have an enjoyable experience too. Head to the north side of the island, which offers more shelter if you keep close to the rock face.

LIMA ROCK

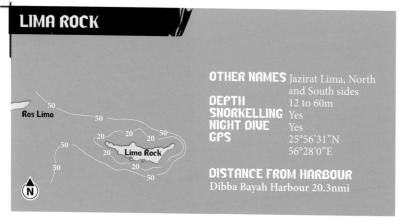

OTHER NAMES Jazirat Lima, North and South sides
DEPTH 12 to 60m
SNORKELLING Yes
NIGHT DIVE Yes
GPS 25°56'31"N 56°28'0"E

DISTANCE FROM HARBOUR
Dibba Bayah Harbour 20.3nmi

MARTINI ROCK

A PLEASING AND COLOURFUL SITE THAT GIVES THE FEELING OF DIVING IN A METICULOUSLY MANICURED AQUARIUM.

Martini Rock is a small, submerged coral outcrop, the top of which is visible from the surface at 3m. The rock has several sandy gullies or alleys and most of it is covered in orange and purple teddybear coral, which makes for a pleasing and colourful dive site. This is an excellent site for divers of all skill levels, and a favourite east coast location.

DIVING

The north side of the rock is the deepest, going down to 22m, while the rest of the site is at about 13m. There's enough time to complete a circuit of the rock in one dive, but note that the site is prone to both thermoclines and strong currents at times.

Martini Rock is an excellent option for a night dive: in the dark, the rock appears completely red because of all the feeding teddybear corals. Look closely into the soft corals to find fish such as juvenile damselfish or hawkfish that use the coral as a safe haven from the larger hunters that are out looking for dinner. You may see sleeping turtles, rays out feeding and perhaps a spotted eagle ray. If you stay near the bottom of the rock on the seabed, you may see large rays sifting through the sand in search of small molluscs and crustaceans.

MARINE LIFE

The variety of fish life is excellent and the top 5m is like an aquarium – schools of snapper, fusiliers, anthias, triggerfish and large-mouth mackerel are present for most of the year. Large sections of the rock are covered in red, purple and orange teddybear corals, with one side swathed in purple whip corals, and green and yellow whip corals in a deep corner. You may be fortunate enough to see the occasional leopard shark, black tip reef shark or guitar shark. There have also been sightings of such unusual creatures as a pygmy seamoth, frogfish and a robust pipefish.

SNORKELLING

The top of the rock is about two or three metres from the surface and the bright colours of the teddybear corals decorating the rock are easily visible. You may also see boxfish, jacks and many shoals of fish near the surface. If you can duck dive down to 5m or more, you may see morays, rays and perhaps even some turtles.

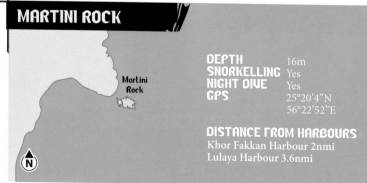

MARTINI ROCK

Martini Rock

DEPTH	16m
SNORKELLING	Yes
NIGHT DIVE	Yes
GPS	25°20'4"N 56°22'52"E

DISTANCE FROM HARBOURS
Khor Fakkan Harbour 2nmi
Lulaya Harbour 3.6nmi

N

138

OCTOPUS ROCK

ANOTHER GREAT MUSANDAM DIVE, THIS FASCINATING SITE IS PRACTICALLY A MARINE ZOO - A MUST FOR ALL UAE DIVERS.

With its distinctive undercut top, this isolated stack lies 3km offshore to the north of Lima and is another great Musandam dive site. The almost perfectly round rock is approximately 50m in diameter and its sides drop more or less vertically to a mixed rock and sand seabed.

The rocky bottom runs in ridges to the west and north, forming sandy-bottomed gullies. The depth of these gullies varies from 15-20m around the base of the rock, when they slope off to the southeast, descending more than 50m.

All in all, the setting makes for a near-perfect dive site teeming with marine life from fanworms to stingrays and leopard sharks, to the backdrop of some stunningly colourful corals.

DIVING

Octopus Rock is practically a marine zoo that can be enjoyed in most weather and tidal conditions, thanks to its sheltered location in Lima Bay. One of the best things about it is that it is also suitable for divers of all levels of expertise.

After reaching the bottom, swim north from the base of the rock and you'll reach a rocky cliff that runs east to west. This leads to the gullies, which are a continuation of the cliff.

Most divers turn back at the cliff and circle around the terraces of rock that surround the stack. If you continue, remember to take note of your bearings, since you can end up a long way from the rock and you don't want to get lost!

MARINE LIFE

The stack is a gathering point for a great variety of shoaling fish life. Close to the rock you'll find numerous reef fish, while further out are jacks, trevally, tuna, barracuda and, if you're lucky, rays and sharks. Soft and hard corals abound; green coloured black coral and purple soft coral whips predominate, and together with the pink and orange teddybear corals, they create a kaleidoscope of colour.

The rocks are home to fanworms, featherstars, juvenile crayfish and anemones. Look under overhangs and in hollows for black or red lionfish, but take care as these fish are poisonous.

Stingrays can be seen feeding in the sand or resting under boulder coral overhangs on most dives. You also have a good chance of seeing nurse and leopard sharks on this site.

SNORKELLING

This is a very good spot for snorkelling. Duck dive down the sides of the stack to make the most of it. Alternatively, you can swim away from the stack to the north-west: there are large outcrops of rock 5 to 8m from the surface that are always alive with reef fish.

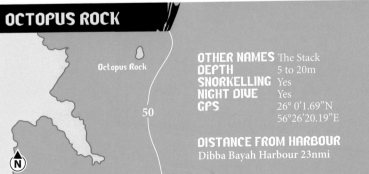

OCTOPUS ROCK

Octopus Rock

50

N

OTHER NAMES	The Stack
DEPTH	5 to 20m
SNORKELLING	Yes
NIGHT DIVE	Yes
GPS	26° 0'1.69"N
	56°26'20.19"E

DISTANCE FROM HARBOUR
Dibba Bayah Harbour 23nmi

TURTLE BARGE

AN EASY-TO-ACCESS SITE THAT IS HOME TO FASCINATING CORALS, FRIENDLY TURTLES AND MYRIAD OTHER MARINE LIFE.

This dive site was discovered by chance some 15 years ago when Blue Planet Divers were training outside the harbour wall in Ajman. The site is formed around three pieces of wreckage which could be parts of one barge or even two or three separate smaller ones. The origins of the wreckage are not known, but that takes nothing away from its appeal to divers.

The wreckage lies just five minutes outside the Ajman harbour, so access is quick and easy and the site is excellent for night diving. This is an ideal site for students, and even well-dived instructors will find something to enjoy on this dive. If you're particularly keen to see many varieties of hard coral in a small area, this is a must.

DIVING

The wreck is fairly flat but full of holes that provide an ideal home for all kinds of marine life. A length of rope stretches about 60m between the two main pieces of wreckage to make navigation easier. There are some large pipes alongside one of the main pieces of wreckage and various bits and pieces littered about. It's easy to become disorientated due to the various pieces of debris, but as it's a nice shallow site you can simply surface and wait for the dive boat to collect you.

Overall, this is an attractive site with an incredibly large number of hard corals spread over the seabed and wreckage. If you look closely, you'll see the corals are almost fluorescent, and glow with hues of orange, green, red and blue.

MARINE LIFE

As you descend the mooring buoy you'll be greeted by a lone clownfish who has made his home under the mooring line. And as the name suggests, you're also likely to encounter a friendly turtle or two that have taken up residence on the wreckage here.

The west coast regulars are all here: yellow snappers, blennies, monos, hammour and barracuda. You may also see nudibranchs, various types of sponges and shells.

SNORKELLING

As the Turtle Barge dive site is rather shallow, this is one of the few wreck sites that snorkellers get to explore as well. When there is little wind, visibility is excellent and you may be able to observe a wide range of fish going about their business in and around the remains of the barge.

TURTLE BARGE

DEPTH	36m
SNORKELLING	Yes
NIGHT DIVE	Yes
GPS	25°13'30"N
	54°13'00"E

DISTANCE FROM HARBOURS
Abu Dhabi Club	43.5nmi
DIMC	51.1nmi
Dubai Creek	58.7nmi
Jebel Ali Marina	46.3nmi

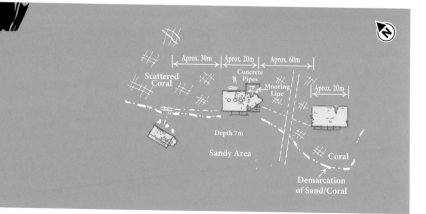

Aprox. 30m | Aprox. 20m | Aprox. 60m
Scattered Coral
Concrete Pipes
Mooring Line
Aprox. 20m
Depth 7m
Sandy Area
Coral
Demarcation of Sand/Coral

East Coast UAE

Home to 65 coral and 930+ fish species, the waters here offer from **A**ngler fish to **Z**ebra moray, from tiny shrimps to seahorses, turtles, colourful reef fish and rays to whale shark. Your gateway to this stunning paradise is only 2 hours away from the busy life in Dubai.

Divers Down

a Dozen Differences...

3 day dives & night dive, 7 days / week
We go to 14 different dive sites
Try-dives in 4 hours. Open Water certificate in 2 days with PADI eLearning
PADI 5-Star IDC Center
Ranked #1 on TripAdvisor
Accommodation packages
Authorized MARES and Dive Rite dealer
Club activities: Travels, Photography, Technical Diving, Coral Conservation
All divers DAN insured
Multilingual instructors
First-aid trained crew & staff
Our values: Safety, fun, flexibility, family-feel

See you on the beach.......

Divers Down, PO Box 10472, Miramar Al Aqah Resort & Spa, Fujairah

Phone +971 (0)9 237 0299, +971 (0)50 553 1688

Email: info@diversdown-uae.com

Website: www.diversdown-uae.com

Divers Down
EAST COAST UAE

SNORKELLING

THE UAE & OMAN'S WARM, CALM WATERS MAKE THIS THE PERFECT PLACE TO GET INTO SNORKELLING.

If you'd like to take a glimpse into underwater life without making the investment to become a certified diver, snorkelling is the way to go. It is a great hobby regardless of your age or fitness level, and the minute you get your first glimpse of bright reef life, you'll be hooked.

WHY SNORKELLING?

As far as hobbies go, this is a great way for the family to enjoy an activity together. Furthermore, with some excellent snorkelling spots literally at your doorstep, there's no shortage of opportunities to fit in a spot of marine life exploration: all you need is some basic equipment and you're ready to go. Divers may get to witness more rare species, but snorkelling has its benefits too. Unlike divers, when snorkellers see something exciting they can call their buddy over to share the sight. Snorkellers are also well placed to get up and close with a variety of fish thanks to the fact that the snorkelling apparatus doesn't make the same kind of noise as dive equipment. Divers often return to the boat to hear of turtles seen coming up for air on the surface, rays jumping out of the water and of shoals of different fish near the surface. In the winter, there are some areas where you're almost guaranteed sightings of sharks and, again, snorkellers often strike it luckier than divers.

EQUIPMENT

All you need is a pair of fins, a tempered glass mask and a snorkel. There are two types of fins: open foot fins and fins meant to be used with booties. It's also a good idea to wear a suit or a 'skin' (which is thinner than a wetsuit but still offers UV protection) to prevent sunburn and to offer some protection from jellyfish stings. If you wear a wetsuit you may need to wear a weightbelt too, especially if you like to duck dive down and check things out.

You can hire snorkelling equipment from most dive shops or centres (see p.244 & p.248) and some hotels. A good dive shop will advise you on how to find a mask that's a good fit; you'll be shown how to attach the snorkel to the mask, and assisted in choosing fins that meet your requirements.

If you'd rather buy your own equipment, a wide variety of masks and snorkels can be found at sports stores and dive shops. Masks and snorkels range in price from Dhs.80 for a generic set to Dhs.300 for a branded, diving-specific set.

BOAT TRIPS

Most dive centres are happy to bring snorkellers along on a regular boat dive. While the divers head down under, you can snorkel on the surface or chill out on a nearby island beach. Prices vary but you can expect to pay around Dhs.50 to 70 for a two-hour trip.

SNORKELLING HOTSPOTS

You can pretty much snorkel anywhere off a boat – all you need is a mask and fins, and you'll probably see something swimming around. However, you're most likely to spot a good variety of marine life by booking a snorkelling tip with one of the local dive schools. What happens is you'll take off on a boat to explore the very same underwater hotspots as the divers; turn back to the previous pages for tips and information on some of the most popular locations.

SPECIALITY DIVES

STEP AWAY FROM THE USUAL DIVES AND TRY SOMETHING DIFFERENT.

In addition to traditional scuba diving, there are a handful of other, quirky ways to explore the region's varied underwater life.

DHOW DIVING

There are a number of companies that offer dhow, boat or yacht charters. They range from a sundowner cruise of a couple of hours, overnight trips with stopovers for snorkelling to liveaboard-type dive excursions. Turn to p.182.

If you want to do your own thing, large independent groups can charter a dhow from the fishermen at Dibba on the east coast, to travel up the coast to Musandam. If you haggle you can usually knock the price down substantially, especially if you know a few words of Arabic. Expect to pay around Dhs.2,500 per day for a dhow large enough to take 20-25 people. Smaller vessels can be hired from just Dhs.100 per hour. Many of the larger dhows come equipped with full-service facilities. For some of the smaller vessels, you may need to bring your own food, water and dive gear.

The beautiful, fjord-like scenery of Musandam makes it a fantastic dive dhow destination. Al Marsa Musandam (almarsamusandam.com) organises a range of trips that let you explore the remote corners and more distant dive spots. Other companies include Al Boom Diving (alboomdiving.com), Freestyle Divers (freestyledivers.com) and Sheesa Beach Dive Centre (sheesabeach.com). For more, see on p.240 & p.247 of the Directory.

If you leave from Dibba on the UAE side, Omani visas are not required even though you enter Omani waters. It's also possible to arrange stops along the coast and it's worth taking camping equipment for the night.

This kind of trip is ideal for diving, although non-divers will enjoy it too as it's pleasant enough to spend the day swimming, snorkelling and soaking up the sun.

PEARL DIVING

Recreational diving in this part of the world is very rewarding in its own right thanks to the myriad of marine life. But dive in the right spot and you may return with something even more precious – natural pearls. Long before recreational divers began exploring the waters that surround the Arabian peninsula, the Gulf's traditional pearl divers were already masters of pearl diving, a craft which involves freediving to depths of several metres in the search of oysters that contain the shimmering creations. Emirates Marine Environmental Group (emeg.ae) organises Dubai pearl diving experiences at Jumeirah Beach Hotel.

FREEDIVING

This modern sport builds on ancient freediving traditions such as pearl diving in the Gulf. Freediving means diving without any breathing apparatus. All equipment you'll need is a mask, fins and a qualified dive buddy. Freediving UAE (freedivinguae.com) organises training courses that are certified by the Worldwide Federation for Breath-holding Diving (aidainternational.org).

SKY & SEA
ADVENTURES DUBAI

WATER SPORTS & DIVING CENTER

Hilton Hotel JBR - Sheraton Jumeirah Beach Resort Dubai U.A.E. P.O. Box 57133

+971 4 399 90 05   +971 50 770 73 48   +971 50 724 61 84
info@watersportsdubai.com   diving@watersportsdubai.com
www.watersportsdubai.com

WATER SPORTS

WATERSPORTS

WHETHER KAYAKING IN THE MANGROVES OF ABU DHABI, OR SURFING THE WAVES IN OMAN, THERE'S PLENTY OF WATERSPORTS ACTION TO KEEP YOU BUSY.

The UAE offers plenty of opportunities for physical water-based fun, from the latest craze of stand-up paddleboarding to the turbo-charged thrills of jetskiing.

The different ocean breaks in the UAE also allow for a wide range of activities to take place within close proximity. The calm waters around Dubai Marina and the creek area, for example, provide glassy waters that are perfect for wakeboarding and waterskiing, especially if you head out early in the morning. The wide open stretches of beach in Al Gharbia and around some of Abu Dhabi's islands are excellent for kitesurfing, harnessing the wind that picks up in these areas. The lush mangroves around Umm Al Quwain, meanwhile, are undoubtedly a kayaker's paradise.

Before grabbing your kayak or board and making a break for the ocean, make sure that the beach is open to the public as certain stretches in Abu Dhabi, Dubai and Muscat are restricted so check the signs before hitting the sand. Similarly, there are beaches that are more suitable to certain sports – these will be identified throughout this chapter. Just remember that beaches in the UAE and Oman are not patrolled as diligently as some European beaches (if at all) so you need to take extra precautions.

If watersports are your thing and you're looking to make an investment, there are a few good stores that sell all the latest gear, gadgets and equipment. Al Boom Marine (alboommarine.com) in Dubai is probably the longest established, stocking a huge range of brands. Al Boom is also one of the few UAE stores to sell the coveted GoPro cameras (gopro.com). Waterproof, shockproof and versatile in every terrain, these lightweight cameras can be mounted onto surfboards, jetskis and oars, or

harnessed on to your chest, head or wrist to capture your most extreme adventures.

Watersports store Beach St (leisuremarine-me.com) is just as water-focused. The large JBR store showcases a whole host of specialist clothing and products, such as wetsuits, ropes and handles, as well as skis, boards and kayaks. Adventure HQ (adventurehq.ae), located in Dubai's Times Square Center is the UAE's largest outdoor adventure superstore. There, you'll find a huge range of gear for active lifestyle pursuits, including kayaks, surf boards, wakeboards and handles, and kitesurf boards, kites and harnesses. Decathlon at Mirdif City Centre has plenty of own-brand watersports equipment and clothing which offer superb value for money, with Intersports also stocking a decent line.

If you don't own your own equipment there are several excellent watersports centres in the UAE that offer rental and instruction to first timers. The UAE's beach front hotels (see p.242 & p.247

for a full listing) usually offer basic watersports, including parasailing and kayaking, but there are a handful of watersports centres (see p.161, p.245 and p.248) that cater more specifically to those looking to improve their skills.

SAIL AWAY

There may be little in the way of skill involved in parasailing, but it's certainly not an activity to be taken lightly. Harnessed to the back of a speedboat and slowly raised into the air connected to a parachute, parasailing can be a nerve wracking experience. But once up in the air, parasailing is a blissful experience, and one that can be enjoyed by all. Try the Sheraton Jumeirah Beach Resort at the end of JBR Walk. 04 399 5533

Kiteboarding in Al Gharbia

CANOEING AND KAYAKING

TAKE ADVANTAGE OF THE GULF'S CALM WATERS AND ENJOY A PEACEFUL PADDLE OUT TO SEA.

Whether you're after a leisurely paddle along the coastline, or want to try your hand at a competitive race out at sea, kayaking is one of the easiest sports to take part in. Many of the UAE's beach hotels such as the Hilton Jumeirah Dubai Hotel and the Hiltonia Beach Club Abu Dhabi provide hourly kayak hire (around Dhs.100 per hour).

In fact, taking to a kayak is just about the best way to get up close to the region's wildlife and wild coastline. With paddle power alone, you can glide silently across pristine lagoons and through gnarly mangrove forests. It is incredibly easy to get started; for a paddle through the mangroves of Abu Dhabi, head to Qasr Al Bahr towards the shore and you can launch your kayak off the jetty. Or try the swamps of Khor Kalba - just head over the bridge towards the Children's Park and head for the conservation reserve. In most locations, you'll come across curious turtles that like to pop up and say hello.

If you're looking for a more challenging and intensive ride, try the white water rapids at Wadi Adventure in Al Ain (see p.150) where hardcore kayak enthusiasts can test their skills down one of three man-made routes.

PADDLE HARD

If you're serious about your canoeing and kayaking – or would like to be – point your boat in the direction of Dubai Surfski & Kayak Club (dskc.hu). This club is for those who want more than just a social splash, organising beginner sessions which take place on Umm Sequim Public Beach; alternatively, you can book a private lesson. A one hour session costs Dhs.250. DSKC is also the place to be if you're already a dab hand with a paddle, with regular training sessions, meet-ups and races.

CALL OF NATURE

Many of the UAE's tour operators (see p.245) organise kayak excursions in some of the country's most rich and diverse marine habitats. Noukhada Adventure Company (naoukhada.ae) is an eco-aware tour operator that has been a pioneer of such kayak tours in the UAE.

The trip to the east coast destination of Khor Kalba, which has the oldest mangroves in Arabia and is home to the incredibly rare and endangered white-collared kingfisher, is highly recommended.

COME PLAY FOR THE DAY
IN ATLANTIS THE PALM, DUBAI

HE LOST CHAMBERS
QUARIUM

DOLPHIN BAY

AQUAVENTURE
WATERPARK

VHERE 65,000 OF OUR
ARE EXHIBITS CAN SWIM

SWIM WITH OUR
FRIENDLY DOLPHINS

THE LARGEST WATERPARK
IN DUBAI

xplore the ruins of the legendary
ty of Atlantis as you wander
he Lost Chambers Aquarium,
ome to one of the most exotic
nd diverse collections of marine
e, including sharks, rays, piranha,
ant arapaima, jellyfish, lionfish,
eahorses and many more.

Wade into crystal clear waters and
come nose to bottlenose for an up
close experience. Choose one of 5
exciting interactions and enjoy the
thrill of spending 30 minutes in the
water at Dolphin Bay. Learn more
about these intriguing mammals,
touch, hug and even kiss your new
friend during an enchanting
experience.

Enjoy the thrill of jumping into the
largest and most exciting
waterpark in Dubai. Aquaventure
is overflowing with 42 fun-filled
acres of rides and slides – water
roller coasters, rivers, rapids,
Splashers children's play area,
lush tropical landscapes as well as
access to a beautiful private beach.

pen Daily:
:00am - 10:00pm

Open Daily:
10:00am - Sunset

Open Daily:
10:00am - Sunset

AE Residents enjoy special rates for select attractions

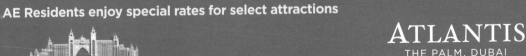

ATLANTIS
THE PALM, DUBAI

or more information, call +971 4 426 0000 or visit atlantisthepalm.com

THE WILDEST WADI

THE MIDDLE EAST'S FIRST MAN-MADE FACILITY WHERE YOU CAN WHITE WATER RAFT, KAYAK AND SURF, ALL IN THE MIDDLE OF THE DESERT.

Located on the lower slopes of Jebel Hafeet is the latest amazing tourist attraction that has visitors and residents from all over the UAE heading to Al Ain. Wadi Adventure is a waterpark with a difference; instead of slides and rides, here you'll find three world-class white water rafting and kayaking runs, totalling more than a kilometre in length. Whether you choose to get stuck in with a rafting session or take a one-on-one kayak session, there are enough options to suit your needs and past experience.

A giant conveyor belt drags you to the summit of the rapids and then it's up to you to complete the course. The beginner rapids are suitable for families (kids have to be taller than 1.2m). Don't be surprised if you capsize on the tougher rapids, though; just make sure you listen carefully to the safety instructions beforehand. Surfer dudes can also get in on the action with a huge surf pool that generates a three metre high wave every 90 seconds; while the more experienced surfers tackle the big waves at the back of the pool, beginners can take lessons nearer the shore. Lessons are available to everyone, including children taller than 1.2m.

If water isn't your thing, then the tree-top obstacles and canyon swings should keep you occupied. There are also a few food and drink outlets for refuelling. Entrance for adults is Dhs.100 and Dhs.50 for children below 1.2m, with each activity then charged separately.
wadiadventure.ae

PRICES

Access
Surf Pool – Dhs.100 (55 mins)
Kayaking – Dhs.100 (All day pass)
White water rafting – Dhs.100
(1.5 hour pass)
Climbing wall – Dhs.40 (20 mins)
Airpark zip line – Dhs.50
(All day pass)
Giant swing – Dhs.25 per swing
Lessons
Kayaking lesson – Dhs.100 (1 hour)
Surfing lesson – Dhs.150 (1 hour)

White water rapids at Wadi Adventure

SURFING

WHETHER YOU'RE AFTER SMALL WAVES TO LEARN ON, OR BIGGER ONES TO PRACTISE YOUR SKILLS, THE UAE AND OMAN CAN CATER TO ALL... AS LONG AS YOU KNOW WHERE TO LOOK!

Surfing at Umm Suqeim Open Beach

Ok, so the United Arab Emirates is not exactly Surfer's Paradise and, a little too often, you can be left with your board in hand as a frustrating lack of waves wash in; but, if you're a beginner, those manageable waves and the year-round warm water make the UAE a great location to pick up the sport of surfing.

If you are looking to catch some waves, you'll find an enthusiastic community of surfers to turn to who are out always whenever there's a swell. If you're already a keen and accomplished surfer, then just sign up for swell alerts through Surfing Dubai (surfingdubai.com) to find out when the waves are coming in. Sunset Beach (Umm Suqeim Open Beach) is a popular beach, with smallish but decent waves, while the beach off JBR, between the Hilton and Sheraton in Dubai Marina, also sees some waves. The islands around Abu Dhabi tend to act as breakwaters and prevent much swell rolling in.

The surfing season in the UAE typically runs between October and April, with the peak months being December to February; surfers also head to the south of Oman for the far bigger waves and cooler temperatures between May and August. Keep close contact with Surf Dubai, as it often organises summer surfing trips to Oman whenever the surfers hear that a big swell is coming.

The surfing community in the UAE also rejoiced at the opening of Wadi Adventure (see p.150), where artificial waves are generated every 90 seconds in a surf specific wave pool.

GET BOARD, STUPID

You can pick up boards relatively easily. Head to Beach St., Adventure HQ (adventurehq.ae) or Decathlon for a new board, while you'll find secondhand gear on dubizzle.com. You can also purchase boogyboards at Beyond the Beach stores throughout Dubai and Abu Dhabi – perfect for the little ones.

BOARDING SCHOOLS

If you're still a bit of a kook who's not quite ready to hang five with the groms, surfingdubai.com is also the online home of the Surf Dubai surf school, which runs group sessions for beginner and intermediate surfers on the public beach next to Burj Al Arab. Lessons last between 60 and 90 minutes and cost around Dhs.200. There are also sessions dedicated to kids who are keen to surf and sessions cost Dhs.300. Surf School UAE (surfschooluae.com) is also a popular option, owned and managed by keen and experienced surfers, and certified by the International Surf Association. Lessons are available in a range of languages, costing Dhs.150 per hour, or Dhs.500 for a group of four.

KITESURFING

IT'S JUST BEEN NAMED AS AN OLYMPIC SPORT FOR THE 2016 GAMES. HERE'S WHERE YOU CAN FLY HIGH AND SURF THE COAST. SEE YOU IN RIO!

You may see kitesurfers showing off along several of Dubai's beaches, but the kiting beach in Umm Sequim is the only place where kiting is officially permitted. The Dubai Kite Forum (dubaikiteforum.com) is a good place to find out the latest on regulations.

In Abu Dhabi, however, there are two main kiting beaches close to the city, one on Yas Island and another at Al Dabayyah, which is a half hour drive west towards Mirfa; although it should be pointed out that neither of these locations boast facilities and

lifeguards so kitesurfing is always done at your own risk. A few hours further west, near Mirfa for example, there are other kiting beaches.

In Oman, the best kitsurfing spot is off Masirah Island; contact kiteboarding-oman.com to arrange a trip there. A lesson in kite surfing is a two step process and it's required that you take a few lessons on land to learn the basic methods of controlling a kite. Then, when your instructor feels you are ready, you'll gradually move into the water and eventually onto a board.

KITESURFING MANIA

Each year, the very best in the kitesurfing business gather for the 10-day Al Gharbia Watersports Festival in Mirfa which takes place in March. Go down and watch the best kitesurfers compete and then stay overnight in the designated camping village. For more information, check out algharbiafestivals.com.

LEARNING THE ROPES

There are several individuals and companies in Abu Dhabi and Dubai that offer kitesurfing lessons, with prices including all the equipment, such as kite, harness and board. Lessons aren't too cheap so, if you're looking to keep the cost down, taking part in small group lessons may be the way to go. Here are some of the best instructors to get you flying.

KITE 4 FUN IKO certified Marc teaches in both English and German. Lessons cost Dhs.300 per hour. Marc is also a dealer for North Kiteboarding equipment, and the website is a good resource for wind and weather conditions, as well as finding out about kiteboarding trips to some of Abu Dhabi's islands. **kite4fun.net**

KITE DUBAI A great place to learn the basics, an introduction to kiteboarding costs Dhs.250 for one hour. Alternatively, you can opt for a complete kiteboarding course which includes eight hours of coaching broken up into four lessons and costs Dhs.2,800. **kitedubai.net**

KITEPRO Offers lessons from several IKO certified instructors, with top equipment such as radio helmets available. Individual lessons start from Dhs.300 per hour, with a 10 lesson package (valid for six months) costing Dhs.2,600. Lessons are available in English and Arabic. The website also has an online store and directions to the UAE's main kite beaches. **kitepro.ae**

KITESURFING UAE A collection of International Kiteboarding Organisation certified instructors who are available for kiteboarding lessons. An hour's instruction starts at Dhs.300 an hour for private tuition including all equipment, going down to Dhs.150 per person per hour for a four person group session. Also a great place to keep up to date on upcoming kitesurfing trips to Oman. **kitesurfinguae.com**

Kitesurfing in Mirfa

STAND UP
PADDLE BOARDING

ROOTED IN POLYNESIAN TRADITION, SUP-ING IS THE PERFECT WAY TO GET OUT ON THE WATER WHEN THERE ISN'T MUCH SURF.

Paddling through the mangroves with Abu Dhabi Stand Up Paddle Club

It began thousands of years ago, out on the Pacific Islands, where natives devised boards and oars that they could use to cross from island to island. Using this elevated position to their advantage, fishermen took to the boards. And then, one day, after a hard day of spearing fish out on the Pacific waters, one adventurous type decided to use his board to ride a wave back into shore and a multitude of sports and industries were born.

In all that excitement, stand up paddle boarding (SUP) was forgotten, until a couple of decades ago when surf superstars like Laird Hamilton started taking to the water on their SUPs again.

SUP is an appealing sport for many reasons. Since the length and width of the board is a generous size, balancing on top of one is far easier than a surfboard and makes it a relatively easy skill to pick up, so for some, it's a nice, easy introduction to board sports; for others, it's a great workout and a good way to get out on the water when conditions are less than ideal for surfing or kitesurfing.

GET UP STAND UP

SUPing is pretty easy and, if you want to just jump on the board and give it a try, you'll find boards and oars available to rent from just Dhs.70 an hour or even less; check out Watercooled Dubai at the Jebel Ali Resort & Spa (p.158). If you already have a paddleboard or plan to purchase one (see opposite for where to get the gear) then there are several places around the UAE and Oman that you can explore. Check out the calm waters of Dibba in Oman just off the shore by the Golden Tulip Hotel, paddle out to Snoopy Island off the coast of Fujairah near the Sandy Beach Hotel before diving in for a snorkelling adventure, or check out the wildlife at the Umm Al Quwain marine reserve; the list of locations is endless. However, like all deceptively simple activities, there is an art and a technique to it; if you decide a lesson or two could be in order to help you get to grips with the basics, try some of the following – they're also all excellent resources for learning more about SUP and the SUP community in the UAE.

ABU DHABI STAND UP PADDLE CLUB

Jen Scully is the capital's tireless SUP advocate and an accomplished instructor. She also arranges tours of the corniche and the mangroves. One hour private lessons cost Dhs.200 for individuals; Dhs.150 each for two people; or Dhs.125 each or three of more. **abudhabisup.com**

SURF DUBAI

Lessons range from a 20 minute express session which costs Dhs.175 (plus 1 hour free rental) to one hour private lessons costing Dhs.350 for individuals (plus 30 minutes free rental). **surfingdubai.com**

SURF SCHOOL UAE

Single lessons for both adults and children cost Dhs.200 and Dhs.175. Alternatively, you can sign up for a tour around the Burj Al Arab for Dhs.125, including equipment and a short coaching session. **surfschooluae.com**

UAE SUP

UAE SUP supports the growing paddling community in Abu Dhabi by offering social paddling sessions on Thursdays. **uaesup.com**

NOUKHADA ADVENTURE COMPANY

This tour operator runs a two hour adventure combining a paddle out to a mangrove island with some quality on-the-board yoga. **noukhada.ae**

GET THE GEAR

As you can do it in almost any conditions and it requires only the one-off purchase of a board and a paddle, SUPing is an easy and convenient way to get out on the water. Unless you don't live near the beach or live in an apartment – as the 12 foot (3.6m) boards can be difficult to transport or get into lifts! One ingenious solution is an inflatable SUP – surprisingly sturdy and robust, with the advantage that they can be inflated quickly and packed into a bag after use. You'll find inflatable SUPs at Adventure HQ (adventurehq.ae), starting at around Dhs.4,500.

MAKING A SPLASH

WHILE MANY BEACH CLUBS OFFER ONLY A HANDFUL OF ACTIVITIES, THIS NEW FIVE-STAR WATERSPORTS CENTRE HAS THE LOT... AND EVEN MORE BESIDES.

A brand new little gem on the shoreline of the Jebel Ali Golf Resort & Spa, Watercooled Dubai (watercooleddubai.com) offers the full range of watersports from wake boarding, waterskiing, wakesurfing and kitesurfing to SUP, kayaks and sailing. Plus, it serves them up with a touch of style, comfort, friendliness and professionalism that makes it ideal for regular watersporters in search of a weekly stomping ground.

THE CENTRE

The clubhouse, which is located right on the beach of the resort, is an open-plan wooden beach chalet with decking and plenty of loungers to relax on before and after indulging in an activity. The stylish club house also features a large plasma screen where you can watch your performance on the water courtesy of GoPro cameras that capture your day. There's even complimentary water, towels and WiFi for guests.

THE EQUIPMENT

All the equipment here is brand new; the boats are top of the range, and the latest in Liquid Force, Starboard, Mastercraft and Hobie equipment is used.

The highly experienced and passionate instructors are all fully qualified to teach at international standards and they are always on hand to guide newbies while also helping to improve the technique of more experienced guests.

THE ACTIVITIES

Whether you're interested in learning how to wakeboard, kitesurf, windsurf, paddleboard, kayak or sail, Watercooled Dubai offers it all. For something a little different, try zapcatting – the ultimate speed demon! With incredible acceleration similar to a Ferrari, and capable of pulling up to 3G whilst cornering, there's nothing quite like these small, inflatable powerboats. When static it is very stable, but give it some power and it's all fast action, high speed and very wet!

STAND-UP AND STRETCH

If being at one with the water is just not spiritual enough, you can also try your hand at a spot of SUP yoga. Not only is it a great form of relaxation, but the unsteady board makes it a challenging but fun core workout with the added advantage that, if things get that bit too sweaty, you can simply jump off the board to cool down.

PRICES

Kayaking – Dhs.90 (1 hour hire)
Kayaking lesson – Dhs.230 (20 minutes; per person)
Waterski/wakeboard – Dhs.250 (20 minutes; per person)
Zapcat experience – Dhs.250 (30 minutes; per person)
Kitesurfing course – Dhs.550 (3 hours)
Windsurfing – Dhs.115 (1 hour, beginner), Dhs.170 (1 hour, intermediate)
Windsurf lesson – Dhs.460 (2½ hours)
Sailing introduction - Dhs.460 (2½ hours)
Bookings necessary for all activities.

TIMES

Watercooled Dubai is open from 09.00 to 17.00 every day.
watercooleddubai.com

WAKEBOARDING & WATERSKIING

SINCE BURSTING ONTO THE SCENE A FEW YEARS AGO, WAKEBOARDING HAS TAKEN THE WORLD BY STORM. HERE'S HOW TO GET INVOLVED LOCALLY.

Waterskiing has long been a firm favourite with thrillseekers, while wakeboarding is the cool, young upstart that has become the newest, hippest watersport around. Which you opt for is just a matter of preference – although if you've excelled at skiing or snowboarding on the slopes, that might stand you in good stead; waterskiing is perhaps slightly easier to pick up initially, as getting up is a little trickier in wakeboarding but, once you're up, it's hard to find a more thrilling experience.

As you don't need any special licence to practise wakeboarding or waterskiing, and the UAE is surrounded by calm waters that are ideal for sliding across, the best case scenario is if you or some close friends own a sportsboat (see buying as boat, p.176), giving you whenever-you-want access that isn't limited to the usual 15 or 20 minute slots. If you are lucky enough to be in that situation, you'll find all you need – from handles and ropes to boards and impact and buoyancy vests at Beach St (leisuremarine-me.com), Adventure HQ (adventurehq.ae) and Al Boom Marine (alboommarine.com).

If you don't have (or can't lay claim to) a boat, you'll find that most of the big hotels' beach clubs (see p.242 & p.247 for full listings) offer the sport with a going rate of about Dhs.140 for 15 minutes.

On the busiest weekend, you could easily find that all the wakeboarding rental centres are fully booked. If that's the case or, in fact, you're looking for a bit more value for money, you should try out cable boarding. A popular sport in the US and Europe, cable boarding allows you to wakeboard while being pulled along by a zip line. The Al Forsan International Sports Resort (see p.164 for more information and prices) has two excellent cable boarding lakes.

Wakesurfing is also an increasingly popular alternative to wakeboarding. This new sport is a soft-impact version of wakeboarding where you let go of the reins, do your best to balance on the board, and surf along to the wake generated by the ski boat. It looks spectacular and offers surfing enthusiasts the opportunity to get their surfing fix without having to rely on the unpredictable Gulf swell.

BEST BEACH CLUBS

The UAE and Oman are home to some great beach clubs and these are often your best bet when looking for somewhere to practise your favourite watersport. Some hotels charge a fee for access to the beach clubs; it usually gives you a full day of access to the beach, pool and other leisure activities, which can be nice for a day out but is frustrating if you only want to book a waterski session or a parasailing trip. The following are some of the best beach clubs that guests are free to access.

AL HAMRA FORT HOTEL & BEACH RESORT

Paradise for watersports fans – not only is it a great escape from the bustling cities, but there's everything on offer, from banana boating to waterskiing and kayaking, and the rates are excellent. A 30 minute wakeboarding session costs Dhs.180. **alhamrafort.com**

BEACH ROTANA ABU DHABI

Great value; offers wakeboarding taster sessions that cost Dhs.55 for two circuits of around 10 minutes each. There's a dive centre onsite, and plenty of other watersports available. **rotana.com**

BRISTOL BOATS

Located next to the Dubai Marina Yacht Club, qualified French instructors offer lessons in wakeboarding, waterskiing, knee boarding and wake skating to both children and adults. Sessions cost Dhs.150 for 15 minutes. **bristol-middleeast.com**

ONE&ONLY ROYAL MIRAGE

Primarily aimed at guests, off-season the beach club here offers sessions to outside guests and the price is fairly reasonable at Dhs.150 for a 15 minute stint. **royalmirage.oneandonlyresorts.com**

SKY & SEA ADVENTURES

This watersports specialist operates at both the Sheraton and Hilton hotels that bookend the main stretch of the beach at Dubai's JBR. You'll find the same huge list of activities on offer at each. Wakeboarding and waterskiing each cost Dhs.200 for 15 minutes. **watersportsdubai.com**

UAQ MARINECLUB

UAQ Marine is one of the United Arab Emirates' best kept secrets. It's only about an hour's drive from Dubai; the water's almost always flat; and the watersports activities are charged at relatively low prices – a one hour session costs Dhs.250. **uaqmarineclub.com**

WATERCOOLED DUBAI

The latest watersports centre offers a plethora of watersports activities with wakeboarding lessons just the tip of the iceberg. See p.158 for more information. **watercooleddubai.com**

JETSKIING

THE MOST HIGH SPEED AND HIGH OCTANE OF WATERSPORTS, THERE ARE SEVERAL BEACHES YOU CAN HEAD TO FOR SOME JETSKI ACTION.

At one time, jetskis flew up and down the entire coastline, however, a few years ago, the maritime authorities clamped down on the use of 'personal water crafts' due to them being dangerous and creating excessive noise pollution along popular beaches.

In the last couple of years, restrictions have eased somewhat; in most of the emirates, PWCs can now be used as long as they're kept away from the main beaches and marinas. In Dubai, however, everyone (tourists included) must have a licence for their PWC and, therefore, there's no possibility of renting a jetski in Dubai as you can in certain places in other emirates (excluding the close proximity of swimming areas or marinas); some of these spots are listed below.

JOIN THE JETSET

There are several places that do offer jetski rental, with prices varying significantly. In Abu Dhabi, Hiltonia Beach Club (hilton.com) counts jetskiing amongst the wide range of watersports that it offers. Head out to the ocean and try to spot the dolphins that regularly pass by – Dhs.180 for 30 minutes.

Looking north, the watersports centre at Al Hamra Fort Hotel & Beach Resort (alhamrafort.com) rents jetskis – the perfect way to explore the Ras Al Khaimah coastline at high speed – for Dhs.160 per 15 minute slot. Although you can't rent jetskis in Dubai itself, there are options nearby. In spite of its name, Jetski Dubai is actually located just on the Abu Dhabi side of the border in Ghantoot; the company rents out jetskis from 09:00-17:50 seven days a week. It's a great, safe area to ride, with the wide manmade channel running from Ghantoot right down to the sea. Prices start at Dhs.250 for 20 minutes.

For residents at the other end of the city, a number of tour operators rent out jetskis from Al Mamzar Beach Park which sits on

the border with Sharjah; Arabian Desert Tours, for example, charges Dhs.275 for a 30 minute session.

For those keen to watch jetskiing in all its glory, the UAE International Jet Ski Championships (dimc.ae) take place every January. The championship is run over six rounds; three in Abu Dhabi and three in Dubai. Both courses are set near the shores, allowing spectators to follow the thrilling races up close.

SAFETY FIRST

While you can now rent jetskis in a number of emirates, as well as in Oman, bear in mind that they can be dangerous to others as well as yourself. Never ride close to beaches.

THE CABLE GUYS

LEARN THE ART OF CABLE WAKEBOARDING AT THIS HIDDEN GEM ON THE OUTSKIRTS OF ABU DHABI.

Sat on the outskirts of Abu Dhabi, near the Abu Dhabi Golf Course, is the fairly recently-opened Al Forsan International Sports Resort. From the entrance, the recently-constructed hotel looks no different than other five-star resort but, as you walk through the grounds, you'll uncover its two greatest assets – two large cable parks – which are arguably two of the UAE's best-kept watersports secrets!

Opened in 2011, Al Forsan is now becoming something of a Disneyland for extreme sports nuts living in the UAE. The site offers some great paintballing fields, clay pigeon shooting and archery, a go-karting circuit and horse riding, but its pieces-de-resistance are without doubt the world-class cable boarding facilities.

If you've tried wakeboarding behind a boat, then you'll already have the general gist of what is required to cable board. The main difference, of course, is that there is no need for a boat and, instead, the strong cable links that are wired around the lakes pull you along. And, if you haven't tried wakeboarding before, then many find cable boarding the ideal way to start thanks to the calm waters and steady tension on the tow line; in fact, one of the lakes at Al Forsan is dedicated entirely to beginner boarders, with a slower cable ride to practice your technique.

Over on the expert lake, meanwhile, wakeboarders and wake skaters zip their way around the outside of the lake, jumping over ramps while practising surface switches and superman tricks. There are also plenty of knee boarders and water skiers out there too.

Both pro and beginner equipment, including the mandatory lifejacket and helmets, are provided at the entrance and the staff are more than willing to give helpful tips to get you up and riding. All riders must be over 140cm tall and there's no need to book in advance; just be aware that it gets busy over the weekends.

Setting up for a jump at the cable park

PRICES

One hour – Dhs.125
Two hours – Dhs.180
Four hours – Dhs.230
All day – Dhs.280

Equipment upgrades (board, wetsuit, safety jacket) vary in price.

TIMES

Al Forsan opens daily from 15:00 to 22:00. 09.00 to 17.00 every day.
alforsan.com

WATER SPORTS

FLIGHT SIMULATOR

EQUESTRIAN

SHOOTING

MOTOR SPORTS

PAINTBALL

ALTERNATIVE WATERSPORTS

WATERSPORTS ARE COOL AND QUICK TO IMPROVISE. WHEN ONE BECOMES MAINSTREAM, ANOTHER DARING ACTIVITY TAKES ITS PLACE.

Clockwise from top-right: Riding a jet pad, skimboarding and sub winging

SKIMBOARDING

When waves are too small for surfing, skimboarding provides a happy medium. Originally created for lifeguards to get across the beaches faster, it uses a thin wooden board, which is dropped on to the wash that rolls up on to the beach. Riders then run up to the moving board and jump on, driving it forward. There are two styles of skimboarding; freestyle and wave riding. You can hire skimboards at Beach St. (leisuremarine.com) in JBR for Dhs.100 for 2 hours or, if you want your own, you can pick up one for about Dhs.1,000. Adventure HQ (adventurehq. ae) also sells boards, ranging from Dhs.450 to Dhs.1,000. For bigger waves, Joe's Point, Sur in Oman is a popular surfing and skimboarding location and is approximately 90 miles south of Muscat.

OTHER LOCATIONS:

Gold Coast – Jumeirah Open Beach
Beach St. – End of the marina, past The Sheraton, close to the overpass
Tea Bags – Next to Burj Al Arab where there are some sand banks
Black Palace – Between Palm Jumeirah and the palaces on Al Sufouh Street

SUB WING

Fancy soaring beneath the waves? This twin-winged device is connected by a tow rope to a speedboat and allows adrenaline seekers the chance to fly and roll underwater like a stingray. Once in motion, riders can steer the Subwing up and down, left and right, or perform spins, by angling or twisting the wings. **subwing.com**

JETPAD

The latest green and family-friendly alternative to the jet ski has recently landed on UAE shores. The battery powered personal watercraft has a maximum speed of 40km/h and costs approximately Dhs.60,000. Check out the awesome Explorer model which includes a glass panel at the base of the craft so you can see all the aquatic life beneath. **jet-pad.com**

WET N WILD WATERPARKS

WITH ITS YEAR-ROUND SUNSHINE, THE UAE IS THE PERFECT LOCATION FOR THE CLASSIC WATERPARK.

Clockwise from top-right: Ice Land, Aquaventure, Dreamland Aquapark and Wild Wadi

Waterparks in the UAE are adventure havens – for both adults and kids – filled with stupendous slides, wonderful wave pools, fantastic flume rides and other amazing attractions. With several excellent water parks in the country, you will never be short of places to cool off when you get too hot. Just don't forget your sunscreen!

AQUAVENTURE

Located at the top of the Palm, Aquaventure is the ultimate destination for thrill seekers. The Leap of Faith gets the adrenaline pumping with a 27 metre near-vertical drop, while the next ride along shoots you through a tunnel surrounded by shark-infested waters. The Rapids here are a whopping 2.3km long tumultuous voyage, complete with waterfalls and wave surges. Entrance for those over 1.2m is Dhs.210 (Dhs.140 for UAE residents), and Dhs.165 (or Dhs.115 for UAE residents) for those under that height. Open daily from 10:00 until sunset. **atlantisthepalm.com**

DREAMLAND AQUA PARK

Dreamland is something of a hidden gem, with more than 25 water rides spread across huge, green and well-maintained grounds. Adrenaline junkies will not be disappointed with rides such as the Black Hole, the Kamikaze and the four Twisting Dragons. The best part about Dreamland, though, is that you can stay overnight in a cabana hut within the confines of the park. Admission costs Dhs.135 for adults and Dhs.85 for children below 1.2m, while children under 3 go free. Opens at 10:00; closing times vary throughout the year. **dreamlanduae.com**

ICE LAND WATER PARK

The latest waterpark, Ice Land, opened in mid-2011. Attractions include Penguin Falls (the world's tallest man-made waterfall), Penguin Bay (a rain dance pool), Arctic Slides and Tundra Baths. You'll also find plenty of aqua games fields and a coral bay reef for snorkelling. General admission costs Dhs.150 for adults and Dhs.100 for kids. Open daily from 10:00 until 18:00 (weekdays) and 19:00 (weekends). **icelandwaterpark.com**

WILD WADI

Spread over 12 acres and right beside Jumeirah Beach Hotel, this waterpark has a host of aquatic rides and attractions to suit all ages and bravery levels – including slides that actually go uphill, thanks to the master blasters. Highlights include Wipeout, a permanently rolling wave that is perfect for showing off your flow riding skills, and the two latest rides, Burj Surj and Tantrum Alley – giant, four-seated flume rides that are sure to get the blood pumping. Admission is Dhs.200 for adults and Dhs.170 for children. Opens at 10:00; closing time varies throughout the year. **wildwadi.com**

YAS WATERWORLD

Scheduled to open by the end of 2012 on Yas Island, the park features a range of 43 rides, slides and attractions including the Water Bomber Roller Coaster that reaches speeds of up to 55 km/h, and the Aqualoop which will spin riders 360 degrees around in a loop. **yaswaterworld.com**

KEEPING FIT

THE UAE PROVIDES HUNDREDS OF REASONS TO GET OUT AND GET FIT, BUT STAYING INJURY FREE IS ALSO KEY TO ENJOYING THAT ACTIVE LIFESTYLE.

'We see all sorts of complaints and, like our patients, they come in all different shapes and sizes; the most common are probably ankle injuries, knee injuries and sprains,' says Dr Moosa Kazim, the Consultant Orthopaedic Surgeon at Orthosports in Dubai (**orthosp. com**), a medical centre that specialises in sports medicine and therapy.

'Impact sports, such as football, rugby and tennis are usually responsible, much more so than gym-based sports and workouts.'

As any sporty type is more than aware, aches and pains are part of the process, so how do you know if you've picked up a run-of-the-mill sprain on the slopes of Ski Dubai or twisted your ankle while out hiking, or if it could be something more serious?

'You need to be diligent. A lot of the injuries we see here started off as just minor grievances. Each case is obviously different but the two things to look out for are, firstly, swelling within the joint and, secondly, little or no improvement within a few days of picking up the injury.

'When patients come here, we'll firstly listen to how the injury was sustained and then try to extract certain other details. We can diagnose 80% of injuries in this way. The next step is to conduct a physical examination, either for confirmation of the initial diagnosis, or for additional information. Finally, we'll investigate using a method such as an Xray or an MRI.'

Once the injury and its extent have been discovered, it's important that a consultant works with the patient, so they understand exactly what the issue is, and are involved in their own course of recovery.

'We'd first want to use a non-invasive treatment, such as physiotherapy. This is the most common treatment required. Then there's a limited-invasive treatment, like an injection, and the final option is some form of surgical treatment.'

If you do pick up an injury while living in the UAE, Dr Kazim insists that you could barely be in better hands. 'When looking for a clinic, make sure it is licensed and then go by reputation – word of mouth is important. However, the calibre of medical care for sports injuries in the UAE is top class and on a par with most developed countries.'

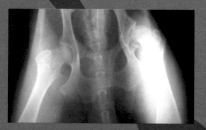

WHAT ELSE?

Traditional exercise isn't for everyone. Award-winning personal trainer, Omar Al-Duri, reveals his top alternatives.

Boxing: great cardio and an amazing de-stressor.
Climbing wall: excellent for strength and endurance.
Kettle bells: excellent tool for weight-loss, especially for glutes and core.
Gravity machine: phenomenal for toning up with thousands of exercises.
ViPR (right): brilliant for movements your body isn't used to, frontal and traverse planes.
Omar runs Platform 3 (p3dubai.com)

AVERAGE CALORIE BURN PER HOUR
(based on a 68kg person)

- Aerobics – 405
- Cycling on a flat surface – 441
- Horse riding – 288
- Jogging – 675
- Walking – 297
- Swimming – 603
- Yoga – 360
- Dancing – 370

PUT YOUR FITNESS TO THE TEST

Whatever your preferred activity, being in the best possible shape not only maximises your ability but also your enjoyment. For many, that means pounding on the treadmill or hitting spinning classes, but one local company says the 'just getting it done' approach may not be the best.

Aerofit uses technology to 'scan' your fitness levels and produce data that can be used to fine-tune your programme. 'It's a fitness coaching service that guarantees effective weight loss and improvement in your sports performance,' explains Aerofit's Sreeya Wiesner. 'It provides individualised 'fact-based' plans based on scientific analysis of your metabolism. Aerofit enables you to get the most out of each training session to make quick and visible improvements.'

Runners and triathletes have been queuing up for an Aerofit scan but its application is far wider; identifying the heart rate at which you should conduct most of your cardiovascular exercise means you can make every minute in the gym or pounding the pavement count. **See aerofit.me for full details and to book a consultation.**

Oman, discover the undiscovered

from Muscat's award winning marina.

23°37'55"N 58°16'03"E

Almouj Marina holds an enviable position along Muscat's coastline. Equidistant between two of the capital's most adored maritime destinations, the jaw dropping Damaniyat Islands and Bandar Khayran, means exploring these diverse environments is incredibly easy. If you can imagine a perfect boating destination, we have a berth for you.

Be the first to explore the unexplored. Berthing enquiries are now being taken. Please contact the Almouj Marina team on **+968 2453 4400** or at **info@almoujmarina.com**

مرسى الموج
ALMOUJ MARINA
THE WAVE MUSCAT · OMAN

BOATING AND YACHTING

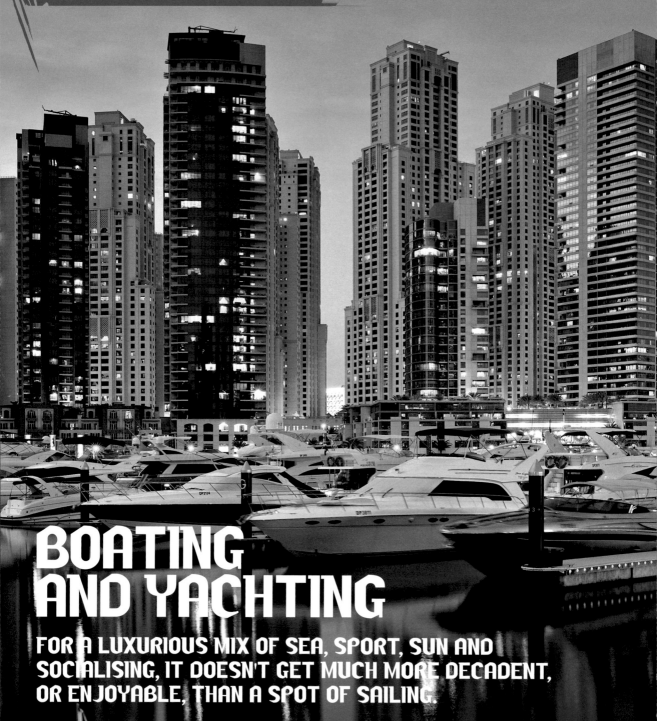

BOATING AND YACHTING

FOR A LUXURIOUS MIX OF SEA, SPORT, SUN AND SOCIALISING, IT DOESN'T GET MUCH MORE DECADENT, OR ENJOYABLE, THAN A SPOT OF SAILING.

With a stunning coastline, calm seas and year-round warm waters, a day out on a yacht has to appear on the itinerary of any wannabe explorer. Whether your intention is relaxing with the family, you'd prefer a fully-organised chartered yacht or catamaran, or you even want to learn how to sail yourself so you can own your very own shiny vessel, there are plenty of options available in the region.

GETTING A BOATING LICENCE

Currently, the UAE follows a similar principal to that of the UK in that no compulsory boating licence is required to own or drive a boat on the waterways (whether open sea or closed canals). Essentially, you can hire a powerboat and be on the seas in next to no time. However, learning what a boat is, how to control it and, more importantly, knowing what to do when things go wrong can very easily be the difference between life and death, just as you could find yourself in hot water should you have an accident – therefore, it is strongly recommended that you take a few short courses on powerboat handling before you head out.

BEGINNERS' COURSES

Both International Yacht Training (IYT) and Royal Yacht Association (RYA) offer a basic powerboat handling course, covering what all skippers should know about engines, launching, knots and basic navigation and manoeuvring.

DUBAI OFFSHORE SAILING CLUB
This RYA-accredited club offers Powerboat 1 and 2 training, all in the club's own boats. dosc.ae

COASTAL SAFETY
Run jointly in the UK and the UAE, and covering all RYA power and motorboat syllabus courses right up to the level of Yacht Master. All practical exams are held on the student's own boat. coastalsafety.com

JPS YACHT & CHARTER SERVICE
This RYA-approved training centre offers shore-based courses in HF radio, radar and marine diesel, as well as the Day Skipper course. jpsyachts.com

MARINE CONCEPT
Offers IYT courses, and students train aboard the company's own charter motor yachts from 38 feet (11.6m) up to 64 feet (19.5m). marine-charter-concept.com

WEATHER WARNING!

Always pay attention to the weather. Even experienced sailors can get caught out by regionally specific conditions, such as the shamal winds, sandstorms and heavy fog.

HOW TO BUY A BOAT

CLOSE PROXIMITY TO THE MEDITERRANEAN, PERFECT WEATHER AND ENDLESS ATTRACTIONS HAVE CREATED A BOATING PARADISE IN THE GULF.

If you intend to explore the Gulf's waterways in great detail, then you may decide to purchase your own vessel. But choosing which boat – or even type of boat – to purchase is no easy task and there are important things to consider before taking the plunge:

BUDGET
It's important to remember that a percentage of your budget should go towards arranging extra modifications, commissioning, initial servicing, surveying, registration fees and berthing.

FINANCE
Even if the funds are there to pay upfront, a good financial advisor can help a potential buyer weigh up the options. For a list of recommended advisors, check out the Directory on p.238.

MOORING
For ease of use, it should be kept somewhere convenient. This may be on a trailer outside your house, in a dry storage unit or in a berth (see Marinas, p.178).

USE
What are your reasons for having the boat? A performance cruiser may seem like fun, but as a fishing boat it would be hopeless, being unstable when not underway; equally, a racing sailing yacht may look great on the course, but will always require a minimum of four experienced crew to sail her.

WAYS OF BUYING
Some people will plough through the internet classifieds, magazines and notice boards to find the right bargains, whereas other may simply register

with a broker to find a boat on their behalf (see p.238 for a list of brokers).

Involving a broker in the purchase process can significantly speed up any potential sale and ensure the boat is purchased legally and with all the correct documentation, especially when dealing

with a foreign marketplace with rules, regulations and official procedures that are not well documented.

Buying through a broker will also cut out a lot of the administration required for the legal transfer of a boat, including the re-registration process.

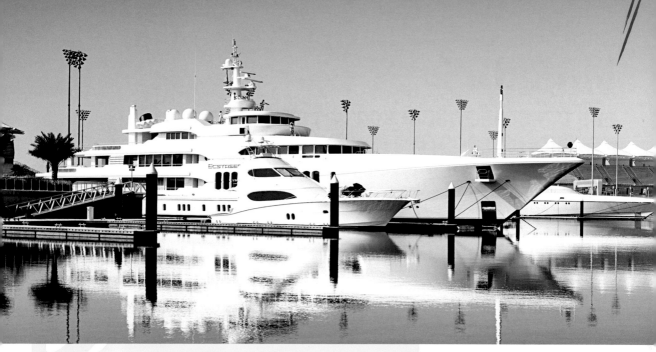

BOAT SHOW BLISS

If you love big boats, then the UAE has a couple of events just for you. The Abu Dhabi Yacht Show (abudhabiyachtshow.com) in February and the Dubai International Boat Show (boatshowdubai.com) in March are the Middle East's largest marine industry exhibitions and a classic showcase of yachts, boats and the latest innovations in marine equipment and accessories.

RULES

All boats, both commercial and private, must be registered with the UAE Coastguard before they may be used, and must display the registration number prominently on the hull or superstructure. The registration number will vary depending on which emirate the boat is registered in, so in Dubai a DP (Dubai Ports) number is issued, Sharjah an SP (Sharjah Ports), Abu Dhabi AP (Abu Dhabi Ports) and so forth.

To register a boat in the UAE, the owner must have a residence visa and, even if a boat is officially registered in another country, it must also be registered in the United Arab Emirates. For more details about rules and regulations, check out explorer's *Boating & Yachting* Guide at askexplorer.com/shop.

ESSENTIAL EQUIPMENT

When buying a brand new boat, it is necessary to also look at setting aside a budget for kitting the boat out with a host of necessary items. In terms of anchors and warp, it is very easy to wander around Deira Creek near the Al Ras metro station or in the Al Meena port in Abu Dhabi and find a multitude of shops selling non-original anchors, rope and myriad other boat equipment.

Similarly, stores such as Blue Waters Marine (bluewatersmarine.com) sell deck hardware, plumbing and ventilation equipment and plenty of other useful marine accessories. For both fixed and handheld GPS systems, chart plotters and radars, visit a Garmin dealer such as AMIT Dubai (amitdubai.net).

WATERSPORTS GEAR

Should you want to kit out your boat with sufficient watersports equipment or fishing gear, there are several stores in the UAE and Oman that sell all the stuff you need. For watersports accessories such as life vests, boards, helmets, and tow sports equipment, try Adventure HQ, Al Boom Marine and Beach St (see Watersports, p.145) where they sell a plethora of well-known brands including Liquid Force, Oakley and O'Neill.

Have you been bitten by the boating bug and now you fancy learning more?

Everything you need to know is available in explorer's *UAE Boating & Yachting* book, which is out now across the region. Or you can pick up a copy from our e-shop at askexplorer.com.

MARINAS

ABU DHABI AND DUBAI BOAST TOP QUALITY MARINAS AND BOATING FACILITIES. HERE ARE JUST A FEW TO CHOOSE FROM.

Should you decide that sailing is the pastime for you and that you want to buy a boat in order to explore local waters on a more regular basis then – more often than not – you're going to need to store the boat somewhere.

While a trailer in front of the house is an option for some (although you should check regulations where you live before making any decisions), for others, berthing in a marina is the logical option.

There are still waiting lists at a few of the UAE's most established and best-located marinas but, by and large, there is availability and rates are competitive throughout the Gulf. Be sure to check what these rates include, however; facilities and benefits can differ greatly.

Dubai Creek Golf & Yacht Club
Tel: 04 205 4646
Email: marina@dubaigolf.com
Website: dubaigolf.com
GPS: 25°14'410.15"N 55°19'54.61"E
Guide Price: Dhs.38-70 per ft per month
Size Range: 4-45m

Dubai Festival City
Tel: 04 232 9316
Email: marina@dubaifestivalcity.com
Website: mourjan-festivalmarina.com
GPS: 25°13'16.92"N 55°21'1.20"E
Guide Price: Upon request
Size Range: 10-35m

Dubai Marina Yacht Club
Tel: 04 362 7900
Email: info@dubaimarinayachtclub.com
Website: dubaimarinayachtclub.com
GPS: 25°4'21.72"N 55°8'9.00"E
Guide Price: Dhs.245 per m per month
Size Range: 8-35m

Al Bandar Complex (Al Raha Beach)
Tel: 02 810 7651
Email: info@aldarmarinas.com
GPS: 24°27'4.10"N 54°35'59.94"E
Guide Price: Dhs.14,688 per year.
Dhs.150 per day
Size Range: 10-35m

Yas Marina
Tel: 02 657 5460
Email: yasmarina@cnmarinas.com
Website: cnmarinas.com/yas
GPS: 24°28´4.66"N 54°36´33.26"E
Guide Price: Dhs,16,445 per year.
Dhs.170 per day (complementary four hours)
Size Range: 8-150m

Al Hamra Marina
Tel: 050 305 4063
Email: claudio@alhamramarina.com
Website: alhamramarina.com
GPS: 25°41'50.51"N 55°46'44.26"E
Guide Price: Upon request
Size Range: Up to 40m

Umm Al Quwain Marine Club
Tel: 06 766 6644
Email: info@uaqmarineclub.com
Website: uaqmarineclub.com
GPS: 25°33'44.19"N 55°33'55.71"E
Guide Price: Dhs.800 per ft per year (wet berth); Dhs.300 per ft per year (dry berth)
Size Range: Dry Berths 5-11m

Marina Bandar Al Rowdha
Tel:+968 24 737 286/+968 24 737 288
Email: marina@omantel.net.com
Website: marinaoman.net
GPS: 23°34'55.78N 58°36'25.73"E
Guide Price: Upon request
Size Range: Less than 8-30m

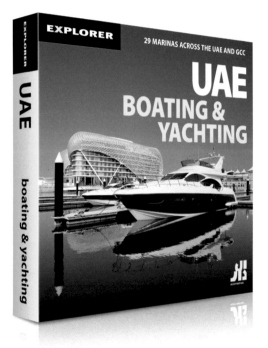

SAILING SPORTS

IF YOU'RE LOOKING TO FIND YOUR SEA LEGS, THERE ARE PLENTY OF CLUBS THAT WILL HELP YOU GET INVOLVED.

A sailing yacht is undoubtedly respected in a different way to motor boats, as there needs to be a certain degree of learning undertaken before a sailing boat will even get going. As a novice, even the basic knowledge of sailing seems an unimaginably large task, but for an intrepid explorer, it's all part of the fun and, luckily, there are plenty of schools and many courses you can take in the UAE.

Membership at one of the UAE's sailing clubs allows you to participate in club activities and to rent sailing and watersports equipment. You can also use leisure facilities and the club's beach, and moor your boat at additional cost.

POWERBOATING

The highlight of the powerboating scene in the UAE are the last two rounds of the UIM Class 1 World Powerboat Championship. These see the stylish heavyweights of the powerboating world (14 metre-long carbon fibre and Kevlar catamarans with twin V12 engines) race their way around a grand prix circuit through Mina Seyahi lagoon at speeds of up to 250km/h, just metres from the beach.

Held at the end of the year, the twin Dubai events are the finale in the European circuit.

Dubai also hosts rounds of the Class 3, 6 litre series, which sees smaller versions of the Class 1 catamarans speeding around at well over 150km/h. The best place to take in the excitement, sound and thrill of watching multimillion dollar boats racing past is on the breakwater of the Mina Seyahi Club Marina, which is opened up for the free festival.

For those who feel the need for speed the world of powerboating is certainly not one that can simply be stepped into lightly, with an average Class 1 campaign running into millions of dollars merely to get the boat.

A cheaper option has popped up with the UAE joining the UK and US as a venue for a P1 Powerstock Championship. The P1 Panther boats can reach speeds of up to 112km/h but can also be run as leisure crafts and cannot be modified, making them more affordable introductions to powerboat racing.

DRAGON BOATING

Training sessions in the ancient eastern sport of dragon boat racing are held most mornings and evenings at Le Meridien Mina Seyahi and the Shangri-La Qaryat Al Beri. It is an increasingly popular sport and there are several teams based in Dubai and Abu Dhabi who regularly compete against each other. Most are more than happy to accept new members with

RACE DATES

November-February: Powerboat Racing & P1 Superstock
March: Mussanah Race Week
April: Dubai Dragon Boat Festival
May: Al Gaffal Traditional Dhow Sailing Race
May: The Commodores Cup

little or no experience. The UAE Dragon Boat Association lists all of the country's principal teams; for training times and joining details visit dubaidragonboat.com.

LEARNING THE ROPES

If you've not found your sea legs but would like to, there are a few places that will teach you how to be your own captain.

Dubai International Marine Club
Offers sailing lessons for children. A 12 hour course sets members back Dhs.1,500. dimc.ae

Dubai Offshore Sailing Club
This Royal Yachting Association Training Centre offers dinghy and keelboat courses. dosc.ae

Abu Dhabi Sailing Club
There are fleets of Kestrels, Lasers and Optimists. Beginner sailing courses are offered for adults and children from the age of 6. adsyc.ae

Noukhada Adventure Company
For those who want to learn how to sail, Noukhada is a perfect starting point. Its Hobie catamarans are light and easy to manoeuvre and the staff have been sailing for years. noukhada.ae

Watercooled Dubai Watersports Centre
Watercooled has a fleet of RS dinghies and Hobie Tattoo 16 catamarans for private hire, individual lessons and group lessons. If you haven't tried sailing before, take the Watercooled 'Introduction to Sailing' course which lasts 2.5 hours and costs Dhs.460. watercooleddubai.com

Oman Sail
The main Oman sailing school is located at Marina Bander Al Rowdha and offers courses for kids. omansail.com

El Mundo
DUBAI
...an affordable luxury.

Celebrations • Corporate functions • Tailored cruises

Enjoy an unforgettable experience cruising the azure waters of the Arabian Gulf on your tailor made charter.

www.elmundodubai.com   info@elmundodubai.com   +971 50 551 7406

BOAT TRIPS

FROM DHOW TRIPS TO LUXURY CHARTERED YACHTS, OPTIONS ABOUND FOR THOSE LOOKING TO GET ONBOARD.

From the traditional abras that snake across the creek and the splendid old dhows that provide dining and sightseeing trips, to speedboats and super yachts that cruise along the coastlines at high speeds, there are several ways to explore the Arabian waters.

THE CREEK

Once the central hub of Dubai, Deira remains an incredibly atmospheric area. Narrow, convoluted streets bustle with activity while gold, spices, perfumes and general goods are touted in its numerous souks. Dubai Creek, beside which Deira sits, was the original centre of Dubai commerce and it still buzzes today with boats plying their transport and cargo trades.

ABRA-KADABRA

Abras (wooden, single-engine boats) have long been the primary method of crossing the creek; don't miss out on the chance to experience a trip across the water on one of these traditional crafts. Each trip across the water costs a mere Dhs.1 and abras can carry around 20 seated passengers. The ride across the creek lasts about 10 minutes and you can just turn up and queue to go on. Alternatively, Dhs.120 will allow you to charter an abra (and driver) for an hour, giving you the chance to explore the whole creek at your leisure.

CREEK FERRY TRIPS

If you fancy a longer time on the water, you can hop aboard the new ferry service that

begins at the creek in Al Ghubaiba and travels through the Bastakiya area and out along Dubai's coastline. The ferry (rta.ae) operates two trips a day (17:00 and 19:00) and lasts one hour. There are more than 100 seats (with standard economy and posh business class seats available) and tickets start at Dhs.50 and can be bought at the booth on the creekside.

COASTLINE

The UAE is blessed with a long and enticing coastline. From immaculate stretches of sandy beach and colourful mangroves to views that include iconic landmarks dotted along the shore line, taking a cruise on the Gulf is an essential experience.

CHARTER YACHTS

If you're a newcomer to the region, or just keen to experience a different kind of boat trip, there are a number of companies that offer charters. These provide activities ranging from sundowner cruises that last a couple of hours to overnight trips with stopovers for snorkelling and swimming. Meanwhile, fishing trips and watersports packages are also available.

Large sailing yachts, speedboats, catamarans and other motorboats can be hired for private charter and corporate events; typically, each chartered yacht is charged for by the hour with hourly rates starting at around Dhs.2,500, depending on the size of the yacht you're after and whether you need a crew.

Try the likes of Arabian Divers & Sportsfishing Charters (fishabudhabi.com), Blue Waters Marine (bluewatersmarine. com), JPS Yacht & Charter Service

(jpsyachts.com), Bristol Middle East Yacht Solution (bristol-middleeast.com) and Xclusive Yachts (xclusiveyachts.com). Remember, like all companies and activity providers mentioned in this guide, you'll find more contact details for these and similar companies in the Directory, which starts on p.238.

THRILL RIDES

If you're after an adrenaline rush, sign up for a turbo jet experience with The Yellow Boats (theyellowboats.com). These guys offer exhilarating tours on board eco-friendly inflatable crafts, which allow you to witness some of the best sights of the Arabian Gulf while you literally fly over the water, twisting and turning along the way. Brace yourself, as you're bound to get wet! Tours take place in Abu Dhabi along the Corniche and in Dubai around The Palm.

COASTLINE FERRY

For a more sedate sailing experience, try the brand new ferry service (rta.ae) that sails along the Dubai coast. Depart from the Dubai Marina Mall and explore the sights of Dubai's famous landmarks. The morning trips cost between Dhs.50 and Dhs.75, taking place at 09:00 and 11:00 and lasting for one hour.

DHOW DINING

For a classier affair, there are numerous dining dhows that sail up and down the creek giving you stunning views while you eat. Hop aboard the Al Mansour Dhow (located at the Radisson Blu Hotel, Dubai Deira Creek), for example, for a two-hour creek trip with dinner included. You'll get great views, atmospheric oud music, a traditional buffet spread and shisha on deck to make it a memorable evening. The ship sets sail at 20:30 and the price is Dhs.185 per adult; however, there are numerous other dhows offering a similar service, both along the creek and also in Dubai Marina. These can be booked through the main tour operators (p.245 & p.248).

In Abu Dhabi, try the well-known Shuja Yacht, which can be booked through Le Royal Meridian Abu Dhabi. The large yacht heads along the Corniche, offering superb views of the Abu Dhabi skyline as you tuck into a tasty seafood buffet.

SAILING THE 'FJORDS OF ARABIA'

One of the most stunningly beautiful parts of Arabia, time spent exploring the myriad inlets and coves of Musandam will be a highlight for any explorer. With its spectacular mountains and deep fjords, Musandam offers some of the most breathtaking scenery in the Middle East. Situated in the northern tip of the Arabian Peninsula, the Omani province has a long, varied history; traders, navies and pirates have all ventured through the Straits of Hormuz into the Arabian Gulf and, thanks to several dhow companies, you can explore the area too.

DHOW CRUISE

Whether it's on a single decker for a day or a triple-deck dhow for an overnight adventure, there are plenty of fantastic options for exploring the Musandam. These traditional dhows often include meals, snorkelling trips and stopovers on deserted beaches. If you choose to stay overnight, you can camp out under the stars, grab a sun-lounger on the top deck, or opt for the comfort of an air-conditioned room. It's one Arabian adventure not to be missed!

SHEESA BEACH TRAVEL

Sheesa Beach HQ is located on the UAE-Oman border and takes just under two hours to reach from Dubai, offering the greatest choice of cruises in the region. With exceptionally friendly service, highly-praised tours and different fleet sizes to suit any group, Sheesa Beach is still one of the favourite options for a Musandam adventure. sheesabeach.com

XVENTURES

Offers full-day dhow cruises from Dibba for Dhs.200 with trips including fishing, swimming, snorkelling and snacks, as well as some amazing views. x-ventures.net

MUSANDAM SEA ADVENTURES TRAVEL & TOURISM

From day trips to three-day excursions, Musandam Sea Adventures will pick you up from Dubai or Abu Dhabi and drive you to the base camp in Oman. Sail 16km through the fjords before jumping on the beach for a barbecue once you've pitched your tents for the night. msaoman.com

FISHING

THE UAE IS A RICH FISHING GROUND. HOWEVER, AS NO FISHERMAN WOULD EVER GIVE AWAY THEIR CHOICE FISHING SPOTS, PART OF THE FUN IS TRYING TO FIND THEM.

Before casting off, not only is it worth researching what type of equipment and bait to pack in your tackle box, but also noting that you need a licence from the relevant department within your resident emirate.

REGULATIONS

If you're caught fishing from a beach, pier or boat without a licence (unless it's an organised fishing trip which does not require individual licences), you face a minimum fine of Dhs.1,000. However, acquiring a recreational fishing licence can be quite tricky and the procedure differs a little from emirate to emirate. In Dubai, for example, you need to contact the Municipality Customer Service Centre for an application form, and then visit the service centre with a completed form, a passport copy, your labour card, your driving licence, your car registration card, two passport photographs, an electricity bill and your tenancy contract…phew! Your application will then be evaluated. On the positive side, it is free if longwinded.

A Dubai licence only grants you permission to fish in Dubai, and not the rest of the UAE. Abu Dhabi residents can apply online at abudhabi.ae for either an annual licence or a weekly renewable licence that can be issued immediately and costs Dhs.30.

FISHING TIPS

It is important to avoid oil installations or anything remotely governmental as fishing is illegal in these areas, but there are plenty of other sites of interest on the charts that will offer a selection of exciting fishing grounds. Look for seabed changes and sources of food such as underwater springs, underwater cliffs, wrecks and areas

where currents will bring in nutrients. The most productive fishing season lasts from September to April, although it is still possible to catch Sailfish and Queenfish in the summer months. Fish commonly caught in the waters off the UAE's coast include king mackerel, tuna, bonito, kingfish, and jacks.
Part of the attraction in owning your own boat is the freedom to explore for yourself what the region has to offer, but if you fancy having your fishing excursion arranged for you, a number of charter firms offer these.

FISHING GEAR

If you're looking to own your own fishing gear, Blue Waters Marine (bluewatersmarine. com) sells tackle, lines, rods and harpoons to get you properly kitted out. Similarly, Arabian Divers & Sportsfishing Charters (fishabudhabi.com) has a small, fully-stocked store in Al Bateen, Abu Dhabi. Dubai Garden Centre (desertgroup. ae) and Adventure HQ (adventurehq. ae) also sell a good range of rods, reels and lures. See p.244 & p.248) of the Directory for more fishing gear stores.

ALTERNATIVE FISHING ADVENTURES

CREEK FISHING

On a Friday, you could hire an abra for the morning (either at the Bur Dubai or Deira landing steps) and ask your driver to take you out to the mouth of the creek for a bit of fishing. Always agree on a price before you leave.

KAYAK FISHING

For something a little different, Noukhada (noukhada.ae) offers catch-and-release kayak fishing in the mangroves of Abu Dhabi and the northern emirates.

ORGANISED FISHING TRIPS

ARABIAN DIVERS & SPORTSFISHING CHARTERS

Operating out of Abu Dhabi, Arabian Divers is one of the best companies for both new and experienced anglers. Captain Greg is a well-known, well-seasoned fisherman and is extremely knowledgeable about where to fish all year. fishabudhabi.com

DUBAI CREEK GOLF & YACHT CLUB

Provides trips on the club's Sneakaway Yacht into the Arabian Gulf to experience big game sports fishing. The fully equipped 32ft Hatteras carries up to six passengers and rates include tackle, bait, ice, fuel and a friendly crew. dubaigolf.com

BARRACUDA DUBAI

As well as being one of the region's main suppliers of fishing rods and tackle,

Barracuda operates a pair of boats from Dubai Marina. barracudadubai.com

LE MERIDIEN MINA SEYAHI BEACH RESORT & MARINA

The custom-built Ocean Explorer and Ocean Luhr are fully equipped with 20, 30 and 50lb class tackle. lemeridien-minaseyahi.com

JEBEL ALI GOLF RESORT & SPA

Four and eight-hour fishing trips are available for up to seven people and tackle, equipment and snacks are provided. jebelali-international.com

SKY & SEA ADVENTURES

Among its varied list of watersports activities, Sky & Sea Adventures offers two hour sport fishing trips and half day deep sea fishing excursions. watersportsdubai.com

ARABIAN SEA SAFARIS

In addition to the standard four and eight-hour fishing trips, you can also try your hand at traditional tuna fishing. Using hand lines, the Omani fisherman will teach you the ancient art of catching yellow fin tuna. A four-hour session costs RO 100. arabianseasafaris.com

WATER WORLD MARINE

If you're a keen sports or game fisherman, this operator is an excellent option. These boats are fully equipped with electronic fish finders, down and outriggers and GPS. waterworldoman.com

Indulge with your loved ones...
at a great location in Musandam, Oman

Exclusive Indulgence

Perched on a rock face, this 4 star resort offers the most panoramic views of the famed Musandam Shoreline. The 60 rooms resort is elegantly furnished with its very own private terrace or balcony offering breathtaking panoramic views on the Gulf of Oman. Your ideal destination for the one's romantic getaway, family vacation, relaxation escape or company retreat.

The Golden Tulip Khasab – Resort offers a wide range of leisure and business facilities delighting the sense of every guest.

- Dhow cruise & Dolphin watching
- Sightseeing Excursion
- Mountain safari
- Fishing Trips

- Dolphin watching
- Diving & Snorkelling
- Barbeque Nights
- Team Building Activities

WEEKEND BREAKS

WEEKEND BREAKS

THERE'S MORE TO THE UAE THAN THE COUNTRY'S FAMED MEGA-CITIES. VENTURE OFF THE URBAN PATH TO DISCOVER A MYRIAD OF FASCINATING DESTINATIONS.

Jumeira Beach Park

FROM THE BEST OF THE EMIRATES...

The UAE's urban areas offer plenty to see and do, but look a little further and you'll find a huge amount of destinations that make for a perfect weekend escape away from the hustle and bustle of city life.

Best of all, it's all within easy reach and, thanks to surprisingly varied landscapes and unique blends of attractions and activities, there's truly something for everyone.

Located a short drive from Dubai, Hatta (p.190) lures visitors with its mix of mountains, wadi pools and dunes; head here for adrenaline pumping desert safaris or sheer relaxation.

Just south of Abu Dhabi, the Pearl Coast (p.192) offers a myriad of watersports as well as pristine beaches and island escapes.

Inland, in the southernmost tip of the country, you'll find the lush Liwa oasis which sits in the midst of the awe-inspiring dunes of the Empty Quarter (p.195), the largest sand desert this side of the Sahara.

Elsewhere, the attractions of inland oasis town Al Ain (p.196) include the region's best zoo, vast palm plantations, plenty of history and culture, as well as the spectacular mountain drive of Jebel Hafeet.

Cross over to the other side of the Hajar Mountains and you'll find the fantastic beach resorts and dive destinations of Fujairah (p.198). In Ras Al Khaimah (p.200), you'll get to combine beach life with the thrills of mountain biking and hiking.

...TO PRISTINE OMAN

Venture just a little further, and you can find yourself in Oman – one of the most beautiful and culturally interesting countries in the region. Oman too can be easily reached and explored by car, with the atmospheric capital Muscat (p.206) just a five or six hour drive away from Dubai and Abu Dhabi. Even closer, at the tip of the Arabian peninsula, the Omani enclave of Musandam (p.204) offers some of the region's best diving and mountain safaris in a scenic fjord setting that has gained Musandam the nickname 'Norway of Arabia.'

HEADING FURTHER OUT - FLY OR DRIVE?

Nearly all of the destinations listed on the following pages are easily within reach by car. However, if you'd like to explore the more remote corners of the UAE and Oman over the weekend, taking a plane may be a smarter choice. This is particularly the case for Desert Islands (p.215), Muscat (p.206) and other parts of Oman (p.12).

Marina Bandar
Al Rowhda, Oman

HATTA

A POPULAR SPOT AMONG OFF-ROADERS, THE MOUNTAIN TOWN OF HATTA OFFERS PLEASING RESPITE FROM THE CITIES THAT ARE JUST A SHORT DRIVE AWAY.

Hatta is located within easy reach of the UAE's biggest cities; by car, it takes less than an hour from Dubai and just under two from Abu Dhabi. With natural rock pools that are easily accessible, an interesting heritage village and the excellent Hatta Fort Hotel, the area is a great spot for a break.

On the way there, along the E44, lies the famed Big Red dune, where you can drive your 4WD over the sand or rent quad bikes and dune buggies. In and around Hatta itself, there are plenty more off-road options, including Hatta Pools, where you can take a cooling dip; to get there, you need to pass Hatta Heritage Village and Jeemah.

If you prefer your action on two wheels, then this is also a popular area for road cyclists looking for a more undulating challenge than the flat roads by the coast provide; the most popular route follows the back roads behind the Hatta Fort Hotel and through Huwaylat and Wadi Al Helo, before meeting up with the S116 all the way down into Kalba. In Kalba, there are plenty of stores for supplies and refilling water bottles before making the return trip. If you follow this full route, the odometer should clock up more than 100km, with climbs of up to 10%. Be aware that other vehicles can come past at some speed, especially on the section that follows the S116 – care should be taken at all times, with lights turned on when passing through the two tunnels.

Back in town is Hatta Heritage Village. It is constructed around an old settlement and was restored in the style of a traditional mountain village. Hatta's history goes back over 3,000 years and the area includes a 200 year-old mosque and the fort, which is now used as a weaponry museum. Entry is free.

STAYING

Hatta Fort Hotel
04 809 9333, jebelali-international.com
This secluded retreat features 50 chalet-style suites which come with patios overlooking the Hajars and the hotel's tranquil gardens; the hotel also doubles as the area's main activity provider, with swimming pools, floodlit tennis courts, mini golf and a driving range, as well as an archery range (instruction is available). The hotel can organise 4WD sightseeing and driving experiences.

PEARL COAST

HUNDREDS OF KILOMETRES OF PRISTINE COASTLINE, STUNNING BEACHES AND REMOTE ISLANDS AWAIT YOU HERE.

Located in the UAE's south-western tip, along a stunning stretch of Arabian Gulf shoreline, the Pearl Coast has everything you need for a fabulous weekend of exploration. If you head west along the coast from Abu Dhabi, the first port of call is Mirfa. A long-established fishing port and pearling centre, Mirfa has a rather quiet feel these days, but this is all set to change following the inauguration of the Mirfa Corniche development in March 2011.

While the works are under way, new life has recently already been blown into the area by the opening of the refurbished Mirfa Hotel (see opposite page), as well as the Al Gharbia Watersports Festival (algharbiafestivals.com). Each year the event wakes up Mirfa with a weekend of crowds, fireworks and competitive kitesurfing, wakeboarding and kayaking.

Watersports are clearly the main attraction for activity seekers exploring this coast and you'll find good facilities, rentals and lessons at hotels like the Jebel Dhanna Resort and Mirfa Hotel, but, if you own your own SUP, kayak or kitesurf gear, then the vast, open beaches here are ideal for camping; sleep under the stars and spend the days on the crystal clear waters – life doesn't get much better.

A hundred kilometres further along the coast is Jebel Dhanna, another stopping point for history's pearl divers. With a great beach and the clear, shallow sea, the Jebel Dhanna Resort now lures travellers to these distant shores. Located a short boat ride off the coast (or a flight from Al Bateen Executive Airport and Jebel Ali) lies Sir Bani Yas island. Once Sheikh Zayed's personal retreat, it is now open to the public as a noted wildlife reserve and an internationally-renowned holiday resort, Desert Islands by Anantara. It's almost easier to list the activities not offered at the Desert Islands resort. You can take tours of the wildlife reserve on horseback or by car to spot animals such as cheetahs, giraffes and oryx. Other activities include archery, falconry, mountain biking, kayaking and sailing; plus, there are the usual facilities like swimming pools and tennis courts.

FOOD & DRINK

The coastline setting means that you'll get to sample exquisite seafood here. Some of the best (and cheapest) food can be found at the small roadside cafeterias. For finer fare, Jebel Dhanna Resort's Zaitoun is highly recommended, as is Samak, the romantic beachfront seafood restaurant at Desert Islands by Anantara.

STAYING

Desert Islands by Anantara
02 801 5400, anantara.com
This stylish resort's attractions range from wildlife safaris to snorkelling, kayaking and mountain biking.

Jebel Dhanna Resort
02 801 2222, danathotels.com
This good-value, five-star resort has a country club feel, great facilities and a decent selection of bars and restaurants.

Mirfa Hotel
02 883 3030, mirfahotel.com
This recently renovated hotel has 114 rooms and wide-ranging leisure facilities in immediate reach of the region's watersports draws.

LIWA & THE EMPTY QUARTER

INCREDIBLE SCENERY AND SOME OF THE MOST ADVENTUROUS OFF-ROAD DRIVING AWAIT IN THE INLAND AREAS OF AL GHARBIA.

For most visitors, all roads lead to Liwa, one of the largest oases on the Arabian Peninsula and a gateway to the magnificent desert. Dotted with date plantations, small towns and ancient forts, Liwa Oasis is the starting point for exploring the Rub Al Khali desert which covers parts of Oman, Yemen, the southern UAE and almost all of southern Saudi Arabia. There is an extraordinary beauty to this harsh, inhospitable landscape and desert driving here is a real adventure.

Camping, dune-bashing or a combination of the two are your principal activities here. The opportunities for camping are endless and sleeping under the stars is a great way to experience the tranquillity of the desert. For more on camping, see p.59. If you don't feel like roughing it, a handful of hotels and luxurious resorts dotted across the dunes now offer all the mod-cons (see right).

Dune-bashing is the other major draw in and around Liwa. The gigantic dunes provide plenty of opportunities to get your adrenaline pumping. You can either turn up in your own 4WD to tackle some of the most thrilling rides anywhere in the country, or book a session with one of the tour operators or local hotels. Tilal Liwa Hotel, for example, offers 90 minute long desert drive adventures which are guaranteed to get your heart pumping.

The Liwa Oasis is a collection of some 50 villages built around a string of natural oases which form a 100km long crescent-shaped area of lushness in the middle of the massive desert. The area is the historic birth place of Abu Dhabi's ruling family, Al Nahyan. Today, you'll find plenty of working farms which provide much of the UAE's local produce.

MOREEB HILL

This huge dune tops out at nearly 300 metres and is the site of several hill-climbing races throughout the year. The area hosts several stages of the UAE Desert Challenge, culminating in the annual championships (usually in January). Even if you're not ready to tackle the steep hill yourself, it's worth turning up as a spectator.

STAY

Liwa Hotel
02 882 2000, liwahotel.com
With a raised location giving fine views across the surroundings, this resort offers a scenic spot plus all mod-cons.

Liwa Resthouse
02 881 2075
This modest option is a little past its prime by now, but the rooms are perfectly clean to make a good budget alternative.

Tilal Liwa Hotel
02 894 6111, danathotels.com
Built to resemble a traditional Arabic fort, this desert hideaway hotel's rooms offer sweeping views of the surrounding dunes.

Qasr Al Sarab
qasralsarab.anantara.com
Easily the most scenic and atmospheric choice, this luxurious resort sits in the midst of stunning dunes and features gorgeous Arabic-style rooms and villas with private pools, as well as a great spa.

AL AIN

GREENERY AND OASIS HERITAGE ARE JUST SOME OF THE DRAWS HERE, BUT AL AIN IS ALSO ONE OF THE COUNTRY'S ADVENTURE HUBS.

For one of the most diverse and action-packed weekend breaks, head inland to Al Ain. The city is a Unesco World Heritage Site thanks to its many fortresses, and a visit to Al Ain National Museum offers a glimpse into the city's ancient trading past. The camel and livestock souk is also well worth a visit – arrive early to soak up the lively atmosphere.

Al Ain makes for a nice family break, with the highlight arguably being Al Ain Zoo (p.215), which is one of the largest and best wildlife reserves in the Gulf region. With ample greenery and shaded pathways, the park makes for a wonderful family day out, while kids will love the white lions and white tigers. Hili Fun City (p.218) is also worth a visit; the spacious, leafy grounds make the 22 acre park a nice destination for family outings. Adults and older kids who enjoy high-speed thrills should head to Al Ain Raceway (alainraceway.com), which has a 1.6km karting track.

But Al Ain is also something of an outdoor adventure paradise. Cross over the border into the Omani side of the city (known as Buraimi), and you'll find yourself 30 minutes' drive or less from a handful of amazing off-roading and hiking routes, such as the Hanging Gardens (p.86), Wadi Madbah (p.32) and Jebel Rawdah. All of these offer great camping spots too, with canyons, springs and pools for taking refreshing dips.

Another focal point for adventure is Jebel Hafeet (p.121). The 13km road that winds through 21 corners to the top of the 1,240m mountain is regularly named one of the world's great driving roads and is worth tackling. For local cyclists and runners, the Jebel Hafeet Mountain Road offers a once-in-a-lifetime challenge; the journey up may be gruelling but the views from the top are exhilarating, as is the journey back down.

Although Jebel Hafeet is home to an intricate cave system and several trails, there is no organised caving, canyoning or climbing on the mountain. Fortunately, for those who like high altitude thrills and spills, at the foot of the mountain lies the superb Wadi Adventure (p.150), which offers a climbing wall, zip line and rope course, as well as a surf pool and white water rafting.

One advantage that Al Ain has over some of the other weekend break destinations is that there is something of a – albeit

AL AIN ZOO

This sprawling park is the Middle East's most progressive nature facility. Around a third of the 180 species on show are endangered and the zoo is actively involved in wildlife preservation and re-release programmes. Other highlights include white lions, white tigers and a fantastic twice-daily bird show.

fairly tame – nightlife. You can follow the lead of locals and pop over to the Danat Resort's Horse & Jockey Pub for a quick drink, for example, or head to the popular Trader Vic's at the Al Ain Rotana for some cocktails before dinner at one of the many good restaurants found in the city's hotels.

STAY

Al Ain Rotana
03 754 5111, rotana.com
A city centre resort with spacious rooms and an attractive garden with swimming pool. Popular restaurants include Trader Vic's and Min Zamaan.

Danat Al Ain Resort
03 704 6000, danathotels.com
One of the most enjoyable inland resorts in the UAE, this hotel's landscaped gardens and pools make it a great choice for families.

Hilton Al Ain
03 768 6666, hilton.com
Located near the heart of Al Ain, this is a particularly convenient choice when visiting the wildlife park and Jebel Hafeet.

Mercure Grand Jebel Hafeet Al Ain
03 783 8888, mercure.com Situated in a spectacular location near the top of Jebel Hafeet, the Mercure offers incredible views of Al Ain.

FUJAIRAH & THE EAST COAST

SCENIC MOUNTAIN VISTAS, PRISTINE BEACHES AND A SPOT OF DIVING OR BIRD-WATCHING AWAIT YOU ON THE EAST COAST.

Located on the UAE's beautiful east coast, along the Gulf of Oman, Fujairah can now be reached in about an hour from Dubai or two hours from Abu Dhabi, thanks to a new highway. The drive cuts through the rugged Hajar Mountains, which provide breathtaking scenery, as well as the backdrop to plenty of high adrenalin activities.

Areas like Wadi Sidr, Wadi Tayyibah and Wadi Asimaf lie on the border between Fujairah and Ras Al Khaimah, and offer diverse terrain ideal for wadi bashing, camping and picnicking; you'll find pools and streams in the area at certain times of year, but the paths and routes lend themselves particularly well to hiking and mountain biking.

The seaside itself is home to smart beach resorts that attract visitors throughout the year thanks to the fact that summer temperatures tend to be a few degrees lower than in Abu Dhabi and Dubai. The hotels offer the usual mix of beachfront facilities and an array of watersports,

but this coastline is particularly popular with divers and snorkelers – the Gulf of Oman is richer in marine life than the Arabian Gulf, with turtles, sharks and whales to discover. There are a number of excellent dive and snorkel spots to check out: for more on diving, see p.125.

The northern tip of Fujairah meets the amazing Omani enclave of Musandam (p.204), so, if you're in search of a longer adventure break, you could combine these two great destinations for all the wadi bashing, climbing, cycling, hiking and diving that even the most committed explorer could possibly dream of.

CAMPER'S DREAM

Try camping on Dibba or Al Aqah beaches; in the morning, you can simply flop into the sea to wake yourself up in the best possible way.

STAY

Fujairah Rotana Resort & Spa – Al Aqah Beach
09 244 9888, rotana.com
Rooms with views, great dining options, an indulgent spa and a private beach.

Le Meridien Al Aqah Beach Resort
09 244 9000, lemeridien-alaqah.com
A classy resort with ocean views, fantastic family features and a spa.

The Royal Beach Al Faqeet Hotel
09 244 9444, royalbeach.ae
A great budget option in Dibba. In close proximity to dive spot Dibba Rock.

Sandy Beach Hotel & Resort
09 244 5555, sandybm.com
Located right opposite Snoopy Island, this is a firm favourite among divers.

Desert Adventure Escapes
at Tilal Liwa Hotel

Spend an adventurous getaway from the bustling city life at stunningly secluded desert hideaway Tilal Liwa Hotel, perched on the edge of Rub Al Khali Desert. Immerse yourself in an authentic Arabian "Oasis of Hospitality," where tantalizing restaurants, an infinity pool and a full range of superb amenities offer the ultimate accompaniment to the natural beauty of the desert.

Discover the wonders of the rolling sand dunes of Liwa and explore adventurous activities such as sand boarding, dune bashing 4x4, quad biking, horse riding, sightseeing visit to the camel farms and camel race arena. Tilal Liwa Hotel beckons you to escape to an unforgettable experience.

Visit www.danathotels.com for exciting packages including accommodation, breakfast and leisure activities or call +971 2 894 6111 for further information.

Tilal Liwa Hotel

Managed by Danat Hotels & Resorts, a Division of National Corporation for Tourism & Hotels
P.O. Box 112723, Abu Dhabi, United Arab Emirates | T. +971 2 894 6111 | F. +971 2 894 6112 | E. info.tilal@danathotels.com | www.danathotels.com

RAS AL KHAIMAH

ACTIVITIES GALORE, SPECTACULAR SCENERY AND A HOST OF NEW RESORTS MAKE RAK ONE OF THE UAES HOTTEST DESTINATIONS.

With the majestic Hajar Mountains rising just behind the city, the Arabian Gulf stretching out from the shore and the desert starting just to the south near the farms and ghaf forests of Digdagga, Ras Al Khaimah has possibly some of the best scenery of any UAE emirate.

Outdoors enthusiasts are spoilt for choice when it comes to the activities on offer in this varied area, but most prefer to start at the awe-inspiring mountains.

The Hajars are at their most rugged, challenging and beautiful along the border between Ras Al Khaimah and neighbouring Fujairah, and it's along this strip that you'll find the UAE's highest named mountain, Jebel Yibir. Not only is Jebel Yibir fairly easy to access, it's the starting point for tens of small wadis and trails that zigzag their way across the mountainside, providing terrific hiking, trekking and mountain biking opportunities. Many mountain bikers head to Jebel Yibir (p.114) in search of a challenge and, if the winding route to the top tests the legs and lungs, the tight switchbacks on the way back down are all about heart and nerve.

Elsewhere along the border, you'll find action-packed routes like Wadi Sidr, Wadi Tayyibah and Wadi Asimaf which also offer hiking, mountain biking and camping. The beauty of outdoor sports in these areas is just how accessible they are to people of all ages, abilities and fitness levels. However, if you're really not sure where to start, a number of tour operators (p.245 & p.248) can organise and guide you through athletic outdoor pursuits, from mountaineering to kayaking.

While out there in the mountains, you can visit the ancient sites of Ghalilah and Shimal, head for the hot springs at Khatt or make for the camel racetrack at Digdagga. Culture-buffs will not go empty-handed either: Ras Al Khaimah boasts several archaeological sites, some dating back to 3000BC. Many of the artefacts can now be found in the Ras Al Khaimah Museum, but some sites are still interesting to visit onsite too: take the Al Ram road out of the Al Nakheel district towards the Hajar Mountains to discover some of the area's history, including the Dhayah Fort, Shimal Archaeological Site and Sheba's Palace.

Elsewhere in RAK, the mountains give way to the Arabian Gulf. Al Hamra Marina

(alhamramarina.com) is the best place for boat excursions, waterskiing and fishing trips; you can also rent jet skis here. Golfers can choose between Al Hamra Golf Club (alhamragolf.com) and the Tower Links Golf Course (towerlinks.com). The latter lies among the mangroves around the creek and features a clubhouse, restaurant and gym.

Ras Al Khaimah makes for a good family escape, as not all the activities are quite so high adrenaline. Guests at the Banyan Tree Al Wadi, for example, are offered relaxing camel or horseback rides through the desert, while there's a fantastic falconry display and course which kids love. They also tend to love the nearby Ice Land Water Park (p.169).

Outdoor attractions aside, there's plenty to do in the emirate's namesake main city, like visiting the souk in the old town and the National Museum of Ras Al Khaimah, which is housed in an old fort.

STAYING

Al Hamra Fort Hotel & Beach Resort
07 244 6666, alhamrafort.com
With traditional Arabic architecture set among acres of lush gardens and a strip of sandy beach, this hotel offers a peaceful getaway.

Banyan Tree Al Wadi
07 206 7777, banyantree.com
Fuses superior luxury with exclusive spa facilities, desert activities and a wildlife conservation area.

The Cove Rotana Resort
07 206 6000, rotana.com
The Cove's sprawling layout is reminiscent of an old Mediterranean hill town.

Golden Tulip Khatt Springs Resort & Spa
07 244 8777, goldentulipkhattsprings.com
Simple and subdued, this resort lures visitors with tranquillity and spa packages.

Hilton Ras Al Khaimah Resort & Spa
07 228 8844, hilton.com
Tucked away on an exclusive bay, this resort is perfect for a beach break.

OFF-THE-WALL

IF YOU ARE LOOKING FOR SOMETHING A LITTLE DIFFERENT, THE UAE AND OMAN HAVE A HOST OF FABULOUSLY QUIRKY ESCAPES TO CHOOSE FROM.

XVA ART HOTEL

This little gem of a hotel is hidden away on the upper floor of the XVA Art Gallery in Dubai's historic Bastakiya district. With just eight rooms, you'll feel like you're part of an elite group of hipsters who have rejected the glitz and glamour of the beachfront resorts in favour of a quiet weekend in 'real' Dubai. The individually-decorated rooms all come with en-suite baths and ample character. If fine art, local culture and a tranquil atmosphere sounds like your cup of tea, this is the perfect weekend hideaway.

SHEESA BEACH

An overnight dhow trip with Sheesa Beach is an unforgettable experience. The traditional Omani style boats, which range from simple open-deck models to air-conditioned triple-deckers, can be chartered for a one or two night cruise for up to 15 people. The rentals include an accompanying speedboat for safety and watersports excursions; scuba diving can also be booked. **sheesabeach.com**

FUJAIRAH TENNIS & COUNTRY CLUB

Names can be deceptive and that is certainly the case for this sporting and leisure haven on the east coast; in addition to tennis courts, this club's other great sports facilities and the cosy boutique hotel make it the perfect setting for a fitness weekend away. During the day, choose between tennis, spinning, basketball or squash, or try a yoga or ballet class. Afterwards, tuck into tasty food or grab a few drinks at the onsite pub or restaurant before retiring to one of the 14 individually-decorated rooms for some well-deserved rest. **fujairahtennisclub.ae**

RAS AL JINZ

This nature lover's paradise is a bit further along the coast from Muscat, but the journey is well worth it to witness the thousands of turtles that invade the pristine beach to lay their eggs. Turtle-watching trips, including an overnight stay in one of the dozen rooms, are available from Dhs.620. rasaljinz-turtlereserve.com

ABSOLUTE ADVENTURES

Located in the northern outskirts of Dibba, the Absolute Adventure camp is an oasis of plantations, barasti lookouts and adjoining dorm-style rooms with bunk beds. It may not be as luxurious as staying in a four or five-star hotel, but a weekend here will provide more outdoor adventures than you can possibly imagine. The activities include mountain biking, sea kayaking, treks through secluded mountain villages, scuba diving, canyoning, exploring caves, hang gliding, mountain safaris and wadi bashing. **adventure.ae**

GREEN MUBAZZARAH

The Green Mubazzarah chalets are a great choice for an outdoorsy family weekend in Al Ain. In addition to an overnight stay in a fully-furnished chalet, you'll gain access to the delightfully green park which has natural hot springs, a boating lake and a toboggan run for the kids. Nearby, you'll find Wadi Adventure's adrenaline-pumping white water rafting facilities, and the fabulously scenic drive up Jebel Hafeet is just around the corner (p.121). **mubazzarah.150m.com**

DREAMLAND AQUAPARK

Make your kids' dreams come true by booking an overnight stay at one of the cabins inside Dreamland Aqua Park (p.169). Located right inside the park, the accommodation may be a little basic, but you'll be too busy enjoying the rides, water fun and barbecue dinner to notice. The affordable rates are inclusive of an overnight stay, meals and 36 hour access to the waterpark.

MUSANDAM

BEAUTIFUL FJORDS, MOUNTAINS AND GREAT DIVING - MUSANDAM IS A MUST.

The mountainous Omani territory of Musandam boasts a distinctive landscape that has earned it the moniker the 'Norway of the Middle East,' thanks to the jagged cliffs that plunge directly into the sea and are punctuated by beautiful fjords. It's not hard to see why this area is becoming the region's outdoor epicentre.

Vast and dramatic, off-piste action is the way forward for adventurous off-roaders, hikers, bikers and campers – just make sure you travel in groups, have fully charged mobile phones and GPS units and plenty of water, then head off into the great open spaces. If you prefer, there are plenty of conventional routes to follow too, like the popular Wadi Bih (p.38).

Natural attractions abound underwater here too; in fact, Musandam's unique marine offerings see it pop up time and time again on global scuba wishlists. Just off the shore are coral beds with an amazing variety of sea life, while the numerous caves that are dotted along the shoreline are also home to all manner of underwater creatures. Depending how lucky you are, you could see morays, stingrays, eagle rays, manta rays, spiny lobsters, white top sharks, leopard sharks, whale sharks, nurse sharks, clownfish, squirrelfish, triggerfish, sunfish, trevally, jacks and dolphins.

The capital, Khasab, is a quaint fishing port largely unchanged by the modern world and this is the best departure point for boat trips into the fjords. If you have your own dive gear, you can usually just charter a local boat; if you need to rent equipment or prefer something a little more organised, try Khasab Travel & Tours (khasabtours.com)to book dhow trips or visits to the remote island of Kumzar. The Golden Tulip Khasab can also arrange dive tours, as well as dhow cruises, 4WD mountain safaris and trekking tours.

Located on the southern end of the peninsula, close to Fujairah, the Omani side of Dibba is home to a number of dive operators and is perhaps the easiest way to take to Musandam's waters. Again, there's a Golden Tulip Hotel here which can arrange all manner of diving and adventurous onland trips. If you've cash to spare, try a stay in the luxurious Six Senses Zighy Bay Resort – although mainly focused on relaxed pampering, Six Senses offers guests the option of hang gliding into the resort from the mountain above.

If you'd like to enjoy several days of diving, teamed with some other activities, Nomad Ocean Adventures (discovernomad.com) organises dive trips with accommodation in its own eco-lodges.

STAY

Golden Tulip Resort Dibba
+968 26 836 654,
goldentulipdibba.com
Simple, clean and with a great beach, this is a good option for an affordable getaway.

Golden Tulip Resort Khasab
+968 26 730 777,
goldentulipkhasab.com
Modern facilities and rooms that boast balconies overlooking the Strait of Hormuz.

Khasab Hotel
+968 26 730 267, khasabhotel.net
This small, friendly place offers basic rooms and a small swimming pool in the centre of Khasab.

Six Senses Hideaway by Zighy Bay
+968 26 735 555, sixsenses.com
An exclusive, ultra-luxurious option in a remote bay near Dibba.

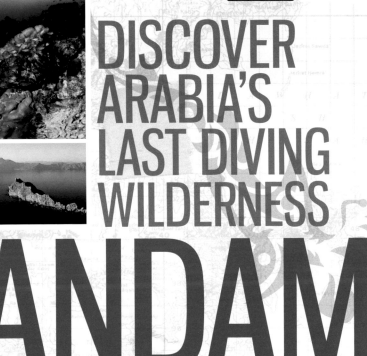

MUSCAT

OMAN'S CAPITAL IS A STRIKING CITY, SANDWICHED BETWEEN SPECTACULAR ROCKY MOUNTAINS AND BEAUTIFUL BEACHES.

Muscat features a lot more greenery than you may be used to if you live in Dubai or Abu Dhabi. With beautiful beaches, bustling souks, a collection of great restaurants and cafes, and some fascinating museums, there's plenty to keep you busy during a weekend trip.

If you're driving, you may want to extend your stay to a long weekend – drive times from Dubai and Abu Dhabi are around five to six hours, depending on border crossings. But if you've only got a regular weekend, despair not: flying is a viable option and this way you can reach the charming Omani capital in a short, one-hour hop with Emirates, Etihad or Oman Air.

Quiet and atmospheric, the old town of Muscat is home to some very interesting museums. Muscat Gate Museum illustrates history from ancient times right up to the present day, while Bait Al Zubair features major displays of traditional jewellery, attire and household items. The Omani French Museum celebrates the close ties between these two countries.

Mutrah rests between the sea and a protective circle of hills, and has grown around its port, which today is far more vibrant than the port of Muscat's old town. Mutrah Corniche is lined with pristine gardens, parks, waterfalls and statues. Nearby, you'll find one of Muscat's most famous

EXPLORER TIP
You'll find some great camping spots south of the Shangri-La Barr Al Jissah Resort and Yiti Beach. For more remote camping, head south to As Sifa, where you will almost always be able to find a secluded spot; pick up a copy of the *Oman Off-Road Explorer* for additional tips.
askexplorer.com/shop

shopping experiences: the Mutrah Souk. It is always buzzing with activity and is renowned as one of the best souks in the region.

Although primarily a residential area, Qurm has some great shopping, good quality restaurants and cafes, the city's largest park (Qurm National Park) and arguably the best beach in Muscat. It is also home to some of the top hotels, all of which have superb leisure facilities.

The villages of Al Bustan and Sidab provide an interesting diversion from the main Muscat areas. Head south along Al Bustan Street out of Ruwi on the spectacular mountain road to get to the village of Al Bustan and the Al Bustan Palace Hotel, one of the most famous hotels in the region.

But it's not all about the urban city break or hotel-hopping down in Muscat. Drive an hour to the west of the city and you'll find yourself in the Western Hajars, an area that offers about the best bang-for-your-buck adventuring as anywhere on the planet. It's here you'll find Wadi as Sahtan (also known as Oman's 'treasure chest'), the ancient Wadi Bani Kharus and Wadi Al Hijayr, the breathtakingly beautiful Wadi Bani Awf and Wadi Mistall – the 'Hanging Gardens' of Oman. Wadi al Abyad makes for a great trip for the first time off-roader. All of these routes beg visitors to camp, hike, picnic and swim in the streams. When you feel ready, head to Wadi Hawasinah for The Chains – nature's very own assault course.

Follow the coast south out of Muscat, and the mountains increase in height as the landscape gets more rugged. Bays here, mostly reachable by roads winding over the mountains, are home to the beaches of Qantab and Jassah, as well as the Oman Dive Center (omandivecenter.com) which is touted as one of the top dive centres in the world.

STAYING

Chedi Muscat
+968 24 524 400, ghmhotels.com
This beautiful boutique resort sits on its own stretch of shoreline and is regularly voted among the best in the region; a truly luxurious escape.

Crowne Plaza Muscat
+968 24 660 660, crowneplaza.com
With its fabulously scenic cliff-top location close to the centre of Muscat, and overlooking a long stretch of beach, this is a great option for families.

InterContinental Muscat
+968 24 680 000, intercontinental.com
Traditional five star luxury, manicured lawns and access to a wide expanse of public beach is on offer here.

Shangri-La's Barr Al Jissah Resort & Spa
+968 24 776 666, shangrila.com
Located in a private, secluded sandy bay, this gorgeous resort offers sheer relaxation and elegant luxury.

Hili Fun City

Unlimited Family Fun in Al Ain

Only 45 DHS

ANNUAL PASS 2012 NOW AVAILABLE

At Hili Fun City, classic and traditional family fun is what we're all about. Enjoy 31 attractions (28 included in the entrance fee) for all ages, with roller coasters, rides, an amphitheatre for 1,400 people, and beautifully landscaped gardens with picnic and play areas.

For more info please call +971 3 784 5542 or visit www.hilifuncity.ae

For admission fees, please refer to our website, Wednesdays are reserved for ladies only. Closed on Sundays.

EXPERIENCES

EXPERIENCES

FROM FLYING AND FLOATING TO FREE FALLING, SHOOTING TO SKATING, AND DRIVING TO RIDING, EVERY DAY IN THE UAE CAN BE A WHOLE NEW ADVENTURE.

When it comes to living the ultimate adventure, the United Arab Emirates is the GCC region's top destination for explorers thanks to the huge number of experiences on offer. From watersports to record-breaking activities, and wildlife to motorsports, the choice is endless.

However, not only are these experiences of interest to residents; recent figures show that tourist numbers are steadily increasing year on year. And while these guests are here, they invest in plenty of outdoor time.

SHOWSTOPPERS

There's no doubt that one of UAE's biggest attractions is the impressive collection of buildings and venues that trump those of the US, Europe of the Far East.

On your Abu Dhabi must-visit list, there should be mention of Yas Island, an impressive 2,500-hectare development that's home to the Yas Marina Circuit (yasmarinacircuit.ae), which hosts the Formula One Abu Dhabi Grand Prix, as well as Ferrari World Abu Dhabi (ferrariworldabudhabi.com), where you can ride the world's fastest rollercoaster.

Another showstopper is the Emirates Palace (emiratespalace.com), a grand luxury hotel that at a cost of approximately $3 billion makes it arguably the most expensive hotel ever built. The 5 star luxury property was also the first to launch the world's first gold vending machine.

The emirate of Dubai, meanwhile, features the tallest skyscraper in the world: the Burj Khalifa. The 829.84-metre high structure offers a viewing experience from its 'At The Top' observation deck (tickets can be booked online via burjkhalifa.ae), where floor-to-ceiling glass walls provide a breath-taking unobstructed 360-degree view of the city, desert and ocean.

An incredibly fascinating structure, the Burj Khalifa has even appeared in a Hollywood blockbuster – Tom Cruise famously shot stunt scenes in and around the building in his film *Mission: Impossible - Ghost Protocol*.

CULTURAL

There's more to the UAE than fancy buildings and flashy venues. It is also home to a wealth of history and culture waiting to be discovered. There are plenty of activities to choose from, including heading to the outskirts and exploring the desert (turn to the Directory for a list of desert tour operators) or visiting the Sheikh Zayed Grand Mosque (szgmc.ae) in Abu Dhabi.

It is well worth checking out the Sheikh Mohammed Centre for Cultural Understanding (cultures.ae), a non-profit organisation established to increase awareness and understanding between the various cultures that live in Dubai and the rest of the UAE. The centre organises activities, such as visits to the Jumeirah Mosque, cultural breakfasts and lunches, tours of old areas such as the Bastakia quarter near Bur Dubai, cultural awareness programmes and even Arabic classes.

ADRENALINE

You don't necessarily need to throw yourself off a mountain to get your adrenaline fix. There are more exciting – and safer – ways to get your blood pumping, and the UAE offers a great variety of thrilling activities – from helicopter rides to Bond-style skydiving. Read on to find out more.

ULTIMATE UAE EXPERIENCES CHECKLIST

Whether you are new in the UAE or have friends or family visiting for the first time, the following experiences are those that you must do during your time in the region:

DUBAI
- ☐ Visit the Burj Khalifa
- ☐ Shop at the biggest mall in the world, the Dubai Mall
- ☐ Enjoy afternoon tea at the Burj Al Arab, the world's only 'seven-star' hotel
- ☐ Head to Atlantis The Palm Jumeirah, and swim with the dolphins at Aquaventure
- ☐ Discover the Dubai-style brunch
- ☐ Spend a day at the Sheikh Mohammed Centre for Cultural Understanding
- ☐ Take an abra from Deira Creek to the textile souk in Bur Dubai
- ☐ Visit Dubai's Bastakia area and the Dubai Museum

ABU DHABI
- ☐ Explore the lobby area of the Emirates Palace (one of the most beautiful)
- ☐ Visit the Sheikh Zayed Grand Mosque in Abu Dhabi
- ☐ Embark on a tour of Yas Island

RAS AL KHAIMAH, FUJAIRAH & AL AIN
- ☐ There is plenty of nature to be explored, with trip options including camping, hiking and diving

NATIONWIDE
- ☐ Go on a desert safari

MOSQUE MANNERS
In line with the UAE's dress code, visitors must be dressed appropriately prior to entering a mosque. Female visitors must wear a traditional robe (abaya) and headscarf (shayla), which can be provided.

JOCKEY FOR THE DAY

UNLEASH YOUR INNER JOCKEY WITH THESE RIDING ADVENTURES.

HORSE-BACK RIDING

Horse riding is a national sport in the UAE, so it comes as no surprise that there are a number of excellent equestrian clubs in the country. That said, many of these are so in demand that they have waiting lists for lessons, so it is highly recommended you call up and book in advance.

One of the latest stables to open is that of Al Forsan International Sports Resort (alforsan.com), which houses indoor and outdoor training areas, show jumping facilities, and a polo field. Al Jiyad Stables near Bab Al Shams (050 599 5866) offers lessons for riders of all levels of experience, and organises individual or group desert hacks, while the Desert Palm Riding School (desertpalm.ae) is a state-of-the-art facility providing classes for all ages.

For longer rides in the great outdoors, the Jebel Ali Golf Resort & Spa (jebelali-international.com) has nine horses, and experienced riders can tackle one-hour desert rides. And if you're in Sharjah, the Sharjah Equestrian & Racing Club (serc.ae) offers a grass show jumping arena, and hacking trails into the desert.

CAMEL RIDING

Apart from great photo opportunities, this is a chance to see a truly traditional local sport up close. Al Ain Golden Sands Camel Safaris (03 768 8006) offers a selection of tours that include a camel ride over the dunes of Bida Bint Saud.

Al Sahra Desert Resort Equestrian Centre (04 427 4055 – also organises horseback desert hacks) runs a full camel experience – including a little information on camels, a taste of camel milk products and a short ride into the desert, followed by Arabic coffee and dates.

THINK PINK & RIDE HIGH

Avid horse riders can trot through the emirates for a good cause with the Friends of Cancer Patients (FOCP) that organise the Pink Caravan campaign each year. The initiative – which involves a lengthy trek throughout the Emirates – aims to spread breast cancer awareness and encourage early detection for all women. Over the course of 10 days, these lone rangers travel over 250km through towns and villages to spread the word about the dangers of breast cancer, while a medical unit performs screenings and education talks at designated stops. If you'd like to join the team on their next campaign, visit pinkcaravan.ae.

SHOOT 'EM UP

INSPIRED BY THE HUNGER GAMES? LOVED DUCK HUNT AS A CHILD? THIS IS THE EXPERIENCE FOR YOU.

SHOOTING & ARCHERY

Over the years, the number of shooting ranges and archery facilities available in the UAE has increased significantly, so there are plenty of places to choose from.

Al Forsan International Sports Resort (alforsan.com) in Abu Dhabi has indoor and outdoor ranges, including the first clay shooting course in the Gulf region. And with simulated game flush shooting, Olympic trap and skeet fields, rifle ranges and a laser shooting simulator, the options are plentiful.

Another popular choice is Sharjah Golf & Shooting Club (golfandshootingshj.com), where the shooting range features indoor pistols, rifles and revolvers, as well as 25m and 50m ranges. It also offers target archery at its indoor facility.

In Dubai, the Jebel Ali International Shooting Club & Centre Of Excellence (jebelali-international.com) has five floodlit clay shooting ranges that consist of skeet, trap and sporting. Indoor and outdoor ranges, as well as a specialised pistol range, are available.

For something out of town, Ras Al Khaimah Shooting Club (07 236 3622) boasts a 50m indoor and 200m outdoor rifle range.

LEISURE WEEKEND AWAY

If you're looking for a hotel that provides shooting experiences, head to the stunning Hatta Fort Hotel (hattaforthotel.com), where

clay pigeon shooting is one of the many activities offered. Meanwhile, the hotel's 25-metre archery range has eight targets, and a 30-minute target practice session costs as little as Dhs.50 per person with all equipment included. Hatta Fort Hotel also hosts an eagerly-anticipated annual archery competition for die-hard fans.

Additionally, UAE-based club The Dubai Archers (see below) holds its annual tournament at this hotel.

JOIN THE CLUB

If you want to dedicate more time to perfecting your craft, then join a local UAE-based group. The Dubai Archers (dubaiarchers.com) meet near Sharjah International Airport and just past Sharjah National Park every Friday. Timings change according to the season, but are usually around 09:00-12:00 in the morning. The sessions cost Dhs.70 for two hours including equipment and instruction for those who require it.

DON'T FORGET YOUR ID!

Most shooting clubs require that you provide a valid UAE Emirates ID or a valid passport/passport copy in order to enter its shooting range, so don't forget to take your ID with you!

EXPLORE WILDLIFE

THE UAE IS HOME TO HUNDREDS OF DIFFERENT ANIMALS AND SPECIES, SOME OF WHICH ARE UNIQUE TO THE REGION. HERE'S WHERE AND WHAT YOU CAN DISCOVER.

AL AIN ZOO

Stretching over 900 hectares, Al Ain Zoo (alainzoo.ae) is one of the largest and best zoos in the Gulf region.

As well as seeing large mammals, reptiles and big cats, you can get up close to some rare and common local species such as the Arabian Oryx and sand gazelle, or pay a visit to the fantastic birdhouse.

Since its founding, the zoo has been a centre for endangered species' conservation and visitors can look forward to spotting true rarities. Nearly 30% of the 180 species are endangered and the park is even home to white tigers and white lions.

One of the most popular attractions is that of the African mixed exhibit, which allows visitors to watch a spectacular concentration of African wildlife. Giraffe, zebra, gemsbok, gazelle, ostrich, wildebeest and rhinoceros roam freely on more than five hectares of open space. The zoo is also one of very few zoos in the world to house and breed the very rare species of Nubian giraffe.

Entry is a bargain – Dhs.15 for adults and Dhs.5 for children.

SIR BANI YAS

Half nature reserve, half luxury resort and spa, Sir Bani Yas Island (desertislands.com) is the centrepiece of Abu Dhabi's Desert Islands.

Home to the Arabian Wildlife Park, and Desert Island Resort & Spa, the island has thousands of free-roaming animals. Hiking, mountain biking and 4WD safaris, as well as snorkelling and kayaking trips, are available, and guests can be delivered to the island by private seaplane.

EMIRATES PARK ZOO

Launched in 2008 as the first private zoo in the UAE, Emirates Park Zoo (emirates parkzoo.com) – formerly known as Kids' Park Zoo – is home to a variety of wildlife, as well as attractions and interactive activities.

Located in Al Bahia, about 35km from Abu Dhabi on the Abu Dhabi-Dubai highway, the zoo allows children to interact with many species by touching or feeding them.

The park is undergoing significant expansion, which will see an increase in the variety and numbers of animals, bringing them to a total of 2,000. These will include the UAE's very first green anaconda, as well as hippopotamus, sea lions and swans.

ANIMAL SANCTUARY

Originally located in Sharjah, the Posh Paws Animal Sanctuary (poshpawsdubai.com) is now in Al Khawaneej, Dubai.

The venue welcomes groups and holds parties at the farm, where children can feed, touch or hold various animals whilst learning some fun facts about each one and how to care for the animals correctly.

The non-profit organisation currently takes care of sloths, porcupines, cockatoos, ponies, deer, llamas, guinea pigs and more.

BYE, BYE DUBAI ZOO

One of the oldest zoos based in the UAE is that of Dubai Zoo in Jumeira. However, the venue has been facing problems over the years due to issues with overcrowding. Thankfully for the animals, at the time of going to print it had been announced that they will get a new home by the end of 2012 as Dubai Municipality starts work on a Dhs.150-million, 400-hectare Dubai Safari in the Al Warqa area on Aweer Road. Dubai Safari will be home to the more than 1,000 animals already at Dubai Zoo, along with many more that will be brought from zoos in other countries. It will also have a butterfly park, botanical garden and golf course, plus entertainment and recreational areas.

UP, UP AND AWAY!

EMBARK ON A UNIQUE DESERT ADVENTURE IN THE UAE.

With its soaring skyscrapers, rolling sand dunes and spectacular man-made islands, the UAE from the air is an impressive and truly unique sight. And there's nothing better than taking in the serenity of the desert from a graceful hot air balloon flight.

The UAE's leading hot air balloon operators are Balloon Adventures Emirates (ballooning.ae) and Amigos Balloons (amigos-balloons.com).

Balloon Adventures organises tours for individuals and groups in four large, advanced balloons, with flights departing before sunrise. All trips are followed by dune driving.

With Amigos Balloons, you can take a dawn hot air balloon flight over the desert out near Fossil Rock and watch the changing colour of the sands as the sun rises. Flights cost Dhs.950 per person.

During trips, it is recommended you wear comfortable loose clothing, and since trips take an average of 4 to 5 hours, it is advisable to carry a light jacket or cardigan (ladies, as you will have to climb in and out of the basket, wearing a skirt or heels can be inconvenient).

A sun hat or cap is also a good idea.

WEATHER WARNING

With temperatures soaring in the UAE over the summer, the above operators only run trips between September and May, therefore it is recommended you book your experience well in advance.

COME FLY WITH ME

IT'S NOT FOR THE FAINT HEARTED, BUT THERE'S NO DOUBT THAT FLYING IS ONE OF THE BEST WAYS TO EXPLORE.

SCENIC FLIGHTS

Not all of us can be captains, so the next best thing would be to enjoy a 30-minute scenic flight exploring the coast line and famous mountains of the UAE's east coast.

Leading operator Seawings (seawings.ae) offers flight tours that depart from either Le Méridien Al Aqah Beach or Fujairah Al Dana and land at Ras Al Khaimah Hilton Beach Resort or Al Hamra Fort Hotel. Prices start from Dhs.795.

For those preferring to stay in Dubai, the Seawings silver package – starting from Dhs.1,325 – is a 40-minute dock-to-dock excursion providing views of Dubai's most iconic landmarks, including the Palm Jumeirah, Burj Khalifa, the World Islands, Burj Al Arab, Dubai Creek and Port Rashid. Absolutely beautiful!

Then there's the Fujairah Aviation Academy (fujaa.ae), which provides enthralling bird's-eye view tours of Fujairah's coastline, rugged mountains, villages and date plantations. The operator's flights can accommodate one-to-three people.

If you are a pilot already, the Emirates Flying School (emiratesaviationservices.com) in Dubai is the only approved flight training institution that offers private and commercial licences, and will convert international licences to UAE. A Private Pilot Licence course costs upwards of Dhs.48,720.

MICROLIGHT FLYING

The Jazirah Aviation Club (jac-uae.net) on the Dubai–Ras Al Khaimah highway is dedicated solely to microlight/ultralight flying and also offers training and pleasure flights.

Meanwhile, Umm Al Quwain's Micro Aviation Club (microaviation.org) offers training courses in microlight flying, paragliding and paramotoring.

Courses start from Dhs.3,500, with an annual registration fee of Dhs.250.

HELICOPTER TOURS

Helicopter tours are also extremely popular in the UAE. Aerogulf Services Company (aerogulfservices.com) provides helicopter tours over the city and its main landmarks. A half-hour tour for four people costs Dhs.3,200, or you can opt to charter a chopper by the hour and choose your route.

THEME PARK MADNESS

AGE IS JUST A NUMBER. UNLEASH YOUR INNER 10-YEAR-OLD WITH THESE UAE-BASED AMUSEMENT PARKS.

HILI FUN CITY

The recently renovated 22 hectare park may not compete with the world's greatest theme parks in terms of the rides on offer, but the spacious, leafy grounds make Hili Fun City (hilifuncity.ae) a perfect destination for family outings. However, don't be fooled by its timid exterior.

Nothing prepares you for the theme park's Sky Flyer - a white-knuckle ride, where you hold on for dear life as you swing like a pendulum until you're completely upside down. You may think the worst is over just before it sends you flying through the sky again – in reverse. Needless to say, get ready to scream your heart out.

Admission to Hili Fun City costs Dhs.45 per adult, while children enter for free. Additionally, new promotions have been introduced for 2012: an annual pass is available for Dhs.200, while a family pass for six people costs Dhs.1,000.

There are plenty of arcade games and refreshment stands, or you could bring your own picnic. Additionally, located on the eastern side of the park is a mammoth 60 by 30 metre ice rink.

GLOBAL VILLAGE

If you've ever driven along Emirates Road during the Autumn-Winter season, chances are you've passed the massive Ferris wheel that's close to Arabian Ranches. So you'd be forgiven for thinking that Global Village (globalvillage.ae) is just your typical fairground.

But there's more to the venue than meets the eye. It is arguably one of Dubai's best-kept secrets for a fun evening out. With food, global market stalls and fairground rides galore, you will be spoiled for choice with what to do first.

CLOSING MONTHS

There's no point planning a trip to Global Village during the summer, as it is only open between October and March. During that time, the venue is open every day from 16:00-00:00, but beware, it gets very busy during Thursdays and Fridays.

At Hili Fun City, special opening hours apply for the June-August period. Also, it is worth bearing in mind that Wednesdays are reserved for ladies and children only, while the park is closed on Sundays. It then closes for the duration of Ramadan (which is when annual maintenance takes place).

STREET SPORT

SKATER BOYS CAN FIND PLENTY OF LIKE-MINDED BOARD PEOPLE HERE IN THE UAE TOO.

LONGBOARDING

If you like to look at the world as your own personal assault course, then longboarding just might be the experience that you crave.

Longboarding is similar to traditional skateboarding but, as the name suggests, the boards are a bit bigger. Although longboards have been around for years, their popularity has really exploded

ROLLER SKATING

Arash Skate Academy (arashskate. com) provides high quality teaching and delivers internationally recognised in-line skating certificates to students. The Acadmey has students with ages spanning from 2 to 70 years old, and also provides lessons for special needs children

since the '90s. These bigger boards are not only a little easier to learn on, and more comfortable for cruising around town, but riding them is more fluid than traditional skateboards, giving them more in common with snowboarding, both in terms of technique and tricks.

'You can pick up cheap imitation boards, of course, but they'll ride like cheap copies too,' explains Simon Hunt of Beach St. (leisuremarine-me.com), which stocks boards by Landyachtz, Rayne and Loaded. 'These are longboards made by longboarders in places like Canada and California, where the sport began. Expect to pay Dhs.850-1,250 for a decent board and that's all you need to get started.

'As you progress, you'll find that there are different boards, various materials, for the different styles of longboarding – cruising, freestyle and downhill – as well as different kinds of wheels suited to certain styles and tricks.'

TIME TO ROCK AND ROLL...

If you're just starting out, get online and you'll find loads of YouTube videos about how to start, and basic foot braking. Then you want to find somewhere flat and, ideally, car-free, where you can practise. Marina Walk or around the lakes in JLT are the ideal places to practise in Dubai; try Khalifa park in Abu Dhabi.

Next, you'll want a small hill; quiet carparks or even some of the UAE's many unfinished flyovers make the ideal locations for mastering carving down gentle slopes. Then it's time to get joined up to the 'Skateboarders of the UAE' Facebook group. There, you'll find details of regular get-togethers, like the weekly meet-up to longboard at Mushrif Park.

Like everywhere else in the world, part of the appeal of boarding is in its extreme and slightly counter-culture nature; keep your eye on the group for news about crazy, pop-up events like the Push Race, Jebel Hafeet descents and multi-storey car park 'Death Races'.

007 ADVENTURE

YOU DON'T NEED TO BE A HOLLYWOOD STAR OR SECRET AGENT TO PULL OFF A STUNT LIKE SKYDIVING.

SKYDIVING

For the ultimate in adrenaline experiences, it doesn't get more exciting – or maybe just plain scary – than a UAE skydive. Obviously, this is not one for the faint hearted, but if jumping out of a plane to catch views of Dubai's Palm Jumeirah is your idea of fun, then head to SkyDive Dubai (skydivedubai.ae).

The centre is the largest in the Middle East, featuring state-of-the-art equipment and facilities, a location offering superb jumping weather and fully qualified staff. In fact, it is an all-turbine dropzone, meaning that you can expect to jump out of two of the cleanest twin otters in the industry, immaculate pilatus porter, and a variety of helicopters and caravan.

First-timers can sign up for the tandem jump, where skydivers are attached to a qualified instructor. Prices start from Dhs.1,750, **which includes digital stills and DVD of the experience.**

This experience is only available for those age 18 and over.

If you are interested in becoming a licensed skydiver, check out the school section of the website to find out about training opportunities.

For the more experienced, SkyDive Dubai also provides freeflying (an expansion of skydiving which includes the traditional belly-to-earth positions, but extends into vertical flight where the flyer is in an upright position, falling feet first); wingsuit flying (where jumpers 'fly' through the air using a special jumpsuit); formation skydiving (where multiple jumpers form patterns by gripping each others' limbs); and finally, canopy piloting (which involves the flight of a skydiving parachute either at high altitude or close to the ground).

DREAMDAYS

UAE experience provider Dreamdays (dreamdays.ae) also organises skydiving experiences. As with SkyDive Dubai, supervised tandem jumps take place along with an experienced professional.

Prices start from Dhs.1,700 per person, which also includes a customised DVD as a memento.

SKYDIVE 101

Due to the nature of this experience, there is a 100kg weight restriction in order to ensure the safety of jumpers at all time. You also must be in good health. Additionally, the experience depends on favourable weather conditions for skydiving, and, for obvious reasons, jumps do not take place after dusk.

During the summer months, the Palm Jumeirah jumps are not operational, but resume in September. From June to August, desert camp jumps are available. Call up and book in advance to ensure you get the experience you want.

RACE LIKE A PRO

FOLLOW IN THE FOOTSTEPS OF FERNANDO ALONSO AND LEWIS HAMILTON, AND GET BEHIND THE WHEEL.

SINGLE-SEATER F1-STYLE EXPERIENCE

Ever dreamed of racing alongside Sebastian Vettel or flying past Fernando Alonso on the last bend of a Formula 1 Grand Prix? The F1-style single-seater experience gets you pretty close. Plus, karting is where many top drivers first honed their craft.

Head to Yas Marina Circuit (yasmarinacircuit.ae) – home of the Abu Dhabi Grand Prix – and strap yourself in for a thrilling race around the track. After being given a briefing by the fully-qualified instructors, you'll take to the track fully in charge of the paddle shifters which shift the gears up and down. Meanwhile, two on-board video cameras will capture your drive and allow you to re-live the action later on – great for uploading onto YouTube and showing off to your friends on Facebook later on! Experiences start from Dhs.1,200.

The Dubai Autodrome (dubaiautodrome. com) also offers a similar experience in the form of its 180bhp Single Seater, available for Dhs.875 per person for 20 minutes.

KARTING

The beauty of karting is that beginners are welcome, and you'll quickly get a taste for the track, so for something easier (and a little more child-friendly), the Yas KartZone offers driving experiences for children aged 8 to 12 years old in Kids Karts, and Senior Karts for those 13 and up. The circuit's fleet can reach up to 70km/h, so it's the perfect introduction to motorsports in a high-energy atmosphere. There's no need to plan in advance; stop by the Yas Kartzone and arrive and drive Tuesday to Sunday 15:00 to 23:00.

Dubai Autodrome's Kartdrome offers a fleet of leisure karts that deliver an excellent racing experience and ensure high safety in a range of specifications to satisfy those aged 7 and up. The venue has both indoor and outdoor karting areas – the 1.2km international standard circuit features no fewer than 17 corners to test the driver's skills, plus a tunnel and bridge to add to the excitement.

HOME TO FORMULA 1

Abu Dhabi is home to the Yas Marina Circuit, which hosts the annual Abu Dhabi F1 Grand Prix.

The fourth edition of the event takes place between 2-4 November 2012, the third from last race of the season, after which the F1 drivers will move from the UAE to the US and then sign off in Brazil.

Schedules and ticket prices vary. To check timetables and book, log on to yasmarinacircuit.ae.

TWO ON-BOARD VIDEO CAMERAS CAPTURE YOUR DRIVE AND ALLOW YOU TO RE-LIVE THE ACTION - GREAT FOR SHOWING OFF TO YOUR FRIENDS LATER.

Do Something Different!

Take a break from the ordinary with a pulse racing trip down the slopes at Ski Dubai.
Whether you're a pro or never seen a snowflake in your life,
Ski Dubai is the perfect place to just hit the slopes and show off your skills in the freestyle zones,
or master the art of skiing and snowboarding at our fun-filled family ski school.
You'll always find something new at Ski Dubai.

SKI DUBAI
سكي دبي

For more information please visit www.skidxb.com and 👍 us on facebook.com/skidxb

INDOOR

INDOOR

NEED A BREAK FROM EXPLORING THE GREAT OUTDOORS, OR IS THE WEATHER TOO HOT TO HANDLE? COME INSIDE FOR SOME AIR-CONDITIONED, INDOOR ADVENTURES.

There's no doubt that the UAE is full of fun and fabulous places that individuals and families can enjoy all year round, and with temperatures reaching beyond 40°C in the summer, the country isn't short of indoor, air-conditioned spaces.

One of the most popular places to spend the long summer days is at one of the country's many shopping malls – where you'll find everything from cinemas and restaurants to cafes and stores providing reason for you to part with your hard-earned cash.

However, there are also plenty of options for kids to keep them busy.

KIDZANIA

This Dubai Mall institution offers kids the chance to become adults for the day. Billed as a 'real-life city' for children, youngsters can dress up and act out more than 75 different roles, from policeman to pilot, and doctor to designer.

The KidZania city even has its own currency, which children can earn and spend. It's intended to be both fun and educational. Prices range from Dhs.95 to Dhs.130, and more information can be found via kidzania.ae.

SEGA REPUBLIC

The Dubai Mall's SEGA Republic (segarepublic.com) is an indoor theme park that offers a range of thrills

and spills, courtesy of the nine main attractions and the 150 arcade games.

A Power Pass (Dhs.140) gets you all-day access to the big attractions, which include stomach-flipping rides like the Sonic Hopper, the SpinGear (the centre's mini indoor rollercoaster ride), and the Halfpipe Canyon.

Unlike many other shopping mall amusement centres, SEGA Republic is for all ages, and features some truly unique thrills.

MAGIC PLANET

Located in several malls around the country (Mall of the Emirates, Mirdif City Centre and Deira City Centre in Dubai, plus Sharjah City Centre, Ajman City Centre and Fujairah City Centre), Magic Planet (magicplanet. ae) offers blaring, boisterous play areas that are hugely popular with kids accompanying their mums and dads on long shopping trips.

There are various rides, including merry-go-rounds, a train, bumper cars and the latest video games. For tinier tots there is a large activity play gym and a small soft-play area.

Entrance is free, and you use the facilities on a 'pay as you play' basis, or buy a Dhs.50 special pass for unlimited fun and entertainment.

PLAYNATION

Playnation (playnationme.com), located in Mirdif City Centre, offers a range of exciting activities (and not just for younger family members), integrating

five fun-tastic experiences: iFLY Dubai (read more on p.228), Soccer Circus Dubai, Little Explorers (advanced edutainment centre), and Yalla! Bowling.

CHILDREN'S CITY

Located in Creekside Park in Dubai, Children's City (childrencity.ae) is an educational project that offers kids their own learning zone and amusement facilities, by providing hands-on experiences relating to theory they have been taught at school.

There's a planetarium focusing on the solar system, as well as a space exploration and nature centre for information on land and sea environments. Discovery Space, meanwhile, reveals the miracles and mysteries of the human body.

It is aimed at 5-to-12 year olds, although items of interest are included for toddlers and teenagers. The centre opens daily from 09:00 to 20:00, except on Fridays when it opens at 15:00. Entrance starts from Dhs.10 per child.

DEFY GRAVITY

YOU DON'T HAVE TO JUMP OUT OF A PLANE IN ORDER TO GO SKYDIVING.

You too can enjoy Superman's ability to fly – albeit for about 30 minutes! Both Abu Dhabi and Dubai offer indoor skydiving/flying experiences suitable for kids and adults. Just turn up and fly, or book in advance (bear in mind that it can get busy during the weekends).

IFLY DUBAI

The ideal place to practise before making the big jump for real, iFly Dubai (iflyme.com) is an indoor skydiving centre located in Playnation Mirdif City Centre. Giant vertical wind tunnels simulate the sensation of jumping from a plane but at a fraction of the cost and with an instructor on hand to help you perfect the technique. It is the region's first indoor double skydiving simulator –

you hover over powerful fans while being blasted up to ten metres into the air by the powerful wind tunnel. If this sounds scary, then fear not; for first-timers, there are experienced instructors on hand to help. While the feeling of weightlessness is similar to that of skydiving, it also feels as if you are flying due to being able to 'float' in the air. A fun experience for kids and adults, it's so realistic that actual skydivers head to iFly for the longer 'freefall' time.

Prices start from Dhs.195 for a regular package and can be booked online. This includes instruction, gear and two flights.

In addition to the regular packages, iFly Dubai also offers a special weekend club for children, priced at Dhs.95 per child (minimum age is 5 years old).

SPACEWALK SKYDIVING

Located at the Abu Dhabi Country Club, Spacewalk Indoor Skydiving (spacewalk.ae) is another place to safely experience the thrill of free falling and skydiving without the petrifying need to actually jump out of an airplane. It is safe, fun for the whole family and an exhilarating experience for beginners (ages 3 and up) as well as those with skydiving experience.

An Intro Flight ticket costs Dhs.180, with a First Class ticket costing Dhs.290.

Your introductory flight includes your training session, use of all flight gear, two one-minute flights (two two-minute flights for First Class), and one-on-one personal assistance from your instructor. You will also learn the basic free fall position.

THIS IS WAR

CHALLENGING, EXCITING AND TOTALLY EXTREME, PAINTBALL IS A FAST-GROWING ADRENALINE-FUELLED ACTIVITY.

It may look easy, but paintballing is actually quite a challenging experience – as anyone who has had ten opponents shoot paintball pellets at them while dashing across the park would testify.

SHARJAH PAINTBALL PARK

For a fun day out, head to Sharjah Paintball Park at the Sharjah Golf & Shooting Club (golfandshootingshj.com), the biggest paintball park in the Middle East, with two air-conditioned indoor arenas and a mammoth floodlit outdoor park that can accommodate up to 150 players per session.

The newly opened indoor arenas consist of playing fields that are replicas of London City (complete with an *Evening Standard* newspaper stand to hide under) and a bank.

For hardcore gamers, the park has a pro-shop selling accessories ranging from clothing to guns and masks. The park has introduced new promotional rates this year, starting from just Dhs.80 for 100 paintballs, gun, mask and suit.

AL FORSAN SPORTS RESORT

Over in the capital, Al Forsan International Sports Resort (alforsan.com) is home to two impressive tournament fields, enclosed in state-of-the-art air-conditioned domes.

Many scenarios can be played out in the themed fields and players can customise their own experience with bespoke packages – be it rescue a hostage from the rival team, defuse a suitcase bomb under fire or protect the saloon from the banditos.

Beginner lessons are available and the pro-shop sells the latest paintballing products. Prices start from Dhs.120 for 200 paintballs; however, players with their own equipment can enter for Dhs.70 per person.

OUTDOOR FUN

Both Sharjah Paintball Park and Al Forsan also have outdoor arenas for even bigger paintballing action. Choose from Jungle or Sahara themes at Sharjah, or World War 2 Pacific Island Zone or Wild West at Al Forsan.

Dubai's Wonderland UAE theme park in Garhoud (wonderlanduae. com) also has an outdoor paintball field where UAE-based club Paintball Dubai (paintballdubai.com) gathers and plays. Visit the site to join the Facebook page.

COLD AS ICE

ONCE YOU GET PAST THE NOVELTY OF SKIING IN THE DESERT, THERE'S PLENTY OF FUN TO BE HAD AT SKI DUBAI.

One of the best things about the UAE is that you can even practice and enjoy activities you wouldn't expect to find in the region!

Take Ski Dubai (theplaymania.com/skidubai) for instance, the Middle East's first indoor ski resort, with more than 22,500 square metres of real snow. The temperature hovers around -3°C, even when it's closer to 50°C outside, to make for a cooling excursion from city life.

With an amazing mountain-themed setting, you can enjoy everything from skiing to snowboarding, and from tobogganing to playing in the snow.

GET ACTIVE

The venue has five runs that vary in difficulty, height and gradient, the longest run being 400 metres with a fall of over 60 metres. Competent skiers and boarders can test their skills on the black run, while beginners can opt for lessons where they can practice turns on the gentle slopes.

Prices range from Dhs.150 and Dhs.180 for adults, depending on entry type, as well as lesson type (optional).

DUBAI SKI CLUB

The Dubai Ski Club (dubaiskiclub.com) has over 1,400 members and meets at 18:00 on the last Saturday of every month, next to Ski Dubai's ticket counter, for social skiing or snowboarding, race training and races, followed by apres ski.

Membership benefits include a reduced fee for the slope pass and use of the 'advance booking' lane when purchasing tickets, plus special offers on equipment, clothing, accessories and holidays. Membership is Dhs.300.

FREESTYLING

If you would prefer to just turn up and do your own thing, Ski Dubai offers a freestylers' night every last Thursday of the month from 20:00 to 23:00, where visitors can enjoy three hours of skiing and boarding for the price of two hours. Prizes will be given away to the best skiers/boarders. Spectators are also welcome.

PLAYING IN THE SNOW

For those that want a more chilled experience, the interactive snow park

– which at 3,000 square metres is the largest indoor snow park in the world – is available for both children and adults.

Stick on your snow boots and enjoy twin track bobsled runs, a snow cavern filled with interactive experiences, and tobogganing hills, or jump on the chairlift for a spectacular bird's eye view of the entire park.

Meanwhile, the upgrade station offers rides inside one of its giant zorb balls (pictured). Tonnes of air-filled fun!

Entry costs Dhs.120 per child and Dhs.130 per adult.

EQUIPMENT

You can hire a large range of ski equipment from Ski Dubai itself, plus you also have the option to purchase gear.

It's worth nothing, however, that slope pass and lesson prices include the hire charge for jackets, trousers, boots, socks, helmets and either skis and poles or a snowboard, but it's worth bringing your own gloves as these are charged extra on top of everything else.

Adventure HQ (adventurehq.ae) in Dubai's Times Square shopping centre also stocks a variety of good quality brands.

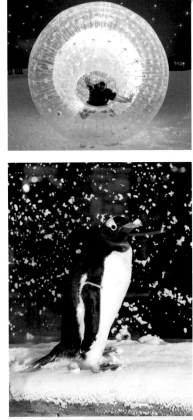

MEET THE PENGUINS!

Ski Dubai is home to several snow penguins, whom you can visit! Guests can get up-close and personal with a colony of gentoo and king penguins, and each experience (priced at Dhs.175 per person) includes underwater viewing, meeting at least two penguins, and optional photos of the experience. Please note that the park does not force the penguins to interact with human guests, so do not be surprised if a tired penguin is allowed to hobble away during the experience.

MEET JAWS

HAVE YOU EVER WANTED TO COME FACE-TO-FACE WITH THE WORLD'S ULTIMATE PREDATOR?

If the beautiful seas around us are not enough for you, then the UAE's indoor aquariums are bound to ignite the adventurer in you.

From mellow experiences to full-on heart-stopping adventures, read on to see what you might tickle your fancy.

DANGER DIVING

Boasting 10,000 pounds of lean muscle and 10,000 razor-sharp teeth, have you ever thought of coming to face-to-face with the world's ultimate predator?

For a taste of the experience – without the risk of being mistaken for food – why not try the Shark Dive at Dubai Aquarium & Underwater Zoo (thedubaiaquarium.com)?

Whether you are an experienced, certified diver, have never dived before, or even do not know how to swim, you can submerge into the depths of the aquarium's 10-million litre tank and interact with the largest collection of sand tiger sharks in the world.

Three shark dives are held daily (each allowing up to four divers), with a dive master and dive instructor supervising every dive, so you'll never feel alone.

ANIMAL SAFARI

Located on the second floor of the Dubai Aqaurium is the Underwater Zoo, a venue perfect for the little ones.

With the zoo consisting of three ecological zones (rainforest, rocky shore and living ocean), there's plenty to see and do, including visiting aquatic creatures such as the otters, piranhas, penguins, caiman crocodiles and water rats.

Kids can also take part in a thrilling jungle night safari throughout the day. Here, they can wear a head lamp and observe exotic animals such as adult carpet pythons, dart frogs and iguanas in a near-natural environment.

LOST IN ATLANTIS

Atlantis The Palm's (atlantisthepalm.com) Lost Chambers allows visitors to explore 65,000 marine animals, including sharks, eels, seahorses and piranhas. There are over 20 marine life exhibits including a touch tank and an interactive aquatheatre show.

Its interactive tour gives further insights into the legend of Atlantis, traditions of the Seven Sages and facts about the marine life that inhabits The Lost Chambers aquarium, while visitors can also come face-to-face with hundreds of indigenous marine animals as they are being fed.

Are you a diver? Visitors can also take part in one of two exclusive dives per day that take place in the largest open air marine habitat exhibit in the world.

Submerge yourself in the depths of the lagoon, enjoy exploring the ancient ruins, and feed stingrays by hand (if you dare!)

GET CERTIFIED

Before taking part in Dubai Aquarium dives, non-certified divers and those who don't know how to swim need to complete a course at Al Boom Diving (alboomdiving.com).

BREAK A RECORD

TAKE ON THE UTIMATE SPEED CHALLENGE AND RIDE THE FASTEST ROLLERCOASTER IN THE WORLD.

If you are an amusement park fan, then it would be a shame not to cross off riding the world's fastest rollercoaster from your list, which can be found at Yas Island's Ferrari World Abu Dhabi (ferrariworldabudhabi. com). The largest indoor and the only Ferrari branded theme park in the world boasts 20 Ferrari-inspired rides and attractions.

Featuring high adrenaline rides, its highlight is no doubt the fastest rollercoaster in the world, the Formula Rossa.

FORMULA ROSSA

The Formula Rossa is a face-distorting, brain-cell-reducing record-breaker that simulates the sensation of driving an F1 car. Riders are catapulted to 240km/h, reaching 0-100kph in less than two seconds – that's an impressive G-force of 1.7.

Harnessing the same technology that powers fighter planes, the rollercoaster travels the ride's 2.07km distance in just 90 seconds.

Needless to say, all riders are given safety goggles to wear for the duration of the ride, just like every other racer that takes on Grand Prix speeds.

FIORANO GT CHALLENGE

For something a little less extreme, challenge your friends by jumping into a Ferrari F430 Spider, and have two GT coasters compete from the starting line on twisting parallel tracks, based on real GT race courses from around the world.

As you reach speeds of 95km/h, feel the thrill and G-forces of a real drag race as you out-manoeuvre and pass the other GT coaster cars, watch out for the hairpin turns then tear ahead through the straight-aways.

General admission tickets to the park start from Dhs.225 per adult and Dhs.165 per child. In case of bad weather conditions, check the availability of rides before going.

KIDS INCLUDED

Ferrari World is not just for the grown ups; there is a host of activities and rides for the little ones too. Junior drivers can even get behind the wheel, learn to drive and cruise through mini streets in Ferrari cars just their size!

Highlights include the Junior GT, where children can learn about the importance of driving safely; the Junior Grand Prix, where they can hone their racing skills; the carousel, Ferrari's version of the traditional carousel; and the Junior Training Camp, where every little racer can play, no matter what their age.

WHERE SPORT IS FRONT PAGE NEWS

SPORT360.COM

SPORT 360°

EXTRA

FIRST AID

IN THE UNFORTUNATE EVENT OF AN INJURY OR ACCIDENT, IT DOES HELP TO BE PREPARED.

All outdoor and adventure sports do, of course, carry with them a small risk of injury but, throughout this book, you will find all manner of safety hints and tips. Your first rule should be to never tackle an experience that you don't feel up to; whether that's off-roading, scuba diving, mountain biking or climbing, we have featured basic routes and easy ways to get started. Step up gradually and, if unsure, the activity providers and tour operators in the Directory (see p.245 & p.248) provide safe ways to get started.

With a little foresight, an accident – if one does happen – need not ruin your trip. If it's serious, stay calm and head for the nearest hospital. If it's less serious, you may be able to treat it on the spot, or at least deal with the accident or injury enough so that a visit to a doctor upon return will suffice.

If you make a habit of heading off into the wild for fun, outdoor adventures, you'd certainly do well to pick up a small first aid book to carry with you.

Can't stand the heat...

The overriding factors that cause many incidents and are elements that very few adventurers have experience of before coming to the UAE and Oman are the sun and the heat. Put simply, no matter how prepared you think you are for them, you're not prepared enough; even short hikes in January can be hot, sweaty, energy-sapping and dehydrating affairs. Whether you're in the desert, in a wadi, on a mountain or at the beach, remember that this region has very little foliage and, therefore, taking shade beneath a canopy of trees simply isn't an option. You're exposed all day and need to prepare accordingly.

Dehydration: Caused by not drinking enough. Remember that your body is already mildly dehydrated by the time you feel thirsty – you need to drink before you even

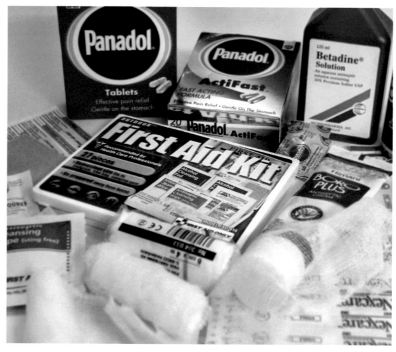

Survival Hamper

- Aches & pains: Paracetamol (such as Panadol). Avoid aspirin or ibuprofen.
- Sprains: Stretch bandage, ice-pack.
- Insect bites: Aspivenin vacuum pump. After-bite stick or xylocaine ointment. Antihistamine tablets in case of allergic reaction.
- Fracture: One roll of strong, wide bandage to apply splint.
- Cuts & wounds: Adhesive dressing

- & tape, plasters, antiseptic cream.
- Dehydration: Salt sachet (such as Dioralyte), isotonic drinks, water.
- Eyes: Sterile eye pad.
- Marine stings: Vinegar, sodium bicarbonate, powdered meat tenderiser or any powder.
- General: Scissors, sterile or saline water, thermometer, tweezers.
- Personal medication
- An up-to-date tetanus vaccination

feel the need. The symptoms are dizziness, headaches, goosebumps and a tingling sensation on the skin. If you (or one of your party) starts to experience these symptoms, head for a cool, shaded area and replenish fluids and salts (isotonic energy drinks are a good solution). Salt and sugar in diluted orange juice make for a good on-the-hop substitute, as does flat cola.

Heatstroke: Prolonged exposure to very hot conditions can cause the body to stop effectively regulating its temperature, resulting in headaches, dizziness, restlessness and confusion. You should also look out for flushed skin and an uncontrollably fast pulse. If the body temperature rises to 40°C (104°F) or more, unconsciousness is usually just minutes away. Get the affected person to the coolest place available. Remove all outer clothing and wrap them in a cold, wet sheet, keeping it constantly damp. Once their temperature has dropped to 38°C (100.4°F) replace the wet sheet with a dry one and observe constantly. Be prepared to repeat the process if their temperature begins to rise again. Get to a doctor as soon as possible.

Sunburn: Over-exposure to the sun causes redness, itching, tenderness and, in extreme cases, blisters. If you're feeling sunburnt, first and foremost you need to get out of the sun and sponge the area with cold water, while drinking regularly. Apply after-sun lotion, calamine, aloe vera or yoghurt to soothe mild burns while extensive blistering or skin damage requires the attention of a doctor.

IN CASE OF AN ACCIDENT...

For less critical incidents, you may find treatment at one of the private clinics in Dubai or Abu Dhabi reassuring. If time is of the essence, aim for the nearest hospital (see p.241 & p.247 of the Directory). In the meantime, uninjured parties can create a beneficial atmosphere of confidence and reassurance by:

- Staying in control of both yourself and the problem.
- Acting calmly and logically.
- Being gentle but firm, both with your hands and by speaking to the casualty kindly, but purposefully.

NO MATTER HOW PREPARED YOU THINK YOU ARE FOR THE SUN AND THE HEAT, YOU'RE NOT PREPARED ENOUGH; EVEN SHORT HIKES IN JANUARY CAN BE HOT, SWEATY, ENERGY-SAPPING AND DEHYDRATING AFFAIRS.

DIRECTORY

UNITED ARAB EMIRATES

AMUSEMENT PARKS & CENTRES & WATER PARKS

Al Ain

Al Ain Zoo	alainzoo.ae
Hili Fun City	hilifuncity.ae

Dubai

Aquaplay	playnationme.com
Aquaventure	atlantisthepalm.com
Ski Dubai	skidxb.com
SplashLand	wonderlanduae.com
Wild Wadi Water Park	jumeirah.com
WonderLand Theme & Water Park	wonderlanduae.com

Ras Al Khaimah

Iceland Water Park	icelandwaterpark.com

Sharjah

Adventureland	adventureland-sharjah.com

Umm Al Quwain

Dreamland Aqua Park	dreamlanduae.com

BIRDWATCHING

Dubai

Emirates Bird Records Committee	uaebirding.com
Ras Al Khor Wildlife Sanctuary	wildlife.ae

BOAT & YACHT BROKERS

Abu Dhabi

Sea Pros Yachts	seapros.com

Ajman

Silvercraft	silver-craft.com

Dubai

Macky Marine	mackymarine.com
Marquis Yachts	marquisyachts.com
Royal Yachting Yacht Agency	royalyachting.net

BOAT, YACHT & DHOW CHARTERS

Abu Dhabi

Abu Dhabi Sailing Club	abudhabisailing.com

Al Dhafra	aldhafra.net
Arabian Divers & Sportfishing Charters	fishabudhabi.com
Belevari Marine	belevari.com
Blue Dolphin Company	050 492 6887
Coastal Safety	coastalsafety.com/me
Le Royal Meridien Abu Dhabi	leroyalmeridienabudhabi.com
Noukhada Adventure Company	noukhada.ae
Sea Tourism	seatourism.net
Shuja Yacht	leroyalmeridienabudhabi.com
The Yellow Boats	theyellowboats.com
Xventures	x-ventures.net

Dubai

4Yacht Arabia	4yachtarabia.ae
Al Boom Tourist Village	alboom.ae
Al Wasl Cruising & Fishing	cruiseindubai.com
ART Marine	artmarine.net
Athena Charter Yacht	dubaimarinayachtclub.com
Bateaux Dubai	bateauxdubai.com
Blue Waters Marine	bluewatersmarine.com
Bristol Middle East Yacht Solution	bristol-middleeast.com
Coastal Safety	coastalsafety.com/me
Cruise With Nakheel	nakheel.com
Divaz	funkyhipvenues.com
Dubai Creek Golf & Yacht Club	dubaigolf.com
Dubai Ferry	rta.ae
Dubai Garden Centre	desertgroup.ae
Dubai International Marine Club	dimc.ae
Dubai Offshore Sailing Club	dosc.ae
El Mundo	elmundodubai.com
J.P.S. Yacht & Charter Service	jpsyachts.com
Jebel Ali Golf Resort & Spa	jebelali-international.com
Khasab Travel & Tours	khasabtours.com
Le Meridien Mina Seyahi Beach Resort & Marina	lemeridien-minaseyahi.com
Marine Concept	marine-charter-concept.com
Ocean Active	oceanactive.com
Ocean Group	oceanindependence.com
Radisson Blu Hotel, Dubai Deira Creek	radissonblu.com
Tour Dubai	tour-dubai.com
UAE Dragon Boat Association	dubaidragonboat.com
Ultimate Charter	dubaiultimatecharter.com
Xclusive Yachts Sport Fishing & Yacht Charter	xclusiveyachts.com

Ras Al Khaimah

Coastal Safety	coastalsafety.com/me

Sharjah

Al Marsa Travel & Tourism	almarsamusandam.com

Umm Al Quwain

Barracuda Beach Resort   barracuda.ae

CAMEL RIDES

Dubai

Desert Rangers	desertrangers.com
Mushrif Park	dm.gov.ae
WonderLand Theme & Water Park	wonderlanduae.com

CAMERA EQUIPMENT

Abu Dhabi

Grand Stores	grandstores.com
National Stores	jk.ae
Plug-Ins	pluginselectronix.com

Dubai

Jacky's Electronics	jackys.com
Jumbo Electronics	jumbocorp.com
MK Trading Co	mktradingco.com
Plug-Ins	pluginselectronix.com
Sharaf DG	sharafdg.com
United Colour Film (UCF)	ucfq.com

CAMPING

Umm Al Quwain

Dreamland Aqua Park   dreamlanduae.com

CANOEING & KAYAKING

Abu Dhabi

Abu Dhabi Ocean Warriors	adowsurfski.wordpress.com
Noukhada Adventure Company	noukhada.ae
Noukhada Adventure Company	noukhada.ae

Al Ain

Wadi Adventure   wadiadventure.ae

Dubai

Desert Rangers	desertrangers.com
Dubai Paddling School	050 640 6087
Dubai Surfski & Kayak Club	dskc.hu
Explorer Tours	explorertours.ae
Sky & Sea Adventures	watersportsdubai.com

Fujairah

Sandy Beach Hotel & Resort   sandybm.com

Ras Al Khaimah

Al Hamra Fort Hotel & Beach Resort   alhamrafort.com

CAR RENTAL AGENCIES

Abu Dhabi

Al Ghazal Rent A Car	adnh.com
Al Raeed Rent A Car	alraeeduae.com
Avis	avisuae.ae
Budget Rent A Car	budget-uae.com
Car Fare Rent A Car	carfarellc.com
Diamondlease	diamondlease.com
Dollar Rent A Car	dollaruae.com
Europcar	europcar-middleeast.com
EuroStar Rent A Car	eurostarrental.com
Fast Rent A Car	fastuae.com
Hertz Rent A Car	hertzuae.com
National Car Rental	national-me.com
Payless Car Rental	paylesscar.com
Sixt Rent A Car	sixt.com
Thrifty Car Rental	thriftyuae.com
United Car Rentals & Wafi Limousine	unitedcarrentals.com

Al Ain

Fast Rent A Car   fastuae.com

Dubai

Avis	avisuae.ae
Better Car	bettercardubai.com
Carlease Rent A Car	carlease.ae
DRC Rent A Car	discountcardubai.com
Fast Rent A Car	fastuae.com
German Rent A Car	germanRAC.com
Green Car Rental	greencardubai.com
Icon Car Rental	dubairentacar.ae
Impala Rent A Car	impalauae.com
Low Cost Rent A Car	lowcostcardubai.com
National Car Rental	national-me.com
OffRoad-Zone	offroad-zone.com
Parklane Car Rental	parklanecarrental.com
Shift Leasing & Car Rental	shiftleasing.com
Travel House Rent A Car	travelhouserentacar.com

Fujairah

Impala Rent A Car   impalauae.com

CAR SERVICING, PARTS, REPAIRS & ACCESSORIES

Abu Dhabi

Ace	aceuae.com
ADM Abu Dhabi Motors	bmw-abudhabi.com
Bosch Service Centre	cmeuae.ae
Central Motors & Equipment	cmeuae.ae

Dubai

4x4 Garage	4x4motors.com
Al Saeedi Total Tyre Solutions	alsaeedi.com
House of Cars	houseofcarsgroup.com
Icon Auto Garage	icon-auto.com
Juma Al Majid Est	hyundai-uae.com
Max Garage	maxdubai.com
OffRoad-Zone	offroad-zone.com
Robbies Motorsport	robbies-ms.com
Specialized Sports Equipment – Polaris	polarisuae.com
Stellar Auto Garage	stellar-auto.com
Trading Enterprises	tradingenterprises.ae
X Service Centre	houseofcarsgroup.com

CAVING

Mountain High Middle East	mountainhighme.com

CLIMBING

Abu Dhabi

The Club	the-club.com

Al Ain

Wadi Adventure	wadiadventure.ae

Dubai

Adventure HQ	adventurehq.ae
Climbing Dubai	climbingdubai.com
Climbing Dubai	climbingdubai.com
Desert Rangers	desertrangers.com
E-Sports	esportsuae.com
Pharaohs' Club	pyramidsrestaurantsatwafi.com

Ras Al Khaimah

Global Climbing	globalclimbing.com

CYCLING

Dubai

Cycle Safe Dubai	cyclechallenge.ae
Dubai Roadsters	dubairoadsters.com

DIVING & SNORKELING

Abu Dhabi

Al Mahara Diving Center	divemahara.com

Ajman

Kempinski Hotel Ajman	kempinski.com

Dubai

Al Boom Diving	alboomdiving.com
Atlantis Dive Centre	atlantisdivecentre.com

Desert Sport Diving Club	desertsportsdivingclub.net
Emirates Diving Association	emiratesdiving.com
Scubatec	04 334 8988
The Pavilion Dive Centre	jumeirah.com

Fujairah

7 Seas Divers	7seasdivers.com
Divers Down UAE	diversdown-uae.com
Freestyle Divers	freestyledivers.com
Sandy Beach Diving Centre	sandybm.com
Scuba 2000	scuba-2000.com

Nationwide

Freediving UAE	freedivinguae.com

Ras Al Khaimah

Abu Dhabi Sub Aqua Club	the-club.com
Arabian Diver	arabiandiver.com

Sharjah

BSAC 406 Wanderers Dive Club	bsac406.com
Sharjah Wanderers Dive Club	sharjahwanderers.com

DUNE BUGGY RIDING

Dubai

Arabia Horizons Tours	arabiahorizons.com
Dadabhai Travel	owtravels.com
Desert Rangers	desertrangers.com
Explorer Tours	explorertours.ae

FESTIVALS, EVENTS & EXHIBITIONS

Abu Dhabi

Al Gharbia Watersports Festival	algharbiafestivals.com
UIM Class 1 World Powerboat Championship	class-1.com

Dubai

Dubai International Boat Show	boatshowdubai.com
UIM Class 1 World Powerboat Championship	class-1.com

FINANCIAL ADVISORS

Abu Dhabi

KPMG	kpmg.com
P.I.C. Middle East	pic-uae.com

Dubai

Holborn Assets	holbornassets.com
Mondial (Dubai)	mondialdubai.com
Prosperity Offshore Investment Consultants	prosperity-uae.com

FISHING

Abu Dhabi
Beach Rotana Abu Dhabi	rotana.com
Hiltonia Health Club & Spa	hilton.com
Noukhada Adventure Company	noukhada.ae
Sheraton Resort Health Club	sheraton.com/abudhabi

Dubai
Al Wasl Cruising & Fishing	cruiseindubai.com
Club Joumana	jebelali-international.com
Dubai Creek Golf & Yacht Club	dubaigolf.com
Soolyman Sport Fishing	soolymansportfishing.com
Xclusive Yachts Sport Fishing & Yacht Charter	xclusiveyachts.com

Fujairah
The Oceanic Hotel & Resort	oceanichotel.com

FLYING

Dubai
Emirates Flying School	emiratesaviationservices.com

Fujairah
Fujairah Aviation Academy	fujaa.ae
Jazirah Aviation Club	jac-uae.net

Umm Al Quwain
Micro Aviation Club	microaviation.org

GUEST/REST HOUSES & HOSTELS

Abu Dhabi
Ghayathi Rest House	02 874 1003
Liwa Resthouse	02 882 2075

Al Ain
Green Mubazzarah Chalets	mubazzarah.150m.com

Dubai
Orient Guest House	orientguesthouse.com

Fujairah
Fujairah Youth Hostel	uaeyha.com

Sharjah
Sharjah Youth Hostel	uaeyha.com

HIKING

Dubai
Absolute Adventure	adventure.ae
Arabia Outdoors	arabiaoutdoors.com
Desert Rangers	desertrangers.com

HORSE RIDING

Abu Dhabi
Abu Dhabi Equestrian Club	adec-web.com
Al Forsan International Sports Resort	alforsan.com
Sir Bani Yas Stables	desertislands.com

Dubai
Al Ahli Horse Riding Club	alahliclub.info
Al Jiyad Stables	050 599 5866
Al Sahra Desert Resort Equestrian Centre	jebelali-international.com
Dubai Polo & Equestrian Club	poloclubdubai.com
Emirates Equestrian Centre	emiratesequestriancentre.com
Golden Stables	goldenstables.ae
Jebel Ali Equestrian Club	04 884 5101
Jebel Ali Golf Resort & Spa	jebelali-international.com
Riding For The Disabled Association Of Dubai	rdad.ae
The Desert Equestrian Club	050 309 9770
The Desert Palm Riding School	desertpalm.ae

Sharjah
Sharjah Equestrian & Racing Club	serc.ae

HOSPITALS

Abu Dhabi
Ahalia Hospital	ahaliagroup.com
Al Noor Hospital	alnoorhospital.com
Al Rahba Hospital	alrahba.ae
Al Sila Hospital	seha.ae
Corniche Hospital	cornichehospital.ae
Dar Al Shifaa Hospital	daralshifaa.net
Delma Island Hospital	seha.ae
Ghayathi Hospital	seha.ae
Hospital Franco-Emirien	hfe.ae
Liwa Hospital	seha.ae
Madinat Zayed Hospital	seha.ae
Mafraq Hospital	mafraqhospital.ae
Marfa Hospital	seha.ae
NMC Specialty Hospital	nmc.ae
Sheikh Khalifa Medical City	skmc.gov.ae

Al Ain
Al Ain Hospital	alain-hospital.ae
Emirates International Hospital	03 763 7777
Oasis Hospital	oasishospital.org
Tawam Hospital	tawamhospital.ae

Dubai
Al Baraha Hospital	albarahahospital.8m.com
American Hospital	ahdubai.com
Belhoul Speciality Hospital	belhoulspeciality.com
Cedars Jebel Ali International Hospital	cedars-jaih.com

Dubai Hospital	dha.gov.ae
Iranian Hospital	ihd.ae
Latifa Hospital	dha.gov.ae
Medcare Hospital	medcarehospital.com
Medcare Orthopaedics &	
Spine Hospital	medcareorthopaedics.com
Neuro Spinal Hospital	nshdubai.com
NMC Hospital	nmc.ae
Rashid Hospital	dha.gov.ae
The City Hospital	thecityhospital.com
Welcare Hospital	welcarehospital.com
Zulekha Hospital	zulekhahospitals.com

Ras Al Khaimah

RAK Hospital	rakhospital.com

Sharjah

Al Zahra Private Hospital	alzahra.com

HOT AIR BALLOONING

Dubai

Balloon Adventures Emirates	ballooning.ae

HOTELS & RESORTS

Abu Dhabi

Al Raha Beach Hotel	danathotels.com
Danat Jebel Dhanna Resort	danathotels.com
Desert Islands Resort &	
Spa By Anantara	desertislands.anantara.com
Dhafra Beach Hotel	danathotels.com
Liwa Hotel	almarfapearlhotels.com
Mirfa Hotel	almarfapearlhotels.com
Qasr Al Sarab Desert Resort By Anantara	anantara.com

Ajman

Ajman Beach Hotel	ajmanbeachhotel.com
Kempinski Hotel Ajman	kempinski.com
Ramada Hotel & Suites Ajman	ramadaajman.com

Al Ain

Al Ain Rotana	rotana.com
Al Massa Hotel	almasahotels.com
Asfar Resort	asfarhotels.com
Ayla Hotel	aylahotels.com
City Seasons Hotel Al Ain	cityseasonsgroup.com
Danat Al Ain Resort	danathotels.com
Hilton Al Ain	hilton.com
Mercure Grand Jebel Hafeet Al Ain	mercure.com

Dubai

Al Maha, A Luxury Collection	
Desert Resort & Spa	al-maha.com
Bab Al Shams Desert Resort & Spa	meydanhotels.com
Hatta Fort Hotel	hattaforthotel.com
Jebel Ali Golf Resort & Spa	jebelali-international.com
Jumeirah Beach Hotel	jumeirah.com

Fujairah

Al Diar Siji Hotel	aldiarhotels.com
Concorde Hotel Fujairah	concordefujairah.com
Fujairah Rotana Resort & Spa – Al Aqah Beach	rotana.com
Hilton Fujairah	hilton.com
Iberotel Miramar Al Aqah Beach Resort	iberotel.com
Le Meridien Al Aqah Beach Resort	lemeridien-alaqah.com
Miramar Al Aqah Beach Resort	iberotel.com
Radisson Blu Resort Fujairah	radissonblu.com
Royal Beach Al Faqeet Hotel & Resort	royalbeach.ae
Sandy Beach Hotel & Resort	sandybm.com

Ras Al Khaimah

Acacia Hotel	acaciahotelrak.com
Al Hamra Fort Hotel & Beach Resort	alhamrafort.com
Al Hamra Palace Beach Resort	casahotelsandresorts.com
Banyan Tree Al Wadi	banyantree.com
Bin Majid Beach Hotel	binmajid.com
DoubleTree By Hilton	
Hotel Ras Al Khaimah	doubletree3.hilton.com
Golden Tulip Khatt Springs	
Resort & Spa	goldentulipkhattsprings.com
Hilton Ras Al Khaimah	hilton.com
Hiiton Ras Al Khaimah Resort & Spa	hilton.com
Mangrove Hotel	mangrovehotelrak.com
Ras Al Khaimah Hotel	rakhotel.net
The Cove Rotana Resort	rotana.com

Sharjah

Coral Beach Resort	coral-beachresortsharjah.com
Corniche Al Buhaira Hotel	cornichealbuhairahotel.com
Golden Tulip Sharjah	goldentulipsharjah.com
Holiday Inn Sharjah	holidayinn.com
Hotel Holiday International	
Sharjah	holidayinternational.com
Lou' Lou'a Beach Resort	loulouabeach.com
Radisson Blu Resort Sharjah	radissonblu.com
Royal Beach Resort & Spa	royalbeachresortspa.com
Sharjah Carlton Hotel	mhgroupsharjah.com
Sharjah Grand Hotel	sharjahgrand.com
Sharjah Premiere Hotel & Resort	sharjahpremiere.com
Sharjah Rotana	rotana.com

Umm Al Quwain

Barracuda Beach Resort	barracuda.ae
Flamingo Beach Resort	flamingoresort.ae

Palm Beach Resort	palmagroup.ae
Pearl Hotel	pearlhotel.ae

INSURANCE COMPANIES

Abu Dhabi

Abu Dhabi National Insurance Company (ADNIC)	adnic.ae
Abu Dhabi National Takaful Company	takaful.ae
Al Ain Ahlia Insurance Company	alaininsurance.com
Alliance Insurance	alliance-uae.com
Arab Orient Insurance Company	insuranceuae.com
Daman National Health Insurance Company	damanhealth.ae
Emirates Insurance Company	eminsco.com
Gargash Insurance	gargashinsurance.com
Guardian Insurance Brokers	gib-uae.com
Nasco Karaoglan	nascodubai.com
National General Insurance	ngi.ae
Oman Insurance Company	tameen.ae
Qatar Insurance Company	qatarinsurance.com
RSA	rsadirect.ae

Dubai

Aetna Global Benefits (Middle East)	aetnainternational.com
AFIA Insurance Brokerage Services	afia.ae
Al Khazna Insurance Company	alkhazna.com
Al Khazna Insurance Company	alkhazna.com
Alfred's Insurance Market	insurancemarket.ae
Alliance Insurance	alliance-uae.com
Allianz SE	allianz.com
AXA Insurance (Gulf)	axa-gulf.com
Gargash Insurance	gargashinsurance.com
Greenshield Insurance Brokers	greenshield.ae
Lifecare International	lifecareinternational.com
MedNet UAE	mednet-uae.com
MetLife Alico	metlifealico.ae
Nasco Karaoglan	nascodubai.com
National General Insurance	ngi.ae
Neuron	neuron.ae
NEXtCARE UAE	nextcare.ae
Oman Insurance Company	tameen.ae
Qatar General Insurance & Reinsurance Co	qgirco.com
RSA	rsagroup.ae

Nationwide

Oman Insurance Company	tameen.ae

MOTOCROSS & MOTORCYCLING

Dubai

Automobile & Touring Club Of The UAE	atcuae.ae
Dubai Motocross Club (DMX)	dubaimotocross.com
Harley Owners Group (HOG) Dubai	hoguae.com
Royal Enfield Dubai	royalenfielduae.com

MOTOR SPORTS

Abu Dhabi

Abu Dhabi MX Club	050 818 4668
Al Forsan International Sports Resort	alforsan.com
Ferrari World Abu Dhabi	ferrariworldabudhabi.com
Yas Marina Circuit	ymc.ae

Al Ain

Al Ain Raceway	alainraceway.com

Dubai

Dubai Autodrome	dubaiautodrome.com
Emirates Kart Centre	emsf.ae
Emirates Motor Sports Federation	emsf.ae

Umm Al Quwain

Emirates Motorplex	motorplex.ae

MOUNTAIN BIKING

Abu Dhabi

Noukhada Adventure Company	noukhada.ae

Dubai

Hot-Cog Mountain Bike Club	hot-cog.com

NEW CAR DEALERS

Abu Dhabi

Abu Dhabi Motors	bmw-abudhabi.com
Al Futtaim Motors	alfuttaimmotors.ae
Al Habtoor Motors	alhabtoor-motors.com
Al Masaood Automobiles	nissan-almasaoodautomobiles.com
Ali & Sons (Volkswagen)	ali-sons.com
Bin Hamoodah Automotive	binhamoodahauto.com
Central Motors & Equipment	cmeuae.ae
Elite Motors	belbadi.com
Emirates Motor Company	emc.mercedes-benz.com
Galadari Automoblies	mazdauae.com
Juma Al Majid Est	hyundai-uae.com
Liberty Abu Dhabi Automobiles	libertyautos.com
Premier Motors	premier-motors.ae
Western Motors	jeepabudhabi.com

Dubai

AGMC	bmw-dubai.com
Al Futtaim Motors	alfuttaimmotors.ae
Al Ghandi Auto	alghandi.com
Al Majid Motors	kia-uae.com
Al Naboodah Automobiles	nabooda-auto.com
Al Rostamani Trading	alrostamani.com
Al Tayer Motors	altayermotors.com
Arabian Automobiles Company	nissan-dubai.com

Autostar Trading	albathagroup.com
Galadari Automobiles	mazdauae.com
Gargash Enterprises	gargash.mercedes-benz.com
Gargash Motors	gargashme.com
Liberty Automobiles	libertyautos.com
Swaidan Trading	swaidan.com
Trading Enterprises	tradingenterprises.ae

OFF-ROAD DRIVING

Abu Dhabi

Abu Dhabi 4x4 The Capital Off-road Club	ad4x4.com

Dubai

Al Futtaim Training Centre	traininguae.com
Desert Rangers	desertrangers.com
Dubai4x4	dubai4x4.com
Emirates Driving Institute	edi-uae.com
OffRoad-Zone	offroad-zone.com

OUTDOOR & SPORTING GOODS

Abu Dhabi

Ace	aceuae.com

Dubai

Adventure HQ	adventurehq.ae
Al Boom Marine	alboommarine.com
Al Hamur Marine & Sports Equipment	04 344 4468
Beach St.	leisuremarine-me.com
Blue Waters Marine	bluewatersmarine.com
Columbia	04 434 1280
Decathlon	04 283 9392
Dubai Garden Centre	desertgroup.ae
Emirates Sports Stores	04 324 2208
Géant	geant-uae.com
Go Sport	go-sport.com
Intersport	intersport.ae
Jashanmal & Co	jashanmal.ae
Knight Shot Inc	knightshot.com
Picnico General Trading	04 394 1653
Quiksilver	quiksilver.com
Ramy Trading	ramy4x4.com
Royal Sporting House	04 295 0261
Sandstorm Motorcycles	sandstorm-motorcycles.com
Specialized Sports Equipment – Polaris	polarisuae.com
Stadium	billabong.com
Sun & Sand Sports	sunandsandsports.com
Timberland	timberland.com
Trading Enterprises	tradingenterprises.ae
Weber	webergrill.ae
Wolfi's Bike Shop	wbs.ae

Nationwide	
Garmin	garmin-uae.com

Ras Al Khaimah

Global Climbing	globalclimbing.com

Sharjah

ULO Systems	ulosystems.com

OUTDOOR & SPORTING GOODS

Nationwide

Carrefour	carrefouroman.com

RECOVERY SERVICES

Abu Dhabi

IATC Recovery	iatcuae.com

Nationwide

Arabian Automobile Association (AAA)	aaauae.com

RUNNING

Abu Dhabi

Abu Dhabi Striders	abudhabistriders.com

Al Ain

Al Ain Road Runners	050 472 1566

Dubai

Dubai Creek Striders	dubaicreekstriders.org
Dubai Road Runners	dubai-road-runners.com
Mirdif Milers	mirdifmilers.com
Nike+ Run Club	facebook.com/NikeRunningMiddleEast
Stride For Life	strideforlife.com

SAILING

Abu Dhabi

Abu Dhabi Sailing Club	abudhabisailing.com
Noukhada Adventure Company	noukhada.ae

Dubai

Dubai International Marine Club	dimc.ae
Dubai Offshore Sailing Club	dosc.ae

SHOOTING & ARCHERY

Abu Dhabi

Al Forsan International Sports Resort	alforsan.com
Caracal Shooting Club	caracalsc.ae

Dubai

Hatta Fort Hotel	hattaforthotel.com
Jebel Ali International Shooting Club	jebelali-international.com

Ras Al Khaimah

Ras Al Khaimah Shooting Club	07 236 3622

Sharjah

Sharjah Golf & Shooting Club	golfandshootingshj.com

SKYDIVING

Abu Dhabi

Spacewalk Indoor Skydiving	spacewalk.ae

Dubai

iFLY Dubai	theplaymania.com
SkyDive Dubai	skydivedubai.ae

TOUR OPERATORS

Abu Dhabi

Abu Dhabi Travel Bureau	abudhabitravelbureau.com
Advanced Travel & Tourism	advancedtravels.net
Al Badeyah Eyes Tourism	abet-uae.com
Al Badie Travel Agency	albadietravel.com
Arabian Adventures	arabian-adventures.com
Cyclone Tours & Travels	cyclonetours.com
Desert Adventures Tourism	desertadventures.com
Emirates Adventures	emiratesadventurestours.com
Emirates Travel Express	eteholidays.ae
Hala Abu Dhabi	halaabudhabi.ae
Kurban Tours	kurbantours.com
Net Tours	netgroupauh.com
OffRoad Emirates	offroademirates.com
Omeir Travel Agency	omeir.com
Safar Travel & Tourism	safar.ae
Salem Travel Agency	salemtravelagency.com
Sunshine Tours	adnh.com

Al Ain

Al Mahboob Travel	03 751 5944

Dubai

Absolute Adventure	adventure.ae
Alpha Tours	alphatoursdubai.com
Arabian Adventures	arabian-adventures.com
Arabian Incentive	arabianincentive.com
Arabian Nights Tours	arabiannightstours.com
Asia Pacific Travels & Tourism	apttdubai.com
Dadabhai Travel	owtravels.com
Desert Rangers	desertrangers.com
Desert Rose Tourism	desertrose-tourism.com

Desert Safari Abu Dhabi & Dubai	desertsafariabudhabi.ae
Dream Explorer	dreamexplorerdubai.com
Dubai Drums	dubaidrums.com
Dubai Travel & Tourist Services	dubai-travel.ae
Flying Elephant	flyingelephantuae.com
Gulf Ventures	gulfventures.ae
Khasab Travel & Tours	khasabtours.com
Knight Tours	knighttours.ae
Lama Tours	lamadubai.com
Net Tours	nettours-uae.com
Oasis Palm Tourism	opdubai.com
Orient Tours	orienttours.ae
Planet Travel & Tours	planettours.co
Quality Tours	quality-tour.com
Seawings	seawings.ae
Sunflower Tours	sunflowerdubai.com

Nationwide

Emirates Holidays	emirates-holidays.com

USED CAR DEALERS

Abu Dhabi

501 Cars	501cars.com
Al Futtaim Automall	automalluae.com
Ali & Sons (Volkswagen)	ali-sons.com
Prestige Cars	prestigecars.ae
Princess Cars	princesscar.com
Reem Automobile	reemauto.ae

Al Ain

Al Ain Class Motors	alainclass.com

Dubai

4x4 Motors	4x4motors.com
Al Futtaim Automall	automalluae.com
House of Cars	houseofcarsgroup.com
OffRoad-Zone	offroad-zone.com

WATERSPORTS

Abu Dhabi

Abu Dhabi Stand Up Paddle Club	abudhabisup.com
Al Forsan International Sports Resort	alforsan.com
Beach Rotana Abu Dhabi	rotana.com
Hiltonia Health Club & Spa	hilton.com
Kite4Fun.net	kite4fun.net
Kitepro Abu Dhabi	kitepro.ae
Noukhada Adventure Company	noukhada.ae
Sheraton Abu Dhabi Hotel & Resort	sheratonabudhabihotel.com
UAE Kitesurfing	ad-kitesurfing.net
UAE SUP	uaesup.com

Ajman

Kempinski Hotel Ajman	kempinski.com

Al Ain

Wadi Adventure	wadiadventure.ae

Dubai

Al Boom Marine	alboommarine.com
Aquaventure	atlantisthepalm.com
Beach St	leisuremarine-me.com
Bristol Middle East Yacht Solution	bristol-middleeast.com
Club Joumana	jebelali-international.com
Dubai International Marine Club	dimc.ae
Jet Ski Dubai	jetskidubai.com
JetPad	jet-pad.com
Kite Dubai	kitedubai.net
Kitesurfinguae.com	kitesurfinguae.com
One&Only Royal Mirage	royalmirage.oneandonlyresorts.com
Sky & Sea Adventures	watersportsdubai.com
Surf Dubai	surfingdubai.com
Surf School UAE	surfschooluae.com
The Flow Club	wildwadi.com
Watercooled	watercooleddubai.com
Wild Wadi Water Park	jumeirah.com

Nationwide

Subwing	subwing.net

Ras Al Khaimah

Al Hamra Fort Hotel & Beach Resort	alhamrafort.com
Iceland Water Park	icelandwaterpark.com

Umm Al Quwain

Dreamland Aqua Park	dreamlanduae.com

OMAN

AMUSEMENT PARKS & CENTRES

Foton World Fantasia	24 537 061
Marah Land (Land Of Joy)	24 562 215

BIRDWATCHING

Muscat Diving & Adventure Centre	holiday-in-oman.com

BOAT, YACHT & DHOW CHARTERS

Al Khayran	alkhayran.com
Al Marsa Travel & Tourism	almarsamusandam.com
ART Marine	artmarine.net
Ibn Qais & Partners	24 487 103
Khasab Travel & Tours	khasabtours.com
Marina Bandar Al Rowdha	marinaoman.net
Moon Light Dive Centre	moonlightdive.com
Musandam Sea Adventure Travel & Tourism	msaoman.com
Muscat Diving & Adventure Centre	holiday-in-oman.com

Oman Charter	omancharter.com
Sheesa Beach Travel & Tourism	sheesabeach.com
Water World Marine	waterworldoman.com

CAMEL RIDES

Desert Nights Camp	desertnightscamp.com
Muscat Diving & Adventure Centre	holiday-in-oman.com

CAMERA EQUIPMENT

Capital Store	csoman.om
Khimji's Megastore	khimji.com
Markaz Al Bahja	albahja.com
OHI Electronics	ohielec.com
Photocentre	photocent.com
SABCO Commercial Centre	sabcogroup.com
Salam	salams.com
Shah Nagardas Manji & Co	shahnagardas.com

CAMPING

1000 Nights Camp	1000nightscamp.com
Al Areesh Camp	areeshcamp.com
Al Naseem Camp	99 328 858
Al Raha Tourism Camp	alrahaoman.com
Arabian Oryx Sanctuary	24 693 537
Desert Camp	99 311 338
Desert Nights Camp	desertnightscamp.com
Jabel Shams Base Camp	jabelshams.com
Luxury Camping Wahiba	alanakatours.com
Nomadic Desert Camp	nomadicdesertcamp.com
Ras Al Jinz Turtle Reserve	rasaljinz-turtlereserve.com
Safari Desert Camp	safaridesert.com
Sheesa Beach Travel & Tourism	sheesabeach.com
Turtle Beach Resorts	tbroman.com

CANOEING & KAYAKING

Muscat Diving & Adventure Centre	holiday-in-oman.com

CAR RENTAL AGENCIES

Al Maha Rent A Car	alhajiryoman.com
Al Masky Rent A Car	almaskry.com
Al Miyasa Rent A Car	23 296 521
Avis Oman	avisoman.com
Budget Rent A Car	budgetoman.com
Dollar Rent A Car	dollaroman.com
Europcar	europcaroman.com
Global Car Rental	24 697 140
Hertz	nttomanhertz.com
Mark Rent A Car	marktoursoman.com
Sixt	sixt-oman.com
Thrifty Car Rental	thrifty.com
Unic Rent A Car	24 691 108
Value Plus Rent A Car	valueoman.com
Xpress Rent A Car	sunnydayoman.com
Zubair Leasing	zubairautomotive.com

CAR SERVICING, PARTS, REPAIRS & ACCESSORIES

Al Khuwair Auto Maintenance	24 602 393
Car Care Centre	99 337 786
Carrefour	carrefouroman.com
East Arabian Establishment	24 815 161
Four Wheel Drive Centre	24 810 962
Hisin Majees Trading	24 811 442
Ibrahim Essa Al Sheti	26 840 720
Mohsin Haider Darwish	mhdoman.com
Sadween Trading	24 837 570
Towell Auto Centre	towellauto.com
Truck Tyre Center	bridgestone-mea.com
Tyre Care Plus	bridgestone-mea.com

CAVING

Al Hoota Cave	alhootacave.com
Muscat Diving & Adventure Centre	holiday-in-oman.com

CLIMBING

Muscat Diving & Adventure Centre	holiday-in-oman.com

CYCLING

Muscat Cycling	new5.muscatcyclingclub.com

DESERT DRIVING

National Training Institute	ntioman.com

DIVING & SNORKELING

Blu Zone Water Sports	bluzonediving.com
Capital Area Yacht Centre	caycoman.com
Extra Divers Leisure	alsawadibeach.com
Extra Divers Musandam	musandam-diving.com
Global Scuba	global-scuba.com
Khasab Travel & Tours	khasabtours.com
Moon Light Dive Centre	moonlightdive.com
Muscat Diving & Adventure Centre	holiday-in-oman.com
Oman Dive Center	extradivers-worldwide.com
Scuba Oman	scubaoman.com
Sheesa Beach Travel & Tourism	sheesabeach.com

FINANCIAL ADVISORS

KPMG	kpmg.com

FISHING

Muscat Diving & Adventure Centre	holiday-in-oman.com
Ocean Active	oceanactive.com
Sheesa Beach Travel & Tourism	sheesabeach.com
Sidab Sea Tours	sidabseatours.com
Water World Marine	waterworldoman.com

GUEST/REST HOUSES & HOSTELS

Al Ghaftain Rest House	99 485 881
Al Qabil Rest House	25 581 243
Extra Divers Villa	musandam-diving.com
Ghaba Rest House	99 358 639
Majan Guest House	25 431 910
Oman Dive Center	extradivers-worldwide.com
Oriental Nights Rest House	onrh-oman.com
Samharam Tourist Resort	shanfarihotels.com

HIKING

Donkey Trekking	99 348 440
Khasab Travel & Tours	khasabtours.com
Muscat Diving & Adventure Centre	holiday-in-oman.com

HORSE RIDING

Al Fursan Stable	99 386 978
Qurm Equestrian School	99 339 222

HOSPITALS

Al Raffah Hospital	asterhospital.com
Badr Al Samaa Hospital	badralsamaahospitals.com
Khoula Hospital	khoulahospital.com
Kims Oman Hospital	kimsoman.com
Lifeline Hospital	w lifelineauh.ae
Muscat Private Hospital	muscatprivatehospital.com
Starcare Hospital	starcarehospital.com
The Royal Hospital	royalhospital.med.om

HOTELS & RESORTS

Al Bustan Palace, A Ritz-Carlton Hotel	ritzcarlton.com
Al Diyar Hotel	aldiyarhotel.com
Al Nahda Resort & Spa	alnahdaresort.com
Al Sawadi Beach Resort & Spa	alsawadibeach.com
Crowne Plaza Muscat	ichotelsgroup.com
Crowne Plaza Resort Salalah	ichotelsgroup.com
Falaj Daris Hotel	falajdarishotel.com
Golden Tulip Khasab Hotel Resort	goldentulipkhasab.com
Golden Tulip Nizwa Hotel	goldentulipnizwa.com
Golden Tulip Resort Dibba	goldentulipdibba.com
Golden Tulip Seeb	goldentulipseeb.com
Grand Hyatt Muscat	muscat.grand.hyatt.com
Haffa House Hotel Muscat	shanfarihotels.com
Hamdan Plaza Hotel	hamdanplazahotel.com
Hilton Salalah Resort	salalah.hilton.com
Hotel Ibis Muscat	ibishotel.com
InterContinental Muscat	intercontinental.com
Jabal Akhdar Hotel	25 429 009
Khasab Hotel	khasabhotel.net
Millennium Resort Mussanah	millenniumhotels.com
Park Inn By Radisson Muscat	parkinn.com
Radisson Blu Hotel, Muscat	radissonblu.com
Salalah Marriott Resort	marriott.com
Shangri-La's Barr Al Jissah Resort & Spa	shangri-la.com
Sheraton Oman Hotel	starwoodhotels.com
Sifawy Boutique Hotel	sifawyhotel.com
Six Senses Zighy Bay	sixsenses.com
Sohar Beach Hotel	soharbeach.com
Sur Plaza Hotel	omanhotels.com

The Chedi Muscat	chedimuscat.com
The Platinum	theplatinumoman.com

INSURANCE COMPANIES

Al Ahlia Insurance Co	alahliaoman.com
Arab Orient Insurance Company	insuranceuae.com
Arabia Insurance Company	arabiainsurance.com
AXA Insurance Gulf	axa.com
Dhofar Insurance Company	dhofarinsurance.com
Falcon Insurance	falconinsurancesaoc.com
MetLife Alico	metlifealico.com.om
NEXtCARE Oman	nextcare.ae
Oman Insurance Company	tameen.ae
Oman Qatar Insurance Company	qatarinsurance.com
Oman United Insurance Co	omanutd.com
Risk Management Services	rmsllc.com

MOTOCROSS & MOTORCYCLING

Oman Automobile Association	omanauto.org
Bikers Oman	sjsoman.com/bikersoman
Harley Owners' Group – Muscat Chapter	hog-muscat.com

MOUNTAIN BIKING

Muscat Diving & Adventure Centre	holiday-in-oman.com

NEW CAR DEALERS

Al Jenaibi International Automobiles	bmw-oman.com
Auto Plus	autoplusoman.com
Bahwan Automotive Centre	saudbahwangroup.com
Daihatsu	daihatsu.com
Ford Oman	fordoman.com
Honda Motor Company	omasco.com
KIA	kiaoman.com
Lexus	lexusoman.com
Mohsin Haider Darwish	mhdoman.com
Porsche Centre Oman	porsche.com
Proton Oman	protonoman.com
Shanfari Automotive Co	shanfari.com
Suhail Bahwan Automobiles	suhailbahwanautogroup.com
Towell Auto Centre	towellauto.com
Toyota Oman	toyotaoman.com
Wattayah Motors	vw-oman.com
Zawawi Trading Company	omzest.com
Zubair Automotive	zubairautomotive.com

OUTDOOR & SPORTING GOODS

Adidas	adidas.com
Carrefour	carrefouroman.com
Home Centre	landmarkgroupme.com
Khimji's Megastore	khimji.com
Lulu Hypermarket	luluhypermarket.com
Magic Cup Sports	24 786 688
Marina Bander Al Rowdha	marinaoman.net
Markaz Al Bahja	albahja.com
Muscat Sports	24 564 364

Oman Dive Center	extradivers-worldwide.com
Sports For All	24 560 086
Sun & Sand Sports	sunandsandsports.com
Supa Sportsman	24 833 192
Toys 'R' Us	toysrus.com
Water World Marine	waterworldoman.com

RECOVERY SERVICES

AAA Oman	24 605 555

RUNNING

Muscat Road Runners	muscatroadrunners.com
Oman Athletics Association	omanathletic.org

SAILING

Muscat Diving & Adventure Centre	holiday-in-oman.com
Oman Laser Association	rahbc.pdorc.com
Oman Sail	omansail.com

TOUR OPERATORS

Al Azure Tours	alazuretours.com
Al Nimer Tourism	alnimertourism.com
Bahwan Travel Agencies	bahwantravels.com
Desert Discovery Tours	desertdiscovery.com
Eihab Travels	ohigroup.com
Empty Quarter Tours	emptyquartertours.com
Golden Oryx Tours	goldenoryx.com
Grand Canyon Of Oman Tours	92 605 102
Gulf Ventures Oman	gulfventures.com
Hud Hud Travels	hudhudtravels.com
Khasab Travel & Tours	khasabtours.com
Mark Tours	marktoursoman.com
Sheesa Beach Travel & Tourism	sheesabeach.com
Sunny Day Tours, Travel & Adventures	sunnydayoman.com
Turtle Beach Resorts	tbroman.com

USED CAR DEALERS

Al Fajer Cars	24 491 111
Al Ittihad Cars Showroom	24 542 990
Al Jazeera Motors	24 600 127
Al Siyabi Used Cars	24 698 195
Al Wathbah Trading	24 421 828
Auto Plus	autoplusoman.com
Best Cars	bestcarsoman.com
General Automotive Company	generalautomotive-oman.com
Modern Cars Exhibition	24 786 011
Mohsin Haider Darwish	mhdoman.com
New Zahra Trading	24 833 953
Nissan	nissanoman.com
Popular Pre-Owned Cars	popularcarsoman.com
Real Value Autos	realvalueautos.com
Wattayah Motors	vw-oman.com

WATERSPORTS

Muscat Diving & Adventure Centre	holiday-in-oman.com

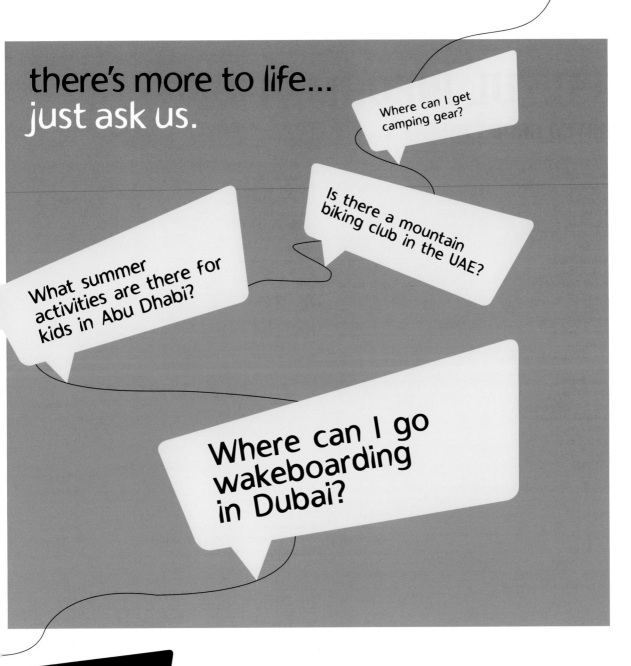

USEFUL INFORMATION

UNITED ARAB EMIRATES

AIRLINES

Aeroflot	aeroflot.ru
Air Astana	airastana.com
Air Arabia	airarabia.com
Air Blue	airblue.com
Air Canada	aircanada.com
Air France	airfrance.ae
Air India	airindia.com
Air India Express	airindiaexpress.in
Air Mauritius	airmauritius.com
Air New Zealand	airnewzealand.com
Air Seychelles	airseychelles.com
Alitalia	alitalia.com
American Airlines	aa.com
Austrian Airlines	austrian.com
Bahrain Air	bahrainair.net
Biman Bangladesh Airlines	biman-airlines.com
British Airways	britishairways.com
Cathay Pacific	cathaypacific.com
China Airlines	china-airlines.com
China Southern Airlines	flychinasouthern.com
CSA Czech Airlines	czechairlines.ae
Cyprus Airways	cyprusair.com
Delta Airlines	delta.com
Eastern Express	flyaha.com
EGYPTAIR	egyptair.com
Emirates	emirates.com
Ethiopian Airlines	ethiopianairlines.com
Etihad Airways	etihadairways.com
flydubai	flydubai.com
Gulf Air	gulfair.com
IranAir	iranair.com
Japan Airlines	jal.com
Jazeera Airways	jazeeraairways.com
Kish Air	kishairline.com/en
KLM Royal Dutch Airlines	klm.com
Kuwait Airways	kuwait-airways.com
Lufthansa	lufthansa.com
Malaysia Airlines	malaysiaairlines.com
Middle East Airlines	mea.com.lb
Mihin Lanka	mihinlanka.com
Nas Air	flynas.com
Olympic Air	olympicair.com
Oman Air	oman-air.com
Pakistan International Airlines	piac.com.pk
Qantas	qantas.com
Qatar Airways	qatarairways.com
RAK Airways	rakairways.com
Rotana Jet	rotanajet.ae
Royal Air Maroc	royalairmaroc.com
Royal Brunei Airlines	bruneiair.com
Royal Jet Group	royaljetgroup.com
Royal Jordanian	rj.com
Saudi Arabian Airlines	saudiairlines.com
Shaheen Air	shaheenair.com
Singapore Airlines	singaporeair.com
South African Airways	flysaa.com
SpiceJet	spicejet.com
SriLankan Airlines	srilankan.lk
Sudan Airways	sudanair.com
Swiss Air	swiss.com
Thai Airways	thaiair.com
Tunisair	tunisair.com
Turkish Airlines	turkishairlines.com
United Airlines	united.com
Virgin Atlantic	virgin-atlantic.com
Yemen Airways	yemenia.com

AIRPORT INFORMATION

Abu Dhabi International Airport:	
Flight Enquiries	02 575 7500
Lost & Found	02 505 2771
Al Ain International Airport	03 785 5555
Al Bateen Executive Airport	02 449 4521
Dubai International Airport Terminals 1, 2 & 3:	
Help Desk	04 224 5555
Flight Information	04 216 6666
Baggage Services	04 224 5383
DNATA Cargo	04 211 1111
Fujairah International Airport	09 222 6222
Ras Al Khaimah International Airport	07 244 8111
Sharjah International Airport	06 558 1111

PORTS & COASTS

DP World	04 881 6048
Jebel Ali Port	04 881 5555
Port Rashid	04 881 5555
Khor Fakkan Port	06 528 1666
Port Khalid Customs Centre	06 528 1666
Sharjah Ports Authority	06 528 1666
Umm Al Quwain Port	06 765 5882
Saqr Port	07 205 6000
Port Of Fujairah	09 222 8800
Mina Zayed Seaport Authority	02 673 0600
Hamriyah Port Authority	06 526 3388

EMBASSIES & CONSULATES

Argentian Embassy	02 443 6838
Australian Embassy	02 401 7500
Australian Consulate	04 508 7100
Bahrain Embassy	02 665 7500
British Embassy	04 309 4444
British Embassy	02 610 1100
Canadian Embassy	02 694 0300
Canadian Consulate	04 314 5555
Chinese Embassy	02 443 4276
Chinese Consulate	04 394 4733
Czech Republic Embassy	02 678 2800
Danish Consulate	04 348 0877
Danish Embassy	02 441 0104
Egyptian Consulate	04 397 1122
Egyptian Embassy	02 813 7000
Finnish Embassy	02 632 8927
Danish Embassy	02 441 0104
French Embassy	02 443 5100
French Consulate	04 408 4900
German Embassy	02 644 6693
German Consulate	04 397 2333
Indian Embassy	02 449 2700
Indian Consulate	04 397 1222
Iranian Embassy	02 444 7618
Iranian Consulate	04 344 4717
Irish Embassy	02 495 8200
Italian Embassy	02 443 5622
Italian Consulate	04 331 4167
Japanese Embassy	02 443 5696
Japanese Consulate	04 331 9191
Jordanian Embassy	02 444 7100
Jordanian Consulate	04 397 0500
Kuwaiti Embassy	02 447 7146
Kuwaiti Consulate	04 397 8000
Lebanese Embassy	02 449 2100
Lebanese Consulate	04 397 7450
Malaysian Embassy	02 448 2775
Malaysian Consulate	04 398 5843
New Zealand Embassy	02 441 1222
New Zealand Consulate	04 331 7500
The Netherlands Embassy	02 695 8000
The Netherlands Consulate	04 440 7600
Norwegian Embassy	02 621 1221
Norwegian Consulate	04 382 3880
Omani Embassy	02 446 3333
Omani Consulate	04 397 1000
Pakistani Embassy	02 444 7800
Pakistani Consulate	04 397 0412
Philippine Embassy	02 639 0006
Philippine Consulate	04 220 7100
Polish Embassy	02 446 5200
Qatar Embassy	02 449 3300
Qatar Consulate	04 396 0444

Russian Embassy	02 672 1797
Russian Consulate	04 328 5347
Saudi Arabian Embassy	02 444 5700
Saudi Arabian Consulate	04 397 9777
South African Embassy	02 447 3446
South African Consulate	04 397 5222
Spanish Embassy	02 626 9544
Sri Lankan Embassy	02 631 6444
Sri Lankan Consulate	04 398 6535
Swedish Embassy	02 417 8800
Swiss Embassy	02 627 4636
Swiss Consulate	04 329 0999
Syrian Embassy	02 444 8768
Thai Embassy	02 557 6551
Thai Consulate	04 348 9550
US Embassy	02 414 2200
US Consulate	04 309 4000
Yemen Embassy	02 444 8457

EMERGENCY & OTHER SERVICES

Police/Ambulance/Emergency Hotline	999
Fire Department	997
Department for Tourist Security	800 4438
Abu Dhabi marine emergencies, accidents or suspicious activity (CNIA)	996
Police Call Centre (Non-emergency)	901
Dubai Police General Department of Criminal Investigations	800 243

PHARMACIES

Sheikh Khalifa Medical City ER Pharmacy	02 819 2188
Lifeline Hospital Pharmacy	02 633 3340
Al Noor Hospital Pharmacy	02 613 9106
Al Ain Hospital Pharmacy	03 763 5888
Liwa Hospital Pharmacy	02 882 2204
Life Pharmacy	04 344 1122
Bin Sina Pharmacy	04 355 6909
Yara Pharmacy	04 222 5503

COUNTRY & CITY/AREA CODES

UAE Country Code	971
Abu Dhabi	02
Ajman	06
Al Ain	03
Dubai	04
Hatta	04
Fujairah	09
Sharjah	06
Umm Al Quwain	06
Ras Al Khaimah	07
Etisalat Mobile Telephone	050/056
du Mobile Telephone	055
Dubai number from outside the UAE	+971 4...
Mobile number from outside the UAE	+971 50 / 55 / 56

USEFUL NUMBERS

du Customer Service:

Mobile enquiries from mobile/UAE phone	155/ 800 155
Mobile enquiries from any phone	055 567 8155
Home enquiries	04 390 5555
Directory Enquiries	199

Etisalat Customer Service:

Within UAE	101
Non-Etisalat Customers within UAE	800 101
Outside UAE	00971 400444101
Directory Enquiries	181
Information	144

International Operator Assistance	100
Speaking Clock	141
Dubai Meteorological Office	04 216 2218
Weather (Abu Dhabi)	02 666 7776
Mastercard International	04 391 4200
American Express	800 4931
Diner's Club	04 316 0355

TAXI COMPANIES

Advantage Taxi	06 544 1938
Al Ghazal Transport	02 635 6060
Arabia Taxi	800 272242
Arabia Taxi	04 285 5566
Cars Taxi	800 227 789
Citi Taxi	06 533 4444
Dubai Ferry	800 9090
Dubai Taxi / Special Needs Taxi / Ladies Taxi	04 208 0808
Emirates Cab	06 539 6666
Emirates Taxi	02 550 9511
Emirates Taxi	03 782 5741
Metro Taxi	600 566 000
National Taxi	600 543 322
Sharjah Taxi	06 568 8444
Union Taxi	06 532 5555
Taxi/Bus	800 1700

BUS & TRAIN SERVICES

Mowasalat	600 522 282
Sharjah Transport	700 067 000
TransAD (Abu Dhabi)	600 535353
TransAD (Al Ain)	03 762 0360
TransAD (Western Region)	02 2 894 5555
Roads & Transport Authority – RTA	800 9090

FERRY SERVICES

Water Taxi & Waterbus	800 9090
Delma Island Ferry Services	8005 5555

OMAN

AIRLINES

Air Arabia	airarabia.com
Air Blue	airblue.com
Air France	airfrance.ae
Air India	airindia.com
Air India Express	airindiaexpress.in
Alitalia	alitalia.com
Biman Bangladesh Airlines	biman-airlines.com
British Airways	britishairways.com
Cathay Pacific	cathaypacific.com
Cyprus Airways	cyprusair.com
Delta Airlines	delta.com
EGYPTAIR	egyptair.com
Emirates	emirates.com
Etihad Airways	etihadairways.com
flydubai	flydubai.com
Gulf Air	gulfair.com
IranAir	iranair.com
Jet Airways	jetairways.com
Kenya Airways	kenya-airways.com
KLM Royal Dutch Airlines	klm.com
Kuwait Airways	kuwait-airways.com
Lufthansa	lufthansa.com
Malaysia Airlines	malaysiaairlines.com
Middle East Airlines	mea.com.lb
Oman Air	oman-air.com
Pakistan International Airlines	piac.com.pk
Qatar Airways	qatarairways.com
Royal Brunei Airlines	bruneiair.com
Royal Jordanian	rj.com
Saudi Arabian Airlines	saudiairlines.com
Shaheen Air	shaheenair.com
Singapore Airlines	singaporeair.com
South African Airways	flysaa.com
SriLankan Airlines	srilankan.lk
Sudan Airways	sudanair.com
Swiss Air	swiss.com
Thai Airways	thaiair.com
Turkish Airlines	turkishairlines.com
United Airlines	united.com
Virgin Atlantic	virgin-atlantic.com
Yemen Airways	yemenia.com

AIRPORT INFORMATION

Muscat International Airport:

Flight Information	24 519 223/456/518 977
Baggage Services	24 519 504/662
Customer Service	24 518 977
Cargo	24 519 291

Salalah Airport:
Flight Information	24 518 072
Customer Service/Baggage Services (Oman Air)	23 294 237
Cargo	23 293 386

Khasab Airport:
Flight Information/Baggage Services	26 731 592
Customer Service	99 027 988
Cargo	26 731 592

EMBASSIES & CONSULATES

Australian Embassy (Saudi Arabia)	00966 1488 7788
Bahrain Embassy	24 605 074
British Embassy	24 609 000
Canadian Consulate	24 788 890
Chinese Embassy	24 696 698
Czech Embassy (Saudi Arabia)	00966 1450 3617
Danish Consulate	24 526 000
Egyptian Embassy	24 600 411
French Embassy	24 681 800
German Embassy	24 835 000
Indian Embassy	24 684 500
Iranian Embassy	24 696 944
Irish Consulate	24 701 282
Italian Embassy	24 695 131
Japanese Embassy	24 601 028
Jordanian Embassy	24 692 760
Kuwaiti Embassy	24 699 626
Lebanese Embassy	24 695 844
Malaysian Embassy	24 698 329
Netherlands Embassy	24 603 706
New Zealand Consulate	24 694 692
Norwegian Consulate	24 526 444
Pakistani Embassy	24 603 439
Philippine Embassy	24 605 140
Qatar Embassy	24 691 156
Russian Embassy	24 602 894
Saudi Arabian Embassy	24 601 705
Spanish Embassy	24 691 101
South African Embassy	24 647 300
Sri Lankan Embassy	24 697 841
Swedish Consulate	24 708 693
Swiss Consulate	24 568 202
Thai Embassy	24 602 684
United Arab Emirates Embassy	24 400 000
US Embassy	24 643 400

EMERGENCY & OTHER SERVICES

CID Services	24 569 501
Police / Fire / Ambulance	9999
Royal Oman Police	24 569 392
Traffic Services	24 510 227/228
Visa Services	24 512 961

PHARMACIES

Abu Al Dahab Clinic & Pharmacy	23 291 303
Hatat Polyclinic	24 563 641
Medident Madinat Qaboos Medical Centre	24 601 668
Muscat Pharmacy & Stores	24 814 501
Scientific Pharmacy	24 702 850
Sultan Qaboos University Hospital	24 147 777/144 615

COUNTRY & CITY/AREA CODES

Oman Country Code	968
Al Musanaah Area Code	26
Barka Area Code	26
Daba Area Code	26
Jabal Al Akhdar Area Code	25
Jebel Sifah Area Code	24
Khasab Area Code	26
Mirbat Area Code	23
Muscat Area Code	24
Nizwa Area Code	25
Salalah Area Code	23
Sur Area Code	25

USEFUL NUMBERS

Friendi Mobile	98 400 000

Nawras Customer Service:
From Nawras mobile	1500
From any phone	9501 1500

Renna:
From Renna mobile	1240
From any phone	800 73662

Omantel Business Call Center	1235
Omantel Directory Enquiries	1318
Omantel Fixed & Internet Call Centre	1300
Omantel International Operator Connected Calls	1305
Omantel Marine & Coastal Radio Services	1302
Omantel Mobile Call Centre	1234
Omantel Payphone Faults & Complaints	1307
Omantel Telex Faults & Complaints	1301

TAXI COMPANIES

Allo Taxi	24 697 997
City Taxi	24 603 363
Hello Taxi	24 607 011

BUS SERVICES

Oman National Transport Company (ONTC)	24 490 046

FERRY SERVICES

National Ferries Company	8007 2000

INDEX

Residents Guides

All you need to know about living in and loving some of the world's greatest cities

Mini Visitors' Guides

The perfect pocket-sized
Visitors' Guides

Calendars

A whole year's worth of
stunning images

Activity Guides

Drive, trek, dive and swim... life will never be boring again

Ultimate Explorer

Maps

Never get lost, no matter where you are

Photography Books

Beautiful cities caught through the lens

Retail Sales

Our books are available in most good bookshops as well as online at askexplorer.com/shop or Amazon.

Bulk Sales & Customisation

All our products are available for bulk purchase with customisation options. For discount rates and further information, please contact leads@askexplorer.com.com

Licensing & Digital Sales

All our content, maps and photography are available for print or digital use. For licensing enquiries please contact licensing@askexplorer.com.com

Check out

Search for information and inspiration, as well as connect with other expats and share your experiences on askexplorer.com

BASIC ARABIC

GENERAL

Yes	na'am
No	la
Please	min fadlak (m)
	min fadliki (f)
Thank you	shukran
Please (in offering)	tafaddal (m)
	tafaddali (f)
Praise be to God	al-hamdu l-illah
God willing	in shaa'a l-laah

GREETINGS

Greeting (peace be upon you)	as-salaamu alaykom
Greeting (in reply)	wa alaykom is salaam
Good morning	sabah il-khayr
Good morning (in reply)	sabah in-nuwr
Good evening	masa il-khayr
Good evening (in reply)	masa in-nuwr
Hello	marhaba
Hello (in reply)	marhabtayn
How are you?	kayf haalak (m)
	kayf haalik (f)
Fine, thank you	zayn, shukran (m)
	zayna, shukran (f)
Welcome	ahlan wa sahlan
Welcome (in reply)	ahlan fiyk (m)
	ahlan fiyki (f)
Goodbye	ma is-salaama

INTRODUCTIONS

My name is...	ismiy…
What is your name?	shuw ismak (m)
	shuw ismik (f)
Where are you from?	min wayn inta (m)
	min wayn inti (f)
I am from…	anaa min...
America	ameriki
Britain	braitani
Europe	oropi
India	al hindi

QUESTIONS

How many / much?	kam?
Where?	wayn?
When?	mataa?
Which?	ayy?
How?	kayf?
What?	shuw?
Why?	laysh?

Who?	miyn?
To/for	ila
In/at	fee
From	min
And	wa
Also	kamaan
There isn't	maa fee

TAXI OR CAR RELATED

Is this the road to...	hadaa al tariyq ila...
Stop	kuf
Right	yamiyn
Left	yassar
Straight ahead	siydaa
North	shamaal
South	januwb
East	sharq
West	garb
Turning	mafraq
First	awwal
Second	thaaniy
Road	tariyq
Street	shaaria
Roundabout	duwwaar
Signals	ishaara
Close to	qarib min
Petrol station	mahattat betrol
Sea/beach	il bahar
Mountain/s	jabal/jibaal
Desert	al sahraa
Airport	mataar
Hotel	funduq
Restaurant	mata'am
Slow down	schway schway

ACCIDENTS & EMERGENCIES

Police	al shurtaa
Permit/licence	rukhsaa
Accident	haadith
Papers	waraq
Insurance	ta'miyn
Sorry	aasif (m)
	aasifa (f)

NUMBERS

Zero	sifr
One	waahad
Two	ithnayn
Three	thalatha
Four	arba'a

Five	khamsa
Six	sitta
Seven	saba'a
Eight	thamaanya
Nine	tiss'a
Ten	ashara
Hundred	miya
Thousand	alf

WHAT TO DO IN AN EMERGENCY

Police and emergency services in the UAE and Oman are efficient, and even equipped with helicopter services for extreme road accidents, beach accidents involving drowning, as well as evacuations from difficult terrain or areas.

However, before setting out on a new adventure, it is advantageous to make yourself aware of the hospitals or medical centres that are near the area you are heading to. There are instances where you may have to get to hospital quickly, so the most reliable method might be to use your own transport or a taxi.

When calling for help (999), most operators understand Arabic, English and even Hindi, but remember to speak slowly and clearly (remember that an operator might not be able to understand a strong regional accent from the UK, for example). State your name, the nature of the accident, address of the emergency and how serious the situation is. And remember to provide them with your telephone number.

In the event of a non-medical related emergency, contact your local embassy (Abu Dhabi) or local consulate (Dubai) for information.

NOTES

NOTES

NOTES

UAE & Oman Ultiimate Explorer Guide – 1st Edition
Lead Editor Matt Warnock
Edited by Laura Coughlin, Jo Iivonen, Rachel McArthur
Contributors Christian Handrich, Carole Harris, Tony Schroder
Proofread by Max Tuttle
Data managed by Amapola Castillo, Ingrid Cupido
Designed by Ieyad Charaf, Jayde Fernandes, Mohammed Shakkeer
Maps by Naisha Raghani, Zainudheen Madathil, Noushad Madathil
Photographs by Michael Estrada, Mark Grist, Pamela Grist, Henry Hilos,
Alistair Mackenzie, Pete Maloney, Rachel McArthur

Publishing
Publisher Alistair MacKenzie
Associate Publisher Claire England

Editorial
Managing Editor Consumer Publishing Matt Warnock
Editor Jo Iivonen
Corporate Editor Charlie Scott
Digital Projects Editor Rachel McArthur
Web Editor Laura Coughlin
Production Manager Therese Theron
Production Coordinator Kathryn Calderon
Editorial Assistants Ingrid Cupido, Amapola Castillo

Design & Photography
Creative Director Pete Maloney
Art Director Ieyad Charaf
Contract Publishing Manager Chris Goldstraw
Designer Michael Estrada
Junior Designers Didith Hapiz, Mohammed Shakkeer
Layout Manager Jayde Fernandes
Layout Designers Mansoor Ahmed, Shawn Zuzarte
Cartography Manager Zainudheen Madathil
Cartographers Noushad Madathil, Naisha Raghani
Photography Manager Pamela Grist
Image Editor Henry Hilos

Sales & Marketing
Group Media Sales Manager Peter Saxby
Media Sales Area Managers Laura Zuffova, Sabrina Ahmed,
Bryan Anes, Adam Smith, Dominic Keegan
Digital Sales Area Manager James Gaubert
Business Development Manager Pouneh Hafizi
Corporate Solutions Account Manager Vibeke Nurgberg
Group Marketing & PR Manager Lindsay West
Senior Marketing Executive Stuart L. Cunningham
Sales & Marketing Assistant Shedan Ebona
Group Retail Sales Manager Ivan Rodrigues
Retail Sales Coordinator Michelle Mascarenhas
Retail Sales Area Supervisors Ahmed Mainodin, Firos Khan
Retail Sales Merchandisers Johny Mathew, Shan Kumar
Retail Sales Drivers Shabsir Madathil, Najumudeen K.I., Sujeer Khan
Warehouse Assistant Mohamed Haji

Finance, HR & Administration
Administration Manager Fiona Hepher
Accountant Cherry Enriquez
Accounts Assistant Sunil Suvarna, Joy Bermejo Belza, Jeanette Carino Enecillo
Admin Assistant & Reception Joy H. San Buenaventura
Public Relations Officer Rafi Jamal
Office Assistant Shafeer Ahamed

IT & Digital Solutions
Digital Solutions Manager Derrick Pereira
IT Manager R. Ajay

Contact Us

General Enquiries
We'd love to hear your thoughts and answer any questions
you have about this book or any other Explorer product.
Contact us at info@ask**explorer**.com

Careers
If you fancy yourself as an Explorer, send your CV
(stating the position you're interested in) to
jobs@ask**explorer**.com

Designlab & Contract Publishing
For enquiries about Explorer's Contract Publishing arm
and design services contact
contracts@ask**explorer**.com

PR & Marketing
For PR and marketing enquiries contact
marketing@ask**explorer**.com

Corporate Sales
For bulk sales and customisation options, for this
book or any Explorer product, contact
sales@ask**explorer**.com

Advertising & Sponsorship
For advertising and sponsorship, contact
sales@ask**explorer**.com

Explorer Publishing & Distribution
PO Box 34275, Dubai, United Arab Emirates
ask**explorer**.com

Phone: +971 (0)4 340 8805
Fax: +971 (0)4 340 8806